THOMAS HOBBES

THOMAS HOBBES

Otfried Höffe

Translated by Nicholas Walker

Thomas Hobbes, Otfried Höffe © Verlag C.H.Beck oHG, München 2010

Published by State University of New York Press, Albany

© 2015 State University of New York

For information, contact State University of New York Press, Albany, NY
www.sunypress.edu

Production, Jenn Bennett
Marketing, Anne M. Valentine

Library of Congress Cataloging-in-Publication Data
Höffe, Otfried.
  [Thomas Hobbes. English]
  Thomas Hobbes / Otfried Höffe ; translated by Nicholas Walker.
    pages cm
  Includes bibliographical references and index.
  ISBN 978-1-4384-5765-9 (hc : alk. paper) — ISBN 978-1-4384-5766-6 (pb : alk. paper)
  ISBN 978-1-4384-5767-3 (e-book)
  1. Hobbes, Thomas, 1588–1679. 2. Political scientists—Great Britain—Biography.
  3. Philosophers—Great Britain—Biography. 4. Political science—Philosophy. I. Title.
  JC153.H66H5813 2015
  192—dc22
  [B]

                                        2014040649

10   9   8   7   6   5   4   3   2   1

Contents

Abbreviations   ix

1. Introduction: Thomas Hobbes: A Pioneer of Modernity   1
   1.1. Three Challenges of the Epoch   3
   1.2. A Pioneer in Three Senses   8
   1.3. The Continuity of Hobbes's Development   14

I.
HOBBES'S CAREER AND
PHILOSOPHICAL DEVELOPMENT

2. Beginnings   21
   2.1. Student, Tutor, and Traveling Companion   21
   2.2. Euclid and Galileo   25
   2.3. The English Civil War   28
   2.4. Exile in Paris   32

3. Leviathan and Behemoth   37
   3.1. A Fractured Relationship to Rhetoric   38
   3.2. The Symbol of Leviathan   42
   3.3. The Return to England   49

II.
THE ENCYCLOPEDIC CHARACTER
OF HOBBES'S PHILOSOPHY

4. Science in the Service of Peace   57
   4.1. The Principal Aim of Hobbes's Philosophy   58
   4.2. The Complex Method   59
   4.3. The Mathematical Paradigm and Its Limits   63
   4.4. Ethics and Political Authority   66
   4.5. Analysis and Composition   73

5. Natural Philosophy and the Theory of Knowledge   77
   5.1. Empirical Realism   78
   5.2. Levels of Knowledge   83
   5.3. On Dreams   84
   5.4. Prudence   85

6. Language, Reason, and Science   89
   6.1. Language 1: The Pre-communicative Dimension   89
   6.2. Language 2: The Political Dimension   95
   6.3. Realism and Nominalism   96
   6.4. The Framework of Language and Reason   98
   6.5. Science   102
   6.6. Hobbes's Division of the Sciences   105

7. An Anthropology of the Individual: The Passions   109
   7.1. A Naturalistic Hedonism   109
   7.2. A Topography of the Passions   113
   7.3. Freedom, Self-Preservation, and Determinism   115
   7.4. Power   117

8. An Anthropology of the Social:
   The Possibility of Peace in a Condition of War   121
   8.1. The Conditions of Peace   121
   8.2. "Man Is a Wolf to Man"   122
   8.3. A Prevailing Inclination for Peace?   128

9. Legitimating the State   135
   9.1. The Laws of Nature   135
   9.2. A Moral Philosophy?   138
   9.3. The Original Contract   143
   9.4. Absolute Authority   146
   9.5. A Right to Rebellion?   152

10. Law   159
   10.1. "Not Truth but Authority"   159
   10.2. The Division of Laws   161
   10.3. A Theory of Commands   164
   10.4. Laws of Nature as a Corrective?   168
   10.5. Authorized Power   170

11. Religion and Church   175
   11.1. A Twofold Political Question   175
   11.2. The Anthropological Foundations of Religion   179
   11.3. The Kingdom of God   181
   11.4. The Principles of a Christian Politics   183
   11.5. A Materialistic Theology   188
   11.6. Hobbes's Critique of Other Churches   191

12. An Excursus: Hobbes's Critique of Aristotle   193
   12.1. The "Vain Philosophy" of Aristotle   193
   12.2. An Aristotelian in Spite of Himself   198
   12.3. Inevitable Strife or the Social Nature of Man?   201

13. History   207
   13.1. Translating Thucydides   207
   13.2. The History of the Church and the Kingdom of God   209
   13.3. Behemoth   210

III.
THE INFLUENCE OF HOBBES

14. From His Age to Our Own   217
   14.1. The Early Reception and Critique of Hobbes's Work   217
   14.2. A Continuing Debate   221
   14.3. The Modern Discussion   225

Chronology of Hobbes's Life and Work   233

Bibliography   237

Name Index   251

Subject Index   255

Abbreviations

B = *Behemoth*
C = *De Cive* (= *Elementa philosophiae*, part III)
Co = *De Corpore* (*Elementa philosophiae*, part I)
D = (*Dialogue between a Philosopher and a Student of the Common Laws of England*)
E = *The Elements of Law, Natural and Politic*
H = *De Homine* (= *Elementa philosophiae*, part II)
L = *Leviathan, or the Matter, Form and Power of a Commonwealth Ecclesiastical and Civil*
Opera = *Opera philosophica*
Works = *English Works of Thomas Hobbes*

The following editions have been used for the texts most frequently cited: Thomas Hobbes, *Leviathan*, edited with an introduction and notes by J. C. A. Gaskin, Oxford University Press, 1996; Thomas Hobbes, *The Elements of Law, Natural and Politic*, edited by J. C. A. Gaskin, Oxford University Press, 1994; Thomas Hobbes, *Man and Citizen* (*De Homine* and *De Cive*), edited by B. Gert, Hackett Publishing Company, Indianapolis, 1991.

Citations from *Leviathan* (L) indicate the chapter number and the pagination of the original edition, which is included in the Gaskin edition and almost all other modern editions of the work (e.g.: L ch. 4: 12). Citations from the aforementioned editions of *The Elements of Law* (E) and from *Man* and *Citizen* (H and C) indicate the chapter number, followed by section number and page reference (e.g.: C ch. 1, §2, p. 110).

ONE

Introduction

Thomas Hobbes: A Pioneer of Modernity

If the philosophy of the state, and of the nature of political authority as such, had long been a neglected, even expressly despised, area of study, there is certainly no doubt about its acute contemporary relevance. In view of an ongoing wave of wars, and particularly of civil wars and internal social conflicts, we no longer simply talk of "prosperity" or "emancipation" as the ultimate ends of political action and intervention. These ends now seem more basic and elementary, namely: peace and freedom, in immediate conjunction with the principle of justice.

The quest for a social order capable of securing such ends has now lost any suggestion of musty irrelevance. The fundamental question for any philosophy of politics—the legitimation and limitation of the public exercise of power—has emphatically passed beyond a merely antiquarian interest in intellectual history and has returned to occupy the place where it has always belonged: the center of a truly political philosophy. And Thomas Hobbes is one of the most important representatives of political philosophy in this sense.

Yet this thinker was concerned with far more than simply "the state" and the nature of law and political authority. For the body of work that Hobbes left us is essentially encyclopedic in character. This philosophy embraces an ontology and a natural philosophy; it examines the nature of language, reason, and knowledge; it investigates human feelings and emotions, and many other issues in what we would now call the philosophy

1

of mind; and, last but not least, it engages with fundamental questions of morality and religion.

If we ignore the field of mathematics, where Hobbes occasionally lost his way (for a judicious account of his views in this respect, see Grant 1996), he addressed his chosen problems in a way that is almost always original, and indeed *radical* in two senses of the word. In his thorough and resolute pursuit of understanding he penetrates below the apparent surface, illuminates hidden corners of experience, and thereby opens up new perspectives that are highly challenging in both substantive and methodological terms. Hobbes is an intellectual revolutionary who undertook nothing less than a fundamental re-grounding of philosophy, one comparable in its radicality with the new beginning proposed by Descartes. But apart from the methodological significance that he assigns to mathematics—something that he shares with the French thinker—Hobbes develops an entirely different revolution in the field of philosophy. He regards the famous Cartesian argument from the *cogito* as fallacious, he repudiates all mind-body dualism, and he replaces ideas with *nomina* or names. Hobbes is an emphatic nominalist. And instead of beginning with an exercise in radical doubt, the English thinker begins by offering a radical new construction of the world.

It is, above all, in his philosophy of the state, of the nature of law and political authority, that Hobbes reveals the full originality, radicality, and consistency of his thought, engaging explicitly with principles and forms of argument (concerning the concept, grounding, and normative criteria of the state and legal authority) that have remained an object of systematic discussion to this day. In this respect too, Hobbes is still our philosophical contemporary.

In the courage that he shows in making full use of his own understanding, Hobbes can be seen as an Enlightenment thinker in the Kantian sense, and one who demands a similar courage on the part of his readers. He struggles against all superstition, derides uncritical reverence for books and supposed authorities, and subjects religious and political communities of every kind to the most thorough critical examination.

This son of an uneducated country priest (who was apparently more interested in drink and cards than in matters of theology), a university student who stoutly rejected the scholastic disputes that were common in such institutions, Hobbes sought to overcome superstition of all kinds by appeal to natural forms of explanation. He is a rigorous naturalist and an equally rigorous materialist, whose views in this regard are not merely intellectually suggestive but remain profoundly challenging. And since he was forced to engage directly with theological questions, he also developed an intimate knowledge of the Bible itself, thus becoming a notable exegete and even a significant theologian.

1.1. Three Challenges of the Epoch

In terms of cultural and intellectual history, Hobbes is very much a philosopher of the seventeenth century. This was an age that witnessed momentous advances in mathematics and the natural sciences, but it was also a period of great political insecurity, marked by numerous wars, social conflicts, and civil wars. In addition, it was an epoch in which many commonly shared moral and religious convictions were beginning to disintegrate. In directly addressing the three challenges created by these specific developments, Hobbes was able to produce an eminently political philosophy that was not merely focused upon political issues in the narrower sense.

In these historical circumstances, especially the situation of political insecurity and the weakening of once shared moral convictions, the philosophers of the time were generally preoccupied with discovering some "firm ground" on which to build. And since they understood this search either under the aegis of mathematics or under that of reliable factual knowledge, the philosophical debate emerged as a struggle between a rationalism that privileges "understanding" or "reason" (*ratio*, in Latin) and an empiricism that privileges "experience" (*empeiria*, in Greek). But the philosophy of Hobbes cannot be understood exclusively in terms of either approach, which only serves to show that rationalism and empiricism are not necessarily mutually exclusive positions after all.

Both the rationalist and the empiricist sides of the debate promoted the notion of a unified and universal science that was supposed to serve the cause of human well-being. There were three fundamental ideas involved here: philosophy must assume a rigorously scientific character and adopt a single unified method (i.e., be a unified science); it must investigate the whole of the natural and social world, including the nature of language (i.e., be a universal science); and it should serve the welfare of human beings (i.e., be an expression of practical interest). To fulfill the first of these demands, philosophy must begin from the simplest possible elements; and to fulfill the second, it must attempt to present the totality of its insights as an organized whole, as a system. This unified and universal science is thus essentially systematic in character. Yet it no longer answers to the classical, and above all, Aristotelian ideal of a pure autarchic *theoria*, and indeed explicitly renounces this ideal. Hobbes's unified and universal science (as we can see from *The Elements of Law*, 1640) is intended to be useful for human beings.

Hobbes seeks this dimension of utility above all in the political state or "commonwealth," an area of reflection that is conspicuously absent from the philosophical system of his outstanding contemporary René Descartes (1596–1650). It was through addressing this theme that Hobbes stepped out onto the contemporary philosophical stage and responded to the challenges in question. He recognized the direct relationship between this novel theme and all of these challenges: in methodological terms, the exemplary character of science and of mathematics as the ideal of rigorous demonstration ("reason is reckoning"); in political terms, the bloody reality of civil war and religious conflict, along with the crisis of received moral convictions and religious beliefs. It is in this context that Hobbes introduced the idea of the "covenant"—the theoretical model of the social contract that is typically mobilized by modern political thought against all established usage and tradition—and thereby also created one of the most important philosophical theories of the state and the nature of political authority in the history of Western thought. Some of the peculiar features, or perhaps even incoherencies, of this philosophy can be explained by reference to the social and economic conditions of the time, and the transition from a feudal to a bourgeois social order. These new conditions can be roughly characterized in terms of the market society of early modern capitalism and the possessive individualism associated with it. Jean-Jacques Rousseau already drew attention to such developments in his *Discourse on the Origin and Foundation of Inequality among Men* (1755), and they have been specifically analyzed and investigated by Franz Borkenau (1934), a thinker close to the Frankfurt Institute of Social Research, and more recently by C. B. Macpherson (1962).

Hobbes himself, on the other hand, ascribed little or no significance to social and economic developments as such, and one looks in vain in his writings for any incipient contributions to a general theory of economic life or social development. The all-defining political experience for Hobbes was the civil wars of the time, or rather simply the English Civil War. For in spite of his early travels in Europe, and his long period of exile in Paris later, he was exclusively interested in the political affairs of his home country.

Nonetheless, Hobbes's theory of the state is significant far beyond the limits of his time, beyond the English Civil War and the emergence of early modern market society. For, after all, it is not only capitalist or bourgeois society that requires an international condition of peace if our material and intellectual powers are to be developed and realized. Furthermore, the English Civil War was only one case of many such political and religious wars in Europe during the sixteenth and seventeenth centuries. As another example, we might recall the Huguenot wars in France that, two generations earlier, had inspired Jean Bodin (1530–1596), the most important theorist of international law in the second half of the sixteenth century, to compose his *Six Livres de la République* (*Six Books on the Republic*, 1576). These writings develop a theory of sovereignty on the part of the prince (that is to say: the French king) and reject any rival authority in relation to pope or emperor, or to the feudal rights defended by the nobility. Hobbes explicitly agrees with Bodin in this regard (E part I, ch. 8, §7).

With his own translation of Thucydides, the English philosopher reached back into the distant past in order to warn his contemporaries of the horrors of civil war. And the things that led to civil war in the early modern period, such as the ruthless rivalry between religious positions each claiming absolute authority for itself, have their later counterpart in the exclusive claims of other competing political and indeed religious factions. Finally, it is clear that the relevance of Hobbes's philosophy of the state is certainly not limited to historical situations of civil war. The position that has often been maintained, under the ultimate influence of Carl Schmitt, that the whole philosophy of Hobbes only acquires its full coherence and plausibility in relation to the civil war (see Kosellek 1959, chapter I.II and Willms 1970, p. 34ff.), is unnecessarily reductive.

The principal question of Hobbes's philosophy is this: Why, and in what form, is a state, an institutionalized order of peace, needed in the first place? Other political philosophers before Hobbes, such as Niccolò Machiavelli (1469–1527) or the aforementioned Jean Bodin, still essentially appealed to the lessons of political experience, to considerations of prudence, and to established historical knowledge, to justify their claims.

But right from the beginning, from his first contribution to political thought onward (*The Elements of Law* of 1640), Hobbes always developed his argument on the basis of general or universal principles. But these most basic principles are confirmed in turn by constant reference to experience. And they are systematically derived from a philosophical anthropology that is itself grounded in a philosophy of nature. It is thus in terms of a rigorously scientific form of argument that Hobbes attempts to resolve the fundamental political problem of his time, that of civil war, in a way capable of commanding universal agreement in spite of the loss of earlier moral beliefs and convictions. Hobbes undertakes to pursue the fundamental questions of politics without appealing to a now problematic system of moral values, and solely by recourse to a truly scientific form of philosophy.

If we ignore the specific way in which he relates it to human experience, this scientific approach to the political belongs, methodologically speaking, to the rationalist tradition. And with a particular variation on the title of Spinoza's principal early work, *Ethica Ordine Geometrico demonstrata* (*Ethics demonstrated in accordance with Geometrical Method*), the entire life work of Hobbes, dedicated as it was to the fundamental questions of politics, could plausibly be described as *Politica Ordine Geometrico demonstrata* (Politics demonstrated in accordance with the Geometrical Method). It is clear, of course, that we should not understand geometry here merely in the narrower sense as the mathematical treatment of space. Since Hobbes also speaks of the "reckoning [that is, adding and subtracting] of the consequences of general names." (L ch. 5: 18; cf. C ch. I, §2) his life work could also be entitled "Politics demonstrated in accordance with the Mathematical Method." Whether geometry or mathematics is taken as the methodological model, Hobbes is essentially interested in the exemplary clarity, coherence, and completeness that they both share, and above all in a process of justification that starts with the most basic possible assumptions and proceeds from here to develop its results step by step.

But in spite of his methodological rationalism, Hobbes argues that all our representations derive from sense experience, and his theory of knowledge is emphatically sensationalist (from the Latin *sensus*: the faculty of sense). And since he also defines "the good" in naturalistic rather than in normative terms, he must be classed as an empiricist. With this singular combination of methodological rationalism and substantive empiricism,

Hobbes effectively undercuts the bald opposition between the two principal philosophical movements of his age.

The political result of Hobbes's reflections also fulfills another fundamental cultural hope of the period, namely the idea of the state as a guarantor of internal peace. Since religious and confessional conflicts also underlie many civil conflicts, so that controversies regarding religious truth endanger the internal peace or security that is the necessary condition of any community, Hobbes expressly removes the political order from any influence or interference on the part of the contending religious confessions. In this way, Hobbes prepares the way for the modern idea of the state as an institution that is supposedly neutral with regard to differences of philosophical outlook or religious belief on the part of its members. It is true, of course, that Hobbes is usually regarded as the philosophical apologist of unlimited state power, and is widely interpreted, not without reason, as the leading theorist of political absolutism. Yet Hobbes clearly thought of himself, as we can see from the dedication of *Leviathan*, as a thinker who sought a middle way between excessive freedom on the one hand and excessive authority on the other. Nonetheless, he hardly expected his theory to be universally welcomed or readily accepted. And as if anticipating the typical reaction that his philosophy of the state has indeed provoked ever since, he expects to find his labors "generally decried," as he says in the dedication. But the real reason for this reaction probably lies in the way Hobbes actually pursues his goal. For in spite of the way he interprets his own work, he clearly adopts a strongly autocratic rather than a moderate or middle way.

The threefold intention behind his thought finds particularly clear expression in *Leviathan*, his most important work. Here Hobbes develops his argument with remarkable methodological rigor. On the one hand, he refuses to weaken his claim to provide a strictly scientific grounding for philosophy. Indeed he reinforces the appeal to mathematical method (*more geometric vel arithmetico*), here reduced to a simple notion of calculation in terms of addition and subtraction that hardly does justice to the thinking actually practiced in the book. Finally, and this is why it is so instructive, Hobbes's work is not governed by any purely theoretical interest but by an essentially practical and political one: that of promoting the power and authority of the state (as the dedication makes clear) on the one hand, and of helping human beings to become obedient citizens of the state on the other (L ch. 2: 17). This already strongly evokes the side of his thought that is so concerned with authority and obedience, while the other side of the coin, the concept of liberty, is rather obscured.

1.2. A Pioneer in Three Senses

When we speak of a pioneer, we usually think of someone who does not simply discover a new field but actually explores and recognizes its significance. In this sense Hobbes deserves to be regarded as a pioneer of modernity, for he did not merely anticipate or prefigure the new epoch that was beginning to emerge, but was an emphatic representative and protagonist of this development, even a crucial part of it. Hobbes was both acutely aware of a fundamental issue and made a fascinating attempt to resolve it, and the heart of his response to this issue has proved relevant and instructive for a considerable period of time, and in a certain sense still remains so. At least as far as political philosophy is concerned, what we understand as early modernity begins in the seventeenth century.

At first sight this claim may seem paradoxical. For both the central issue and the proposed solution, and the specific way in which they are presented, are obviously prompted and influenced by the particular historical time in which they arose. They thus appear to be limited to this time and place, rather than directly relevant in the present. But the claim only appears paradoxical as long as we regard the time in question as utterly different from our own. In fact, the differences are not so fundamental after all.

Of course, Hobbes's repeated, and indeed copious, reference to the Bible is a reflection of the age. In a period that was obsessed with adducing scriptural support and justification of one kind or another, Hobbes appealed with remarkable frequency to both the Old and the New Testament, even if he often cites Scripture for purposes quite different from the usual ones (as he himself points out in the dedication of *Leviathan*). The emblematic figures that furnish the titles for two of his most important works, Leviathan and Behemoth, are monsters from the pages of the Old Testament. And in *Leviathan,* the two parts of the work that directly concern the philosophical system itself, namely his anthropology and his philosophy of the state, are followed by two further parts that deal with religious and ecclesiastical questions. And it is above all here that we find the most frequent references to biblical figures: Aaron, Adam, and David,

John the Baptist and Moses, Paul, Peter, Solomon, Samuel, and Saul. Finally, Hobbes also appeals to "the law of the Gospel"—the so-called Golden Rule—as confirmation at a particularly important point of his argument regarding the second law of nature (L ch. 14: 65).

Since some version of the Golden Rule can be found in many different cultures, it can be regarded as a core element of a cross-cultural morality. It thus serves to support Hobbes's principal interest in providing a universally convincing justification for the authority of the state even in times when generally shared values and beliefs can no longer be presupposed. It is striking that Hobbes does not introduce the Golden Rule as an expression of cross-cultural validity (which he probably did not recognize as such), but simply as a citation from the New Testament.

Hobbes's contemporaries not only possessed considerable biblical knowledge of this kind, they were also educated in a deeply humanistic culture. And this culture encouraged the facility to express ideas in terms of images and to decipher the message communicated in this way. The famous engraving on the title page of *Leviathan* is a masterpiece of emblematic depiction and a consummate expression of political iconography. Hobbes also revealed himself as a highly cultivated humanist through his profound knowledge of the ancient Greek and Roman authors, from Homer to Thucydides, Plato, and Aristotle, from Cicero and Juvenal to Augustine and Justinian. And some of Hobbes's most celebrated and eloquent sayings—such as *homo homini lupus* (man is a wolf to man) or *sed auctoritas, non veritas, facit legem* (it is authority, not truth, which makes the law)—can be traced back to classical sources.

While a systematic evaluation of Hobbes's philosophy may largely pass over his knowledge of Scripture and his humanistic cultural background, it certainly cannot ignore the three fundamental intellectual provocations that we have already mentioned, and these remain as topical as they ever were: the quest for a philosophy that can legitimately claim the status of a science, the threat to peace posed by war in general and civil war in particular, and the absence of generally shared and well-established moral beliefs and convictions.

Hobbes's system of philosophy possesses a threefold structure. It begins with a natural philosophy (*De Corpore*: On Body), proceeds with an anthropology (*De Homine*: On Man), and culminates in a philosophy of the state and political authority (*De Cive*: On the Citizen). By way of introduction to each of these three parts, we can simply indicate Hobbes's pioneering achievement in each case. The last two of these achievements, in particular, have proved so influential, and indeed so plausible, that the history of subsequent Western philosophy could, to a significant degree, be read as a series of footnotes to Hobbes. And this judgment would not require that much qualification even with respect to the first of these achievements.

Hobbes expressly described his philosophical system as *Elementa philosophiae* (Elements of Philosophy) after the example of the most celebrated work in the entire history of mathematics, Euclid's handbook of geometry composed around 300 B.C. (the *Elementa*, according to its Latin title, or *Stoicheia* in the original Greek). Since he also endorsed a Euclidean conception of method, he developed a philosophy we would now call "scientistic": one that derives its ideal of knowledge and the type of arguments it deploys exclusively from the realm of science (from the Latin *scientia*: a body of knowledge). A philosophy is described as scientistic in the strong sense of the word when it regards mathematics and, under the influence of Galileo in particular, the type of causal explanation pursued by the natural sciences as the ideal of all genuine knowledge. It is in this strict and narrower sense that Hobbes can be said to pursue a scientistic program in philosophy.

Thus Hobbes analyzes the state, the essential object of his investigations, into its ultimate constituents, namely the individual human beings that compose it. Then he undertakes, in turn, to trace their activity—their action and interaction—back to the underlying laws of motion. Hence the first part of his system, a "natural philosophy" in the broadest sense, culminates in the concept of "matter in motion." In his theory of nature itself, of human knowledge, and of the objects of knowledge, Hobbes defends a rigorous materialism or, more precisely, a mechanistic position based upon the elementary laws of motion. And "mechanistic" here also implies calculability and potential controllability, since everything is ultimately subject to causal explanation. The world appears to Hobbes like a great clock or "engine." He denies any special or independent status to the realm of mind or spirit, and resolutely defends this mechanistic materialism, rejecting the notion that "there be in the world certain essences separated from bodies" as mere "jargon" and nonsense (L ch. 46: 371).

The second part of Hobbes's system extends and elaborates this materialism as a naturalistic anthropology. As far as living things are concerned, the movements of the body are geared to self-preservation, and find expression in (the higher) animals as feelings and sensations. In human beings we also find "reason" as the ability to conceive or anticipate the end, the means, and the content of our behavior (L ch. 6: 23). This scientifically defined naturalism is the first of Hobbes's pioneering achievements in natural philosophy. This position, of course, is hardly uncontroversial from a philosophical point of view, and this pioneering thinker is also a deeply provocative one. Today, in an intellectual world that is predominantly influenced by an empiricism shaped by analytical philosophy, such pioneering and provocative achievement deserves greater recognition than ever. One should be prepared to look back beyond David Hume, and even beyond John Locke, and recognize Hobbes as the ultimate pioneer in this regard.

In accordance with this naturalistic perspective, the "normative" foundation of Hobbes's fundamental project—the construction of a convincing philosophy of the state—is provided by a purely hedonistic and individualistic concept of the good that has been deprived of any ideal or normative considerations. Here everyone identifies the good as what he desires, and the bad or evil as what he avoids, and happiness as enduring success in obtaining the object of desire (L ch. 6: 23–24 and 29–30). The skeptical attitude that this approach embodies, the doubt regarding the possibility of furnishing any objective judgments with regard to good and evil, reflects a fundamental suspicion of the authoritative rules or principles that the modern age has continued to share and endorse in the political sphere at least. The skepticism that finds expression in this moral, political, and anthropological context is thus Hobbes's second pioneering achievement.

There is no doubt that modernity has also explicitly pursued the opposite approach, namely attempting to ground objective assessments and judgments regarding what is good or bad/evil without recourse to any given or external forms of authority. But even if this attempt proves plausible or convincing, we may still ask whether the legitimation of political power can be justified in this way. If we renounce this particular path and instead follow Hobbes's second pioneering approach, we shall have to defend an individualistic model of political legitimation. This approach, as distinct from individualism as a social theory, does not need to reject the argument that human beings are essentially social. But instead of simply claiming that this is why human beings require a state or political community invested with coercive power, this approach subjects this claim to careful examination. In the course of this examination we recognize, according to the individualistic theory of legitimation, that the political community (or "commonwealth," as Hobbes would say) must justify itself in the eyes of every individual involved. For if political authority cannot justify itself in this way, it remains nothing but a case of mere force in relation to each individual. Thus the individualistic theory of legitimation is only properly satisfied if political authority assures a distributive advantage that is applicable to every individual. It is quite true that Hobbes does not explicitly defend this individualistic theory of legitimation, but the "egoistic" argumentative strategy that he adopts certainly brings him very close to this position.

In the contemporary debate on questions of right, law, and political authority, we encounter a broad family of theories regarding the nature of consensus and agreement in the social and political context. The individualistic theory of legitimation, which also belongs to this family of ideas, relies on a strict notion of consensus that requires universal agreement and presupposes the distributive capacity to participate in creating it. Thus the theory systematically begins by positing a basic freedom that implies an equally basic equality among the participants. Given the premise that each individual must be capable of freely giving consent, every individual must be regarded as a free and equal person. It is with this premise that Hobbes grounds the social contract theory that has provided a preeminent model of legitimation for the public exercise of power. And the theory of contract, or "contractualism" as it is also known, furnished the fundamental conceptual framework of political thought from Locke through to Kant and Rousseau, and after a considerable period of neglect, has been revived in the work of John Rawls and Robert Nozick, of James Buchanan and David Gautier, and in my own contributions to this area. Hobbes is the first and most outstanding defender of the contractualist approach, and he has therefore rightly been recognized to this day as an exemplary and fundamental partner in any discussion of the subject.

It is quite true that Hobbes, unlike Locke or Rousseau, does not typically speak of a "contract" in the crucial passages of his work. He prefers to employ the term "covenant," a word used to translate the "agreement" or relationship (*berith* in Hebrew) established between God and the Israelites on Mount Sinai according to the Old Testament. And the Scots, as Presbyterians who opposed the imposition of the Anglican form of worship, also described their own ecclesiastical union in terms of a "covenant," namely a covenant with God.

Perhaps Hobbes wished to enhance the "plausibility" (Krause 2005, p. 11) of his own abstract contractualist proposal by exploiting an analogy with a concrete expression already well established in the literature

of the period. But one should not ascribe too much systematic significance to the term "covenant." Hobbes actually redefines the concept by
introducing other equivalent terms that derive from jurisprudence rather
than the Bible. Thus he can speak of a "pact or covenant." And although
Hobbes refers abundantly to the Scriptures in *Leviathan*, he does not do
so when he introduces the notion of the "covenant." He does not contrast
the idea of a covenant with that of a contract, but regards it as a specific
form of the latter (L ch. 14: 66). What defines the contract-character of
the covenant is that one party—for Hobbes this is the "Sovereign"—may
"perform his part at some determinate time after, and in the mean time
be trusted" (ibid.).

The alternative to this pact or covenant model of human association
is a model of social cooperation that goes back to Aristotle. This approach
had provided for centuries the almost canonical way of legitimating the
social order, and in emphatically rejecting it Hobbes accomplished nothing less than a revolution in social and political philosophy. In accordance
with the second pioneering achievement that we have indicated, "reason"
plays a purely instrumental rather than autonomous role in this connection. Here too, in responding to our fundamental aspirations for peace
and security, Hobbes belongs in the "empiricist" tradition of contemporary philosophy to which so many increasingly are drawn today.

But the substantive "absolutist" direction of Hobbes's thought represents only one strand in the development of modernity, and one that in
the context of political philosophy is directly opposed to the "republican"
tradition that was inspired by the example of ancient Rome and believed
that the freedom of the citizen was undermined by the arbitrary exercise
of state power (see Brugger 1999).

Hobbes's third pioneering achievement lies in his theory of law and
his defense of the claim *sed auctoritas, non veritas, facit legem,* as he puts
it in the Latin version of *Leviathan* (Opera, vol. III, p. 6). In the light
of this claim, he seems to side with positivism in the modern dispute
between legal positivism and the theory of natural law. But in fact the
formula "it is authority rather than truth that makes a law" discovers the
appropriate conceptual form for the phenomenon of positive law. In fact,
Hobbes recognizes the concept of natural law, and thus does not defend
a positivist theory of law. What the formula does do is effectively capture
the minimal conditions for a proper concept of positive law.

One should not exaggerate the immediate relevance of Hobbes's
thought, and he cannot simply be turned into our philosophical

contemporary. One major deficiency of his thought is particularly evident to us: there is no global dimension to his philosophy of law and the state. We could explain this deficiency in historical terms, namely by stressing the distance that separates Hobbes from our epoch of globalization. But since significant elements of this development were already beginning to appear in his time, we can speak of an early modern form of globalization in this connection. At the height of his life Hobbes was in a position to witness the international repercussions of the religious wars, the effects of the Thirty Years' War, and its final conclusion with the Treaty of Westphalia (1648) and its idea of establishing a lasting peace for Europe as a whole. In Hobbes's time we also see how England was already beginning to develop an empire of potentially global reach. And even before his birth we recognize an exemplary "age of discovery" that would soon turn into the age of colonization, thus generating the many questions that mark the beginning of the notion of international law in the European context.

Nonetheless, it is clear that Hobbes's philosophy of law and the state does not open up directly to a properly international or supranational perspective. In this regard perhaps his particular understanding of sovereignty obstructs his own governing preoccupation with establishing peace among human beings. For it is even more difficult, as far as global relations are concerned, to imagine something that is already difficult enough in the context of an individual state: the idea of the absolute sovereignty of the state. But since Hobbes believes that a condition of war obviously prevails between individual states (L ch. 13: 63), he would have to reflect upon the problem of establishing a peaceful order here too.

1.3. The Continuity of Hobbes's Development

There is a certain break in the evolution of Hobbes's thought, namely that marked by his "conversion" from a rhetorical humanistic culture to a rigorously scientific form of argument inspired by Euclid's *Elements*, even if this approach is not itself entirely devoid of rhetorical aspects. But once he had fundamentally committed himself to this method, around the age of forty, Hobbes's philosophy remained remarkably constant throughout all his significant philosophical texts. The basic features of his theory of law and political authority in particular remain the same, but this is also true for the other parts of his philosophy. In contrast to the claims advanced by Skinner (1996) with respect to the role of rhetoric, or the position of Ludwig (1998) with regard to different theoretical accounts of obligation, I do not believe that we can identify any significant ruptures or discontinuities, any subsequent intellectual conversion or "turning" that would allow or even encourage us to distinguish between a less "enlightened" or "pre-critical" outlook and the more enlightened and critical position of Hobbes's mature work.

From *The Elements of Law*, through *De Cive* (the final part of his *Elementa philosophiae*), down to *Leviathan*, and even *Behemoth* and the *Dialogue*, we can identify an impressive range of shared features throughout: (1) the same basic method that is derived from mathematics and the mathematical investigation of nature, although the manner in which the argument is presented also permits significant scope for rhetoric; (2) the same basic issue regarding the legitimation of the state and its authority; (3) the same basic thesis that the sovereignty of the state also has the last word where confessional conflicts of religion are concerned; (4) the same logical structure of argument, one that starts from an empiricist philosophy of nature, develops an anthropology based upon the concept of self-preservation, and culminates in a philosophy of political sovereignty and a corresponding theory of religion; (5) the same two leading strategic arguments based on a twofold philosophical realism: (5a) a realist anthropology that takes "men just as they are," although the precise execution of the project admittedly reveals a certain one-sidedness (E part I, ch. 1, §2; cf. L ch. 13) and (5b) this one-sidedness should be understood as a strategic argument from "egoism," which eschews moralistic or even altruistic claims and recognizes only what such egoism would be prepared to concede (see the epistle dedicatory in E); and finally, (6) the same fundamental claim that philosophy should be at once rigorously scientific and useful or beneficial to human beings, and here above all politically beneficial. Hobbes hopes to gain recognition for views that will bring an "incomparable benefit to commonwealth" (ibid.). Thus while there are certain changes in the presentation of Hobbes's argument, with regard to the theory of freedom for example, his basic philosophical assumptions remain predominantly unchanged throughout. And as Skinner (2008, p. 123) concedes himself, these changes in his account of freedom do not affect his crucial argument for submitting to the authority of the state, namely our desire for security and protection.

The remarkable continuity of Hobbes's thought probably results from the long period of preparation and gestation that preceded its explicit

philosophical formulation. The intellectually precocious Hobbes was
exposed to the world of science, learning, and politics from an early age,
but he only made his presence felt in the area of political philosophy at
the relatively advanced age of fifty-two, by which time he had developed
a range of carefully considered views that were no longer so open to challenge or significant revision. Even if we prefer an alternative explanation
in this connection, the notable continuity of his thought allows us to
present Hobbes's philosophy effectively by reference to a single text, his
philosophical masterpiece *Leviathan*, although we shall also draw on some
of his other important writings in the course of our interpretation. Like
Plato's *Republic* and Kant's *Critique of Pure Reason*, Hobbes's *Leviathan*,
his most mature and comprehensive work, resembles an "encyclopedia"
of the philosophical sciences. If we consider the specific organization of
the text, it is quite true that it only officially presents us with parts II
and III of the philosophical system (the anthropology and the political
philosophy), supplemented by two further parts entitled "Of a Christian
Commonwealth" and "Of the Kingdom of Darkness." But the first part
of the text, "Of Man," begins with a discussion of themes (such as sense,
imagination, speech, reason, and science), which belong thematically to
part I of Hobbes's system. The relevant text of *De Corpore* is itself divided
into four parts, but many themes of the first part on "Logic" (on philosophy, on names, on method) and some themes of the second part on "The
First Grounds of Philosophy" are also addressed in chapters 4, 5, and 9
of *Leviathan*. And some of the material treated in the first chapter of the
fourth part of *De Corpore*, on "Physics or the Phenomena of Nature," is
also taken up in the discussion of sensation and animal motion in chapters 1 and 6 of *Leviathan*.

Our description of Hobbes as a pioneer of modernity is not simply
intended to emphasize his outstanding contribution to philosophy, but
also indicates the intentions of the present work, which has no interest
in promoting a purely historicist or archival approach to its subject. For
to take a philosophical work seriously means acknowledging the double
claim that it raises: that it addresses fundamental problems presented by
the natural and social world, and that it seeks an answer to these problems
that is not merely consistent or internally coherent but genuinely extends
our knowledge.

In accordance with this hermeneutical premise, the reading that follows cannot content itself with providing a merely historical reconstruction of the intellectual background, with simply understanding Hobbes's

philosophy while eschewing any further substantive assessment. Such an approach may serve to shield the "great masters" of the past from presumptuous criticism of posterity, but this protective and devotional attitude only reduces the intellectual challenge and potential of its subject. Instead, we shall attempt to uncover our own concerns within the political philosophy of Hobbes, given that it certainly addresses problems that remain very much alive. They may be encapsulated in two questions: firstly, why do we need a "state" at all?; and secondly, what is the appropriate basic structure of such a state?

Hobbes's answer to the second question in particular (involving an established church and, especially, an absolute conception of sovereignty that does not depend on the separation of powers or the idea of fundamental rights) naturally provokes not only significant reservations but downright rejection on our part. But a suitably differentiated reading of Hobbes's work would do well to resist the widely shared view that his philosophy as a whole and the philosophy of the state that it involves is so stringently developed that we must often reexamine its basic foundations if we are to challenge the general chain of the argument. In fact the problems encountered in the overall argument are not confined to its initial starting point. For the way in which the argument is subsequently developed is by no means as free of difficulties or inconsistencies as Hobbes and many of his interpreters would like to claim.

Assuming the continuing substantive relevance of his thought, I shall argue that we should distinguish—at least analytically—the two aforementioned questions involved in Hobbes's attempt to justify the necessity of the state: the justification of the state as such, and the justification of an absolute and undivided sovereignty on the part of the state. I shall claim that Hobbes's answer to the first question remains basically convincing. Political rule or dominion is indispensable, and it is legitimated, formally speaking, through the consent of those who are affected, and, substantively speaking, through the shared concern for security and prosperity, which we can identify with Hobbes in the guarantee of free self-preservation. The third claim, defended in the course of our interpretation, is that even the specific failings of Hobbes's thought prove highly instructive, through a kind of "determinate negation," for any attempt to furnish an appropriate justification for the authority of the state.

Although enlightened thinkers like Hobbes desire to challenge all forms of arbitrary or external authority, they would also like to become an authority in their own right (cf. L ch. 31: 193). And this naturally involves them in a performative contradiction. It is true that sometimes, as in the "The Author's Epistle to the Reader" with which he introduces *De Corpore*, Hobbes rhetorically professes a certain modesty: "For I do but propound, not commend to you anything of mine." But in fact this theory, which challenges all authorities, must present itself as an authority, indeed as the decisive court of judgment. Hobbes expects his theory to be acknowledged not just temporarily, but for all time ("eternally"). For it contains a truth that is supposed to be unassailable on account of the strictly scientific method that grounds it.

By way of conclusion to these preliminary observations, I should like to add a further personal word. In my previous writings on central thinkers of the Western philosophical tradition I have principally concentrated, apart from the work of Kant, on the thought of Aristotle. It may appear astonishing that I should turn here to a consideration of Hobbes, certainly one of the most famous critics of the Aristotelian tradition. But ever since I began as a professional teacher of philosophy, and indeed from the time of my own earliest studies in philosophy, I have engaged intensively with the thought of Hobbes. Thus on the occasion of the three-hundredth anniversary of Hobbes's death (December 4, 1679), I was able to arrange a symposium on Hobbes's philosophical anthropology and his philosophy of the state (Höffe 1981), and have subsequently published a number of articles that also touch on Hobbes's contribution to political philosophy (see bibliography below, 3.3, and 4). It is against the background of an interest in Hobbes that has persisted for more than forty years now that I have here undertaken to assess the broader significance of this pioneering thinker of modernity who has often been neglected outside the sphere of political philosophy. In what follows I have not attempted to present or introduce the now enormous body of secondary literature that has grown up around Hobbes, although I have often discussed disputed points of interpretation that have arisen in this connection. Rather, in order to take Hobbes seriously as a philosopher, I have undertaken to consider his fundamental claims and the kinds of arguments he deploys from a systematic point of view, and have attempted to examine their philosophical significance and their intellectual plausibility in this light.

I should like to take this opportunity to thank my students, my secretarial staff, and my academic assistants and colleagues, in this case Axel Rittsteiger, M.A., Giovanni Rubeis, M.A., and in particular, Dr. Dirk Brantl.

                                            Tübingen, October 2009

I

HOBBES'S CAREER AND PHILOSOPHICAL DEVELOPMENT

TWO

Beginnings

2.1. Student, Tutor, and Traveling Companion

Thomas Hobbes was born in the momentous year of 1588, when the Spanish Armada sailed up the English Channel in order to facilitate a military invasion of England from the Low Countries. He was the second son of an ill-educated rural Anglican clergyman and a peasant's daughter, and came into the world on Good Friday, April 5, in Westport, near Malmesbury, in the county of Wiltshire (in the southwest of England). He was very proud of his birthplace, and would always publish his works under the name "Thomas Hobbes of Malmesbury."

Hobbes is not only an important philosopher but also a brilliant writer. Exercising his considerable rhetorical gifts, he would later recount that his mother bore him prematurely, shocked by news that the enormous Spanish fleet was sailing up the channel. "Fear and I were born twins" (Opera, vol. I, p. 86).

And fear would accompany Hobbes, if not throughout his entire life, as people often like to say, then at least from the age of fifty-two onward. It was his fear of persecution at the hands of Parliament that drove the philosopher into exile in France in 1640. After the publication of *Leviathan* he no longer felt safe in France and returned to England in 1652. Even after the restoration of the monarchy, from 1660 onward, he found it impossible to live in his own country without a degree of anxiety and insecurity. And after the Great Plague, in 1665, and the Fire of London, in 1666, Hobbes was accused by Parliament of propagating atheism and heresy, and was no longer legally permitted to publish his works in England.

Once he had experienced fear directly in his own life (after the circulation of his work *The Elements of Law, Natural and Politic,* which was his first contribution to political philosophy and was composed in 1640 before his exile in France), Hobbes the philosopher was so impressed by the significance of this emotion that he interpreted it as an essential feature of human existence. According to the argument presented in *De Cive* (ch. 1, §2), stable social relations derive from our fear of one another rather than from any sense of mutual benevolence. And Hobbes will claim of course in *Leviathan* (ch. 13: 98) that the fear of violent death is the most important of the three passions that promote the establishment of peace.

Yet Hobbes spent the earlier period of his life largely free of fear and care. His youthful years fell in the reign of Queen Elizabeth I, in a time of remarkable economic, cultural, and political development. After the defeat of the Spanish Armada, and not least through the freebooting activity of English vessels, which was actively encouraged by the government, England dramatically expanded its power and influence in seafaring and commerce, and began to lay the foundations of its future colonial empire. Government finances were reorganized and placed on a much more secure footing, while the power of the established church was renewed and consolidated. The art of music flourished at the hands of "the Virginalists," a group of composers who specialized in writing for the principal solo instrument of the period, the virginal or spinet. And the literature of the period could boast the outstanding sermons, satires, and lyric poetry of John Donne (1572–1631) and especially the plays of William Shakespeare (1564–1616), widely regarded as the greatest European dramatist since classical antiquity. The natural sciences also witnessed remarkable developments during this period. Thus William Harvey (1578–1657), the personal physician of King Charles I, would soon discover the principle of the circulation of the blood, while the philosopher Francis Bacon (1561–1626), who also served as lord chancellor, exerted considerable influence as the "prophet" of a new conception of science.

The precociously gifted young Thomas Hobbes grew up in the household of his uncle, Francis Hobbes, who was a successful glove maker in Malmesbury. After attending elementary school in nearby Westport,

Thomas moved to a private school in Malmesbury, where he acquired an extremely thorough knowledge of Greek and Latin languages and literature. In 1603, at the age of fifteen, he went to Magdalen Hall in the University of Oxford, where he studied scholastic logic, physics, and metaphysics, and five years later gained his degree as *Baccalaureus artium*, roughly equivalent to a modern Bachelor of Arts from a philosophy faculty. Although this conferred the right to deliver public lectures on logic, Hobbes made very little use of the opportunity.

As with many other philosophers of the early modern period—such as Bacon and Descartes, Spinoza, Locke, and Hume—Hobbes became a major thinker essentially outside and independently of the university system. Repelled by the spirit of Puritanism and by scholastic philosophy alike, Hobbes would retain a lifelong antipathy toward the academics and teachers of the university establishment. From the age of twenty onward, Hobbes's "profession" would have to be described as that of tutor, traveling companion, private secretary, and friend to the extremely wealthy and intellectually enlightened family of Sir William Cavendish, who would later become the earl of Devonshire. (The Cavendish family remains one of the greatest private landowners in England to this day.)

It appears that between 1610 and 1615 Hobbes was engaged to accompany William Cavendish, the eldest son of his employer and only two years younger than himself, on the kind of cultural Grand Tour that was then obligatory for the English nobility, and which took both of them to France, Germany, and Italy. Once Hobbes had returned to England, it is thought that sometime between 1619 and 1623, in his role as private secretary, he made the acquaintance of Francis Bacon, who was a frequent guest of the Cavendish family. Hobbes translated some of Bacon's Latin essays and this can only have strengthened his contempt for the scholastic philosophy that still prevailed in the universities. Bacon's conviction that "knowledge is power" may well have influenced the passage in *De Corpore* (ch. I, §6 f.) where Hobbes claims that "the end of knowledge is power," that "the scope [i.e., purpose] of all speculation is the performance of some action, or thing to be done," and that even geometry should serve "for the commodity [i.e., utility] of human life" (*Works*, vol. I, p. 7). Nonetheless, Bacon's rationally motivated commitment to observation and experience would ultimately prove insufficient, given its lack of theoretical grounding, for Hobbes's own conception of scientific knowledge.

In the meantime, following the death of the William Cavendish, the second earl of Devonshire, in 1628, Hobbes had established cordial relations with another noble family, the Cliftons of Clifton, and in

1629–30 he accompanied the son of the family on another European journey, probably to France and Switzerland, which lasted over a year. In the course of this trip Hobbes visited a "gentleman's library" and came across an edition of Euclid's *Elements* (see Aubrey 1987, p. 230). Whether he only seriously began his own mathematical and scientific studies at this time, or was thereby merely encouraged to pursue them more intensely, remains a matter of debate.

During these years Hobbes began to immerse himself in the work of the classical writers and historians. In 1620 there appeared an anonymous collection of twelve "essays" and four lengthier "discourses" under the title of *Horae subsecivae* (*Hours of Leisure*), and three of these discourses have been ascribed to Hobbes. From the methodological point of view these texts are rather traditional in character and show no interest in the geometrical issues that would later absorb him, and strike the reader in large part as exercises on classical themes of humanistic culture. The first treatise is concerned with the *Annals*, a historical work of Tacitus, but turns the commentary into a kind of Machiavellian "mirror for princes," drawing on the example of the emperor Augustus to set out the rules for the prudent pursuit of power politics. The third discourse, *Concerning Laws*, argues in favor of "the rule of law" and, in contrast to Hobbes's later writings, ascribes great importance to legal precedent and tradition.

A text of much greater significance is Hobbes's translation of the exemplary classical contribution to critical history, Thucydides' *History of the Peloponnesian War* (published in 1629 under the title *Eight Books of the Peloponnesian War*). Shortly afterward it seems that Hobbes composed his first expressly philosophical text, *A Short Tract on First Principles*, although this remained unpublished. It should be pointed out that Hobbes's authorship of the *Horae* and the *Short Tract* is by no means universally accepted.

A few years later Hobbes found himself on a third tour in Europe (1634–36), this time as companion of the young third earl of Devonshire. In the course of this journey he gained more than the sort of worldly and political experience he had gathered on his earlier travels. For he now made the acquaintance of some of the leading men of science of the time, beginning with Marin Mersenne, a French mathematician and musical theorist, who was in active correspondence with all the important scientists and philosophers of his age.

It was Mersenne (discoverer of the Mersenne numbers now named after him) who introduced Hobbes personally to the French mathematician, physicist, and philosopher René Descartes (1596–1650) and later invited him to compose one of the official "Responses" to Descartes's *Meditations* (published in Latin in 1641, and in French in 1647). Through Mersenne Hobbes also became acquainted with the physicist and mathematician Gilles Personne de Roberval (1602–1675) and, above all, with one of Descartes's principal opponents, Pierre Gassendi (1592–1655), also a scientist, mathematician, and philosopher.

Hobbes and Descartes conceived a strong personal dislike for one another, and even the respect they entertained for each other in a scientific and philosophical context was strictly limited. Nonetheless, each recognized the abilities of the other in those specific areas where they did not enter into such obvious conflict. Hobbes thought that Descartes's work on geometry was more significant than his contribution to philosophy. For his part, Descartes esteemed Hobbes as a moral philosopher (and as a political thinker), but certainly not as a "metaphysician," that is, as a philosopher dedicated to uncovering the ultimate principles of things.

Given that Hobbes also met the seventy-year-old mathematician, physicist, and astronomer Galileo Galilei (1564–1642) in Florence, we can say that he was personally acquainted with almost all of the leading intellectual figures of his time. And he entered into personal correspondence with others, discussing questions of geometry, for example, with the physicist and mathematician Christian Huygens (1629–1695). It is, however, rather remarkable that later on, after Hobbes had begun to develop his philosophical analysis of law and the state, he made no attempt to establish contact with the Dutchman Hugo Grotius (1583–1645), an extremely important contemporary theorist of natural law and international law. And it is also true that he established no intellectual contact with three other significant, though much younger, philosophers of the time, namely John Locke, Samuel Pufendorf, and Baruch de Spinoza (all born in 1632). It is interesting to note that Leibniz addressed two letters to Hobbes (in 1670 and 1674), although it seems that the latter never received them.

2.2. Euclid and Galileo

For Hobbes there was one crucial experience, from the scientific and methodological point of view, in this otherwise rather typical career of a scholar of the early modern period. Prepared perhaps by his earlier interest in mathematics, this was his life-changing discovery in 1629 of Euclid's work on geometry, the *Stoicheia*, which was translated into Latin under the title of *Elementa*.

The *Elements* of Euclid is presented in an axiomatic-deductive fashion, and this immediately became the paradigm of a strictly demonstrative science in Hobbes's eyes. Methodologically speaking, his own philosophy thus belongs to the strictest form of rationalism, adopting the *mos geometricus*, the geometrical method of axiomatic-deductive reasoning, which Descartes already considered and Spinoza (1632–1677) would also later regard as the ultimate ideal of rigorous or scientific philosophy. Starting from a small number of fundamental assumptions, the axioms, one then proceeds to derive or "deduce" all the other relevant propositions step by step.

In contrast to the approach of Bodin and Machiavelli, his two great predecessors in modern political thought, Hobbes's political philosophy is modeled on Euclid and thus abstracts from actual political history and its contingencies. Nonetheless, this process of methodological abstraction does not in fact govern all of Hobbes's work. Thus he will also compose a history of the English Civil War, along with texts on ecclesiastical history and a dialogue on the subject of English law. Even his principal contribution to political philosophy, *Leviathan*, does not simply content itself with axiomatic procedures. Here too, albeit more rarely, Hobbes introduces a range of historical and pragmatic arguments. And a considerable part of the text is taken up with interpretation of biblical texts, above all those of the Old Testament. But in spite of this, geometry remains the paradigm of true science in Hobbes's eyes. Stimulated by Euclid and encouraged by Galileo, Hobbes undertakes to develop a philosophical system that first presents the natural, scientific, epistemological, and anthropological foundations for a political philosophy that is free of all traditional metaphysics, and then proceeds to develop the corresponding political philosophy itself.

After the model of Euclid's *Elements*, Hobbes's first contribution to political thought was entitled *The Elements of Law, Natural and Politic*, and his three-part philosophical system (consisting of *De Corpore*, *De Homine*, and *De Cive*) similarly bore the title *Elementa philosophiae*. And Hobbes's fascination with mathematics explains why he will continue throughout his work to describe "reason" as a process of "reckoning," as he says in *Leviathan* (L ch. 5: 18).

Hobbes's "conversion" to Euclid finds its first expression in the unpublished text we have already mentioned, the *Short Tract on First Principles*. He follows a Euclidean method and derives conclusions from his initial definitions or principles, and then proceeds to sketch a theory of perception and a corpuscular theory of light and sound. If the text is indeed from Hobbes's hand, it shows that he is already a materialist in that he essentially traces natural phenomena back to one fundamental element, namely body or matter, and one fundamental principle, namely motion. He also defends the "sensationalist" position that our mental representations are all initially generated through the processes of sense perception, specifically as a result of pressure on the sense organs which is then further communicated to the heart and brain, where it finally produces a kind counterpressure. For Hobbes all matter is of exactly the same kind, and the different material properties of things arise through the specific configuration, arrangement, and movement of particles.

A few years after he had discovered Euclid's *Elements* Hobbes also became acquainted with Galileo's principal work, the *Dialogo sopra i due massimi sistemi del mondo* of 1632 (*Dialogue regarding the Two Principal World Systems*, namely the Ptolomaic and Copernican systems of astronomy). Hobbes now familiarized himself with Galileo's new conception of physics and its emphatically non-teleological approach to nature, and from then on this strictly causal approach to the world formed the essential counterpart to his idea of hypothetico-deductive argument.

Hobbes also adopts Galileo's "resoluto-compositive" method as his own. This proceeds by analyzing or breaking down some complex object into its elementary constituents (*resolutio*) and then reconstituting or putting it together again (*compositio*). Hobbes undertakes to extend this method, which seems so successful in the context of physics, to the field of political philosophy, where it seemed never to have been applied before. And he illustrates his method by appealing to the model of a machine, specifically a watch: "For everything is best understood by its constitutive causes. For as in a watch, or some such small engine, the matter, figure, and motion of the wheels cannot well be known, except it be taken insunder and viewed in parts; so to make a more curious search into the rights of states and duties of subjects, it is necessary, I say, not to take them insunder, but yet that they be so considered as if they were dissolved" (C, the preface, pp. 98–99).

Hobbes was unaware that the resoluto-compositive method, which had been developed in the "School of Padua," (see Watkins 1973[2], §9) actually looks back to an Aristotelian tradition, and was indeed identified and specifically applied by Aristotle at the beginning of his *Politics* (book I, ch. 2). Thus the application of the resoluto-compositive method to the field of political philosophy is not entirely new after all, although the characteristic appeal to the metaphor of the machine certainly is (see chapter 4, below).

In order to prepare the proper scientific foundations for his theory of society and the state, foundations defined exclusively in mathematical, physical, and mechanical terms, Hobbes undertook extensive research in the field of natural science. This is why, up until the 1640s, Hobbes was widely regarded as a scientist rather than as a philosopher (see Grant 1996, p. 108f.). And he enjoyed a considerable reputation in this regard, especially on account of his contributions to the field of optics (see Malcolm 1988 and Prins 1996). But after the publication of *De Cive* (1642) he would soon become known principally as a political philosopher.

2.3. The English Civil War

After these relatively peaceful years of foreign travel and intellectual apprenticeship, Hobbes eventually found himself embroiled in the political confusions of his time, in the political-religious conflicts that finally resulted in the English Civil War. The controversies and antagonisms that had disturbed the whole of mainland Europe since the Reformation were reignited in Britain with the accession of James I (1603–1625), who, as the son of Mary Stuart, was already King of Scotland and now succeeded to the English crown on the death of Elizabeth I. The ensuing conflicts in Britain revealed a twofold character—one that was more religious-confessional and one that was far less so.

The more non-confessional conflict essentially involved the struggle between the old nobility, headed by a king who exhibited absolutist tendencies, and Parliament, which insisted on established rights (such as the right to levy taxes and to participate in the legislative process). Parliament was supported by most of the important commercial towns, especially London, and by large sections of the gentry, namely the prosperous bourgeois class and the rural nobility. Among other points of contention, there was indeed also a confessional issue in play, for Parliament wanted the king to show greater tolerance towards the Puritans.

This broadly non-confessional conflict was thus overlaid by a further confessional one, which also implicitly involved some solid political interests. This is the conflict waged by the leadership of the Anglican Church (the established church in England founded by Henry VIII and strengthened under the reign of Elizabeth I) against both the Roman Catholics and the Puritans, and particularly the Presbyterians, the English Protestants who were influenced by Calvin. The Gunpowder Plot, instigated by Catholics in order to destroy King James I along with Parliament itself, was uncovered in 1605. And later, in 1620, a group of Puritans, the "Pilgrim Fathers," landed in New England in search of a place where they might freely practice their own religion.

The Puritans (within the Anglican Church) wished to purify the Anglican liturgy of various persisting Catholic elements they considered superstitious. The Presbyterians, on the other hand, wanted to abolish the bishops, the institution of episcopacy itself, and replace them with a more democratic system in which the elders (*presbuteroi* in Greek) would be freely chosen. In this regard, most but not all of the Puritans were Presbyterian. While it is true that James I was open to a degree of liturgical reform, he completely rejected the idea of major ecclesiastical reform since he believed the monarchy was essentially bound up with the episcopate: "No Bishop, no King." Hobbes himself was even more liberal with regard to liturgical reform. As far as prayer and thanksgiving are concerned, he simply says that they should "be made in words and phrases, not sudden, nor light; but beautiful, and well-composed" (L ch. 31: 192). But since Hobbes regarded the Presbyterians as one of the causes of the English Civil War (see L ch. 18: 93), he vehemently rejected them as partly responsible for what he called the "Kingdom of Darkness" (L ch. 47: 382). For his part, James I commissioned a new translation of the Bible, which appeared in 1611 and is now known as the "Authorized Version" or the King James Bible.

Not long after the death of James I, during the reign of his more cultivated successor Charles I (1625–1649), these conflicts became even more acute. Despite the fact that it was dissolved on several occasions, Parliament succeeded in maintaining the Petition of Right (1628) against the king. The petition listed the established rights that were supposed to protect the citizens from arbitrary arrest and arbitrary taxation. In the

period that immediately followed, the petition became a bulwark of civil
freedom that was subsequently confirmed and consolidated by the act
of habeas corpus (1679) and the Bill of Right (1689). The English Civil
War was sparked in March 1642 when the king contravened the petition
by attempting to arrest certain leading members of the parliamentary
opposition.

This complex political and confessional constellation of forces furnished the crucial historical context within which, on account of which,
and against which Hobbes certainly developed his theory of the state, if
not his philosophy as a whole. As a result of the Civil War, Hobbes felt
the effects of fanaticism in his own life, for both after the publication of
his first work of political philosophy, the *Elements* (1640), and after the
publication of his last, *Leviathan* (1651), he certainly feared political persecution, which he avoided by fleeing the country. *De Cive* appeared while
he was in exile (in 1642), and *Leviathan* was dedicated to a friend whose
brother was killed by an unknown hand at the beginning of the war (cf.
L: 390). And *Behemoth or the Long Parliament* (1666), one of the principal works of his old age, is also dedicated to the subject of the Civil War.

In what might well be called his first contribution to political
thought, his translation of Thucydides' *History of the Peloponnesian War*,
Hobbes offers this account of internecine conflict among the Greeks as
a warning to his contemporaries regarding the imminent threat of civil
war in Britain. At the same time he clearly wishes to exhibit the dangers
and deficiencies of democracy as a particular form of government. But
his attempt proved a failure. The political situation only worsened and in
1642 finally led to open war between Parliament and the Crown, which
was only concluded in the winter of 1648–49 with Oliver Cromwell's
victory over the Scottish Presbyterians, and the defeat and finally the
execution of the king.

Although political philosophy would soon become the principal focus
of Hobbes's work, he continued for the moment to pursue other interests.
Thus in 1637 he published an abbreviated version of Aristotle's *Rhetoric,*
which he had probably composed the year before. Hobbes regarded this as
one of the best of Aristotle's works, and his *A Briefe of the Art of Rhetorique*
represented the first English translation of the text. Here Hobbes actually
expresses admiration for Aristotle, a philosopher whom he would subject
to such merciless criticism in the areas of metaphysics, moral philosophy,
and political philosophy.

While Hobbes was an intellectually precocious individual, it was only relatively late in his career, when he was in his early fifties, that he began to emerge as a significant philosophical author in his own right. Two years before the outbreak of the Civil War, encouraged to defend the position of the Crown by his friend the duke of Newcastle, he produced the outline of a systematic philosophical treatment of law and the state. Hobbes allowed his outline, *The Elements of Law, Natural and Politic*, to circulate in handwritten copies. It is remarkable how closely this work resembles his later masterpiece, *Leviathan* (1651), in its basic features. The earlier text is divided into two parts, the first expressly anthropological ("Human Nature") and the second expressly political ("De Corpore Politico"). And in chapter XXVI of this second part ("That Subjects are not Bound to Follow the Judgment of any Authorities in Controversies of Religion which is not Dependent on the Sovereign Power"), Hobbes discusses some of the questions that are also addressed in the third part of *Leviathan*.

The similarities between the two texts go even further. Like *Leviathan*, the text of the *Elements* begins with reflections on the theory of knowledge and the philosophy of mind. Hobbes also underlines that he proceeds likes a mathematician, or *more geometrico*, presenting his argument in a rigorously scientific and objective manner. And he emphatically repudiates the "dogmatists" who approach the fundamental questions with preconceived views based on an appeal to traditional authorities and end up by defending subjective positions rather than ones that are unassailable and objectively well grounded.

Hobbes appeals to mathematical arguments derived from "the rules and infallibility of reason" and are thus free from all "controversies and dispute" (E, the epistle dedicatory, p. 19). He therefore hopes that such purely objective and dispassionate arguments will convince all interested parties of the necessity of a form of power that will ensure peace and security and thus avert the threat of civil war. But again, his highly ambitious political intentions in this regard were unsuccessful. The *Elements*, a work that was offered to support the cause of "government and peace" (ibid., p. 20), only seemed to fan the conflicts that led to war.

As in his later writings on the philosophy of the state, Hobbes does not investigate the precise character of any existing political community. Concentrating his attention on the state as such rather than the concrete situation of the English or British state, Hobbes asks why a political community is required at all and what principles are needed to sustain one.

But on the basis of his hedonistic and materialist anthropology he argues in favor of a much more emphatic form of political sovereignty, and one also capable of deciding on religious conflicts. Thus instead of assuming a position above the contending parties, Hobbes endorses one side of the argument. He defends the cause of the Crown against the parliamentary opposition, and also the Anglican Church against the Roman Catholics and against the Protestants who are remote from the established church. Thus his theory of the state can only strengthen the forces it would contain and control.

If Hobbes's political philosophy fails to realize its own political intentions, it is not because this follower of Euclid and Galileo subscribes to scientism, the belief in the normative supremacy of mathematics and the mathematical natural sciences; nor because as a consistent materialist he denies the supposed autonomy of the mind; nor again because on these assumptions he underestimates the concretely historical character of law. Scientism, materialism, and an inadequate appreciation of historicity may all merit legitimate criticism. But what merits and rightly receives genuine political criticism is the fact that Hobbes thinks he can only defend the institution of the state by defending a notion of absolute monarchy. His diagnosis of his own time may partly be responsible for this, for it appears to be problematic in various respects.

Thus for Hobbes the causes of the Civil War lie not in the violation of established rights but in the political claims of certain social groups. Against the opinion that "powers were divided between the King, and the Lords, and the House of Commons" (L ch. 18: 93), he defends a position that can be described as reactionary from the perspective of constitutional history. For Hobbes wishes to renew a power of the Crown that is not bound by legal principles or the separation of powers, the kind of monarchy which, strictly speaking, had only prevailed in England *before* the Magna Carta (1215), namely more than four hundred years before.

Hobbes could hardly be surprised that his writings only caused anger and consternation: the House of Commons was so incensed that he felt obliged to flee to Paris to avoid the threat of imminent persecution, and there he remained, from November 1640, for the next eleven years.

2.4. Exile in Paris

In his next work concerned with the theory of the state Hobbes once again confronts what we have called the three great challenges of his time. He now attempts to connect the ideal of a truly exact scientific philosophy with the practical and political interest in securing peace on the basis of universal convictions that will not occasion constant conflict. Thus, during his exile in Paris, he quickly composed *De Cive* (*The Citizen*) in 1642, which was first published in that city and then in a second edition of 1647 printed in Amsterdam, one of the most important sites of publication at this time. Although his natural philosophy (presented in *De Corpore* of 1655, the English version of 1657) and his philosophical anthropology (presented in *De Homine* of 1658) would naturally come first from the systematic philosophical point of view, Hobbes actually began with the third and final part of his projected system, on the theory of the state, on account of the threat of civil war, which in fact immediately came to pass.

The first edition of *De Cive* appeared without the writer's name on the title page. Since Hobbes did not even allow friends such as Mersenne to acknowledge him publicly as the author of the text, some contemporaries actually ascribed the work to Descartes. In today's world, where a certain desire for publicity prevails, Hobbes's extreme caution in this regard may seem difficult to understand. But Hobbes was well aware of the originality and revolutionary character of his doctrines and probably feared that an open confession of authorship would merely earn him the sort of hostility that might once again prove life threatening.

Although *De Cive* only appeared in two editions with a tiny distribution, the book immediately turned Hobbes as a political philosopher into something of a European celebrity once his authorship was generally recognized. In 1649 a French version of the text appeared in Amsterdam, and two years later, in the same year as *Leviathan*, an English translation appeared in London under the title of *The Citizen: Philosophical Rudiments concerning Government and Society*.

In Paris Hobbes renewed his contacts with the circle around Mersenne and devoted himself to further studies in the field of natural science, and especially the field of optics. Like many other philosophers of the seventeenth century, although less gifted in this area than Descartes, Gassendi, and Mersenne or, later on, than Leibniz and Pascal, Hobbes worked on a *Tractatus opticus* (written in 1644 but only published in its entirety in 1963) and composed *A Minute or First Draught of the Optiques* (1646). In various fragmentary texts Hobbes also abandoned the corpuscular or emission theory of light and sound that he had previously defended in favor of a theory which can be traced back to Mersenne's own *Tractatus opticus* of 1644. In opposition to the thesis defended by Descartes in *La Dioptrique* of 1637, Hobbes explains light as a motion of infinitesimally small elements that are released through impulses, so that the previously accepted notion of the "ray" (*radius*) is here replaced by that of "radiation" (*radiatio*).

In 1646 Hobbes accepted the invitation to instruct the Prince of Wales in mathematics. The prince, the next in line to the throne who would later be crowned as Charles II, had also fled to Paris during this period. This is a field where Hobbes (in contrast to his philosophical contemporary Descartes, and later to Leibniz and Pascal) certainly did not show exceptional abilities. As far as more politically sensitive questions were concerned, on the other hand, it seems that Hobbes was not to be trusted.

During his exile in Paris, when he was barely fifty-nine, Hobbes fell so ill that he was even administered the last rites. But he recovered and in fact still had thirty-two years of life before him. In spite of all Mersenne's entreaties he refused to convert to Roman Catholicism. And while he was working on *Leviathan* he took the opportunity to express his views on the art of poetry in *An Answer to Devenant's Preface before Gondibert* (1650). It was in Paris that he completed his *magnum opus*, the work that would finally compel the attention of the learned world throughout Europe and which was published in London in April 1651 under the full title of *Leviathan, or The Matter, Forme, & Power of a Common-Wealth Ecclesiastical and Civill.*

It has been claimed that Hobbes personally presented his royal student, who was already describing himself as Charles II, with a luxuriously bound copy of his new book, although one scholar doubts this story (Martinich 1995, p. 16). But there is no doubt about the fact that Hobbes, the defender of monarchy (cf. L ch. 19), was no longer received at court after October 1651. Thus one contemporary observer reports that all sincere friends of the monarchy were delighted that the king had finally banished this father of atheism from his court (Sir Edward Nicholas in a letter of 8/12/1651 to Sir Edward Hyde, in: Clarendon 1786, vol. III, p. 45; for a good account of the proceedings, see Parkin 2007, p. 103ff.).

Since Hobbes's fundamental ideas had not significantly changed in the meantime, he was able to publish an English version of *De Cive* in the same year as *Leviathan*. But his purposes had changed in some respects with regard to his various texts. In the *Elements* Hobbes was principally concerned with law, and in *De Cive* with the citizen (although the full

English title puts the emphasis on "Government and Society"). But it is really only in *Leviathan* that the state or, as Hobbes calls it, the "commonwealth" (or in Latin the *civitas*, the "community of citizens") becomes the central focus of attention.

THREE

Leviathan and Behemoth

The text of *Leviathan*, Hobbes's masterpiece, exists in two versions. The original English version, published in London, contains numerous historical and also contemporary references and examples, and the style is often somewhat ironic, even sarcastic, in character. But there is also a Latin version, produced by Hobbes himself, which reveals certain differences with regard to the English text. (Latin was still widely employed in the learned world, and Hobbes also presented the three parts of his philosophical system in this form.) The Latin translation of *Leviathan* initially appeared in 1668 within the context of a complete edition of Hobbes's philosophical writings (the *Opera omnia*), and then again two years later as an independent book.

In comparison with the original English edition of his book, Hobbes uses the Latin version to make his observations on the position of the monarch more precise, and probably for two reasons. Thus in order both to secure the favor of the king and to counter the charge of atheism, Hobbes somewhat tones down his attacks on the churches. (For the question of how far the different versions of Hobbes's political theory reflect or respond to specific political conditions and developments of the time, see Metzger 1991 and Sommerville 1992.) In the Latin version of *Leviathan* Hobbes's formulations are often more succinct, the argumentation is more concentrated, and parts III and IV of the text involve significant omissions. It is also true that the style of the Latin version is more dryly erudite in character. Nonetheless, it is from this version that we have the famous and striking expressions "*bellum omnium contra omnes*" ("the war of all against all") and "*sed auctoritas, non veritas, facit legem*" ("authority, not truth, creates the law").

3.1. A Fractured Relationship to Rhetoric

Political iconography likes to regale us with mythical creatures representing superior forces and powers of one kind or another. Yet it has often been asked why a rationally inclined thinker such as Hobbes, profoundly mistrustful of word play and rhetorical exaggeration as he was, should have invoked the name of "Leviathan," the mightiest creature of the Bible, and thereby introduced what may be the most powerful and influential image in the history of political thought, a field already rich in such images, symbols, and allegories.

We may begin to answer this question by considering Hobbes's fractured relationship to the rhetorical tradition. As one of the greatest polemical authors of the seventeenth century, Hobbes avails himself of the whole range of literary means for challenging and belittling his philosophical adversaries, although here he also reveals a certain tendency to self-righteousness and sometimes runs the risk of overreaching himself, as we shall see in the case of his controversy with the mathematician John Wallis. Nor does he always avoid the danger of occasionally launching overly blunt claims or counterclaims where subtle arguments are really required. At any rate, as an extremely well-schooled stylist and Latinist, as a translator of Homer, Euripides, Thucydides, and Aristotle, Hobbes is a true virtuoso in the use of ironical and sarcastic language. Despite this, in all Hobbes's work there is hardly a stronger reproach one may level at an opponent than to castigate him as a "rhetorician," unless it is to call him a "dogmatist" or a "schoolman."

It is necessary to provide a differentiated account of Hobbes's intellectual development in this regard (Skinner 1996 seems one-sided here; see also Johnston 1986). The crucial experience for Hobbes was his discovery of an appropriate method for philosophy. It is true that Hobbes was already interested in mathematics even in his early "pre-geometrical" phase before the encounter with Euclid. But he also applied the fruits of his entire humanistic background and education, including his knowledge of classical rhetoric, to the development of the new science of politics, to "civil science" as he calls it. As we have mentioned, Hobbes even translated Aristotle's *Rhetoric*, and it is true that he exploited contemporary contributions in the field of rhetoric as well.

In a further intermediate phase of his thought—which already emerges in the foreword to his translation of Thucydides, clearly reveals itself in the *Elements*, and culminates in *De Cive*—we observe an increasing number of pointed attacks on rhetoric. Thus Hobbes claims that the nature of rhetoric or "eloquence" is "to make that seem just which is unjust, according as it shall best suit with his end that speaketh: for this is to persuade. And though they reason, yet take they not their rise from true principles, but from vulgar received opinions, which are for the most part erroneous . . . whence it happens that, opinions are delivered not by right reason, but by a certain violence of mind." Hobbes's decisive objection here is that the end of eloquence is "not truth (except by chance), but victory," and its "property is not to inform, but to allure" (C ch. 10, §11, p. 231) This is likely, of course, to remind us of Plato's critique of rhetoric in the dialogue *Gorgias*.

But the methodological breakthrough we have mentioned is more significant for Hobbes's rejection of rhetoric than his engagement with the work of Thucydides. For once Hobbes expressly takes Euclid as his real model he is inevitably driven to repress, if not entirely to abandon, the humanistic form of thought that was so strongly marked by the rhetorical tradition. In fact, Hobbes emphatically displays his contempt for rhetoric, without thereby actually renouncing rhetorical elements such as metaphors. And then, finally, in a third phase of his development we see Hobbes moderating this explicit contempt for rhetoric. In this regard one could therefore describe Hobbes's intellectual biography, in a simplified way and with the emphasis upon his conception of method, in a threefold dialectical fashion: the thesis would consist in the effective praise of rhetoric, the antithesis in the explicitly expressed contempt for rhetoric, and the synthesis in a renewed but still fractured and conflicted recognition of rhetoric.

In the first youthful phase Hobbes enthusiastically displays his humanistic learning, including his familiarity with the rhetorical tradition. As soon as he subscribes to the geometrical method, in the second phase, he despises and condemns this humanistic and rhetorical culture, and this implicitly includes his own earlier intellectual development. After he has fully appropriated the new "geometrical" mode of thought he is

able, in the third phase, to make renewed use of his humanistic knowledge and his rhetorical gifts. But these can no longer furnish the methodical core of his thought as they had in the first phase. They thus come to
acquire a subsidiary, but by no means inconsiderable, meaning in his
work. Neither the title *Leviathan*, nor the engraving on the title page, nor
again the metaphors of the machine or the state as an artificial man are
insignificant. But this significance finds no recognition in Hobbes's own
"theory" of rhetoric as it is developed in *Leviathan* itself.

It is true that Hobbes finds a place for rhetoric in his schema of the
philosophical sciences, as he also does for poetics (L ch. 9: 40). But since
he hardly ascribes any philosophical significance to the latter, though
he sees it as a legitimate object of reflection, his schema of the sciences
may simply confirm that while rhetoric is also a potential theme for
philosophical investigation, it cannot be regarded as a valuable form of
argumentation.

Nonetheless, as far as the presentation of Hobbes's argument in *Leviathan* and subsequent works is concerned, rhetoric effectively undergoes
an impressive rehabilitation. In order to convince his readers, Hobbes
deploys a copious array of images, symbols, and figures of argumentation
(*topoi*), and uses all the eloquent language at his disposal to make his
case, often furnishing powerful aphoristic formulations of his thought in
the process. But his explicit evaluation of rhetoric has not really changed
or improved in the meantime. He complains about the "inconstancy"
or vacillating meaning of the metaphors and pictorial images so beloved
of rhetoric (L ch. 4: 17). He certainly concedes: "Eloquence is power;
because it is seeming prudence" (L ch. 10: 41), and this is why "eloquent speakers are inclined to ambition" (L ch. 11: 49). But "simili-
tudes, metaphors, examples and other tools of oratory" are directed not
toward insight but rather to human passions (L ch. 25: 132). Hobbes
thus directly contrasts solid human reason with the specious and misleading culture of the humanists. And mindful of his own rhetorical talents
Hobbes expressly says: "There is nothing I distrust more than my elocution [i.e., eloquence]" (L: 394). The only time Hobbes suggests anything
positive about rhetoric is in the context of his philosophy of language.
Thus when he describes four "special uses of speech," he tells us that the
last of these is "to please and delight ourselves, and others, by playing
with our words, for pleasure or ornament, innocently" (L ch. 4: 13; see
also his *Answer to Davenant's Preface before Gondibert*, and our discussion
in chapter 6.4, below).

Hobbes's relationship to rhetoric remains a fractured one. From the *Elements* onward his central concern was to secure political peace by philosophical means, i.e., through a science that is "free from controversies and dispute" (E, the epistle dedicatory, p. 19). Philosophy, the path required to secure this end, must obviously be free from such controversy. This demands a form of argumentation that will be able to eliminate the "civil war" at the meta-level, namely the intellectual conflict that rages between different philosophical parties. This is why Hobbes repudiates rhetoric so emphatically. He does not indeed banish it entirely, but its only value lies outside the philosophical argument itself, in the dedicatory epistle to *De Cive* for example. Thus he can compare the various disciplines of philosophy with the different seas, which "notwithstanding all together make up *the ocean*" (C, p. 91). In *The Elements of Law,* rhetoric is comparatively rather than absolutely repudiated, for Hobbes says that "whilst I was writing I consulted more with logic, than with rhetoric" (E, p. 19). Again, in a chapter discussing political power, Hobbes distinguishes between two kinds of eloquence—between the "elegant and clear expression" of thought that is aimed at truth and the "commotion of the passions," which seeks only victory and is called "rhetoric" (C, ch. 12, §12, p. 253).

It is not without justification that Hobbes sees mathematics as an exemplary and unsurpassable form of argumentation capable of securing unanimous agreement, for mathematics "consisteth in comparing figures and motion only" (E, the epistle dedicatory, p. 19). There is little place for rhetoric here. And since it can only corrupt mathematics, an uncompromising contempt for rhetoric is demanded as far as the theory of argumentation is concerned. But Hobbes is not pursuing mathematics here, but rather a philosophy of the state, and indeed with a directly practical and political intention, for "it would be an incomparable benefit to commonwealth, that every man held the opinions concerning law and policy here delivered" (ibid., p. 20). From the beginning, therefore, Hobbes is pursuing an end for which rhetoric proves indispensable even after his crucial discovery of mathematical method. For the task is one of "persuading," of convincing and winning people over (even if by appeal to arguments).

Given the persisting significance of rhetoric it is clear that in the final mature period of his thought Hobbes himself continues to practice what he expressly rules out in the field of mathematics and natural science. But this practice is not itself reflected in his "theory" of rhetoric, and nowhere does Hobbes explicitly offer the more differentiated account that one might expect. Only at the very end of *Leviathan*, in "A Review and Conclusion," does he concede that "reason and eloquence, (though not perhaps in the natural sciences, yet in the moral) may stand very well together" (L: 389–90). And apart from this observation, we may say that Hobbes's practice of rhetoric is wiser than his theory of it.

3.2. The Symbol of Leviathan

A closer examination of the image of the "Leviathan" may be more useful than a discussion of Hobbes's general relationship to rhetoric. The point of this examination is not to suggest, for example, that Hobbes merely wished to provide additional support for his rational philosophy of the state by recourse to biblical mythology. For the figure of Leviathan is not intended to enhance the argument, but to furnish a vivid illustration, and in the famous frontispiece even a striking pictorial image. Although we cannot speak of a "visual turn" or an "iconic turn" as so many do today, Hobbes recognizes that the role of visualization is by no means incidental. True to his general demand that science prove useful, from the mid-1640s Hobbes pursued his studies of optics, among other things, with a view to finding genuinely visual and convincing means of presentation over and beyond the usual linguistic means.

According to Carl Schmitt (1938, p. 8), a highly influential interpreter of Hobbes, his invocation of Leviathan created a mythical symbol of "inexhaustible significance" that effectively shatters "the framework of every solely conceptual theory or construction." One can only agree with the first part of the claim here, regarding the "inexhaustible significance" or suggestiveness of Hobbes's image, but we should be more skeptical about this reference to a "solely conceptual theory or construction." For we can certainly verbalize and thus appropriate the conceptual content expressed by the image. As Hobbes himself rightly points out, "of all metaphors there is some real ground, that may be expressed in proper words" (L ch. 38: 243).

The Leviathan that furnishes the title of Hobbes's masterpiece derives from the name of the biblical sea monster in the Book of Job, a creature interpreted sometimes as an enormous serpent, sometimes as a gigantic crocodile, and occasionally simply as a great whale. Perhaps this may ultimately be traced back to a Babylonian-Assyrian myth that recounts the struggle between the light god Marduk and his enemy Tiamat, an archaic personification of the ocean, or perhaps a great snake or dragon (Schmökel 1985², p. 107).

Hobbes himself refers simply to the Book of Job, the protagonist of which is an exemplary Jew, at once upright and God-fearing. In the King James Bible (41:33) we read of the great Leviathan that "Upon earth there is not his like, who is made without fear." In the next verse Leviathan is described as a "king over all the children of pride." The message here is unmistakable. For Hobbes the figure of Leviathan symbolizes the insuperable power that is embodied in the state and represented in the person of the sovereign as monarch.

It is rather remarkable that the name of Leviathan, which furnishes the title of the book, actually occurs only three times in the entire text. According to the introduction, Leviathan is "an artificial man; though of greater stature and strength than the natural" (L: 1). Here we have three images combined in one: the biblical Leviathan is fused with the technomorphic image of the machine, of something artificially constructed or fabricated, and with Plato's image of the magnified object of inquiry. For according to a famous passage in the *Republic* (book II, 368d), while justice in the individual and justice in the state are analogous with one another, its nature is easier to read when it is "writ large" in terms of the *polis* (Höffe 2005²). The first dimension of Hobbes's image is the most important. The artificial and machinelike character of the image certainly captures the functional apparatus of power in a state, and Plato's image of justice in "larger letters" aptly reveals the existential relevance of the state for every individual. But it is only the biblical image of Leviathan that captures the ambivalent character of the state: thanks to its preponderant power it is a kind of monster which at once overcomes the ever-present threat of civil war and incorporates all citizens within itself. Hobbes does not draw the appropriate conclusion from this ambivalence: that the state should not remain a monster that is simply to be feared, but recognized as something that must also be tamed.

Yet according to the second passage in which the figure of Leviathan is named (ch. 17: 87), such taming appears superfluous anyway. For the contract that each individual concludes with every other individual gives rise to that representative person who unites the contracting parties into a unified person or body, into the state. In order "to speak more reverently," Hobbes describes the Leviathan, this new and artificial person, as "that Mortal God" to which we owe our peace and defense under "the Immortal God" (this being the only sense in which Hobbes recognizes something like a taming of the state).

The element of divinity in this mortal God stands for that obedience to the laws that the political sovereign demands of his subjects. This divinity must be recognized as mortal in two respects: sovereignty is transient and subject to time; and, above all, it promulgates purely positive laws that are subject to the higher authority of the immortal God, before whom the positive laws must answer to the normative standards, which are natural laws. Thus Hobbes's state is also bound or obligated in a way, although this obligation only holds in an extra-political, indeed extra-institutional sense, solely in the conscience that is responsible to God. In terms of earthly criteria the state remains an authority without equal (L ch. 28: 166–67). Yet although, as a kind of God, Leviathan appears as something sacred, it is still weaker than the true God. Thus political or "civil" power has a Lord and Master beyond itself, though not here on earth.

In this third passage Hobbes expressly cites the Book of Job and its description of the Leviathan as "king of all the children of pride" (L ch. 28: 167). In the context of Hobbes's philosophy of the state, this implies that the problem the sovereign is required to solve is not simply the contemporary one, for example, of curbing the arrogance and vanity of the nobility and the leading clerics. Rather, the sovereign is confronted with the universal human task of containing the implicitly unlimited and unrestricted freedom of every individual human being. To fulfill this task the sovereign must become the highest, strongest, and therefore also wholly undivided power.

For Carl Schmitt (1938, p. 124), Hobbes is a sorcerer captivated by his own art and by his image of Leviathan. On this reading, the figure that furnishes the title of Hobbes's book is very well chosen. The philosopher desires to show his contemporaries, well versed in the Bible as they were, that there is a single power that is indeed superior to all human beings, but superior only to them, since the greater power of God stands over it in turn. There is certainly no denying that the figure of Hobbes's title has contributed to the lasting impact of his book, and has even, independently of the work itself, established itself as a telling symbol of all threatening state power.

However, the biblical image of the monster Leviathan is not well suited to capture a distinctive characteristic of the commonwealth, namely that the state is a body that embraces all the citizens within itself. And it is here that the engraving on the title page comes into play, at once the most famous and most notorious pictorial image that has ever introduced a philosophical work, even though we do not know for certain the name of the artist who designed it (for the interpretation of this image, see Brandt 1928, Bredekamp 1999, and Burger 2005).

Along the top edge of the engraving we read a quotation from Job 41:24, "*Non est potestas Super Terram quae Comparetur ei*" ("There is no power upon earth that is comparable to him"). In the King James Bible, where this is numbered verse 33, the English translation reads: "Upon earth there is not his like." The Latin formulation effectively alludes to the core doctrine of Hobbes's theory of the state as a sovereign power, which, within this world, has nothing standing above it.

But of course, far more than the line from Job, what immediately captures our attention is the image to which the quotation here refers. The engraving is not dominated by a Leviathan in the sense of some monstrous sea creature. Rather than the image of an enormous serpent, dragon, crocodile, or whale, the upper half of the picture shows a gigantic human figure rising up behind a town and some mountains with a castle and a few villages. The figure is an image of the state that Hobbes describes, as we have seen, as a great, artificial man. If we look closely, we can see that the body of this giant is composed of myriad tiny human figures—more than three hundred for the most part precisely delineated figures with their backs turned—although they do not look as if they have anxiously congregated in any servile or fearful manner. Thus the giant figure symbolizes two things: on the one hand, that the citizens are perfectly incorporated into the all-powerful state, and on the other hand, that the state or sovereign is indeed the representative of all the citizens, but also leaves them to themselves, albeit only within the limits prescribed by the state.

But if we simply confine our attention to one half of the picture, and largely ignore the other lower half, we are liable to produce a distorted interpretation that sees only the power that is superior to every individual, but not the power that is itself subject to God. And in the giant we may see only human beings who lose their individuality and are swallowed up in the state, that is, citizens absorbed in an omnipotent state and who have forfeited their freedom to this all-consuming political power. We no longer perceive the individuals who are united into a community or commonwealth and live together in a peaceful landscape.

Regarded as a whole, the engraving on Hobbes's title page represents a carefully articulated balance between the ruler, the state, and the subjects. The ruler wears a crown, which reveals his role as worldly sovereign. And the features of his face are not perhaps unlike those of Hobbes himself. We might see this as a variant of Plato's famous remark about philosophers and kings: the philosopher as such is not supposed to rule, but may yet lend his intellectual features to the ruler in the shape of a developed philosophy of the state. In one prominent passage in *Leviathan*, in the last paragraph of the last chapter of the second part, which is dedicated specifically to the philosophy of the state ("Of Commonwealth"), Hobbes does allude to Plato's "opinion that it is impossible for the disorders of the state, and change of governments by civil war, ever to be taken away, till sovereigns be philosophers," and concludes with the hope "that one time or other, this writing of mine, may fall into the hands of a sovereign, who will consider it himself" and "by the exercise of entire sovereignty, in protecting the public teaching of it, convert this truth of speculation, into the utility of practice" (L ch. 31: 193). But Hobbes was perhaps less immodest in this regard, for the features of the sovereign in the engraving are also said by some to have been modeled on a portrait of King Charles II.

It is not merely that the gigantic figure wears the royal crown upon his head. The engraving also shows him holding two other symbols of dominion: in his right hand the sword, which symbolizes the power that decides over life and death, and in his left hand the bishop's staff, which reveals the authority of the sovereign where religious doctrines are concerned. Since a certain priority is traditionally ascribed to the right hand, this pictorial representation of the two symbols of dominion also has a specific meaning. The fact that the figure bears the sword in his right hand and the bishop's staff in his left hand expresses the priority of his worldly decisions in relation to his spiritual ones.

Many reproductions of the engraving show only the upper half of the whole image. But the neglected lower half is certainly not without significance. Five sections on each side give concrete visual expression to the exercise of power and authority in different fields. Thus directly beneath the "worldly" right hand of the sovereign we see a castle, a crown, a cannon, then a variety of firearms, spears, drums, and banners, and finally, right at the bottom, a battle. The sovereign is thus seen to triumph over the civil war represented by the various weapons below. What we see directly beneath the "spiritual" left arm of the sovereign are not symbols of religious piety, ritual, or spirituality, nor indeed of divine revelation or of some higher world beyond, but merely the insignia of earthly power. They show institutions, arrangements, and intellectual procedures that symbolize the worldly dimension of the spiritual life: a church, a miter, an image of anathema, subtle (scholastic) distinctions represented by a variety of sharp-pointed instruments, and an ecclesiastical council. Thus the sovereign also prevails over the civil war that is waged by spiritual and ecclesiastical weapons in their worldly and political form. While it is true that the ruler does not decide the matter of religious truth itself, he does decide upon the binding public interpretation of that truth.

The fact that the engraving of Hobbes's title page clearly abstracts from any genuinely religious context or background bespeaks a major step in the process of secularization. Close consideration of the engraving itself should already lead us to question A. E. Taylor's claim with regard to Hobbes's legitimation of the state that a "certain kind of theism is absolutely necessary to make the theory work" (Taylor 1938, p. 420). If Taylor's thesis were correct, this would effectively destroy the basic foundations of Hobbes's theory of the state. The axiomatic claims developed in the opening chapters of *Leviathan*, the theses regarding the nature of the human mind (from sensation and imagination through to language, reason, and science), would then simply distract from the ultimate theistic basis of his thought, and perhaps even consciously or unconsciously disguise it.

Given the fundamental constitutional and religious conflicts of the time, the decisive question for Hobbes is actually this: *Quis interpretabitur, quis iudicabit?* (Who shall interpret, who shall decide?). And he answers this question with uncompromising bluntness: the power to interpret and decide lies solely and utterly with the sovereign. Standing even above the laws he has promulgated, he is an "absolute" ruler in the radical sense of the word (as *legibus solutus*: absolved from the laws). Hobbes does not even consider a possible alternative to this twofold exercise of power, namely the modern state, which is neutral with regard to such religious and philosophical issues and represents the fulfillment of the process of secularization.

Any interpretation of the engraving must remain incomplete if it fails to acknowledge the peaceful landscape with its towns and villages, which the figure of Leviathan effectively embraces within his outstretched arms. This aspect points to the principal task of the sovereign's twofold power, for the giant man who is composed of all the smaller ordinary human beings serves the welfare and benefit of those smaller human beings, the chief benefit of which is the maintenance of peace.

But there are two aspects that are not represented in the visual image. While the sovereign is indeed represented as a gigantic person, he is also depicted in a very human rather than monstrous fashion. He is certainly not such a figure that "terror leaps before him," as Luther put it in his rendering of Job 41:14. But on account of the attentive yet relaxed countenance, and the calm posture, of the figure itself we do not see that sovereignty, the very authority meant to banish the dangerous proclivities of human beings, is itself dangerous. But Hobbes was surely aware of this difficulty, which is why he unfolds the biblical quotation from Job right above the head of the central figure. For a power that can be compared to no other is undoubtedly dangerous. The other aspect, which is an important dimension of the message of the symbol of Leviathan, is not visually represented in the engraving either. It is suggested only in the verse from Scripture: the sovereign is superior only to all earthly power, not to all power, for the more than earthly power of God still stands above him.

And there is yet another aspect that is completely absent from the image, namely the creator of this Leviathan. For the giant man who is composed of all the smaller human beings is himself created by human hands. And the constituent parts of this creation are not so many things that are simply taken up and used without more ado, as the metaphorical image of the machine in Hobbes's introduction (L: 1) rather suggests. Rather, they are elements, namely human beings, which come together of themselves, and they ultimately do so freely, through a contract, and thus by free consent.

A careful examination of Hobbes's engraving shows therefore that the evocative figure of Leviathan is entirely appropriate to his book. Nonetheless, almost as soon as the work was published, and indeed right up until this day, the image has provoked such misunderstanding that the author himself could be cast as "the monster of Malmesbury." Part of the reason for this may lie with the fact that in the medieval and early modern period, "Leviathan" was still understood as a name of the Devil, and thus as the "Prince of the World" in the negative sense of the one who is not subject to God, as the Antichrist (Imschodt/Hornung, p. 1250). But what is principally responsible for such misunderstanding is a partial and selective reading of Hobbes's two images, that of the biblical Leviathan itself and the celebrated engraving on the title page, something that also often recurs elsewhere, in interpretations of the state of nature, for example (L ch. 13).

3.3. The Return to England

Such partial and reductive interpretations of Hobbes's thought already began to emerge during the period of his exile in Paris. In Catholic France, *Leviathan* was read specifically as a rejection of the political claims of the Catholic Church, which is why the French clergy actively encouraged the judicial prosecution of Hobbes at this time. In order to avoid this danger, but perhaps also from a yearning to return to his home country after more than a decade in exile, in the winter of 1651–52 the now sixty-three-year-old Hobbes undertook the arduous journey back to an England that had been ravaged by civil war. In order to live undisturbed in London he accepted the authority of the Puritan Oliver Cromwell, the supreme commander of the forces of the commonwealth, who for his part clearly recognized Hobbes's intellectual stature. So the philosopher could now write: "Then home I came, not sure of safety there, / Though I cou'd not be safer anywhere. / Th' Wind, Frost, Snow sharp, with Age grown gray, / A punging Beast, and most unpleasant way" (*Opera omnia*, vol. I, p. 93; see also E, p. 260). Following the execution of King Charles I in 1649 a form of republic was established in Hobbes's homeland, though this was effectively a military dictatorship under the control of Cromwell, who became lord protector in 1653, although he rejected an offer of the crown in 1657.

Soon after Hobbes's return to England his close contemporary Robert Filmer (1588–1653) published a work under the title *Observations concerning the Original of Government upon Mr Hobbes's Leviathan* (1652). Filmer, an influential Royalist of the period, expressed reservations about the details of Hobbes's thought but welcomed his discussion regarding "the rights of sovereignty, which no man that I know, hath so amply and judiciously handled" (Filmer 1999, p. 184). But in the very next year Hobbes was openly attacked by Henri More in *An Antidote against Atheism* and by Alexander Ross in *Leviathan drawn out with a hook*. And the year after that Hobbes's *De Cive* was placed by the Vatican on the Index of Forbidden Books, a ban that was subsequently extended to the Latin edition of Hobbes writings, the *Opera omnia* published in Amsterdam in 1668. (For more on the reception of Hobbes's work in his own lifetime, see chapter 14.)

Hobbes himself proceeded to publish the two remaining parts of his *Elementa Philosophiae*: *De Corpore* (*Of Body*), dealing principally with natural philosophy, in 1655, followed three years later by *De Homine* (*Of Man*). Ensconced as a permanent guest of the Cavendish family, Hobbes also found time to pursue the numerous disputes and controversies in which he was now embroiled.

Thus he conducted a rather acrimonious theological polemic with Archbishop Bramhall regarding the concept of freedom. In response to the latter's text *A Defence of True Liberty* of 1655, Hobbes published *The Questions concerning Liberty, Necessity and Chance clearly stated and debated between Dr. Bramhall, Bishop of Derry, and Th. Hobbes of Malmesbury* in 1656. Bramhall responded in turn with his *Castigations of Mr. Hobbes*, containing an appendix entitled "The Catching of Leviathan," a phrase that would soon prove influential. Hobbes continued the polemic with his customary vigor, accusing the author of willful misunderstanding, in *An Answer to Bishop Brahmhalls Book, called: The Catching of the Leviathan*, written in 1668 but only published posthumously in 1682.

When the monarchy was restored in 1660 under King Charles II, Hobbes succeeded for a while in reestablishing the cordial relations he had formerly enjoyed with the heir to the throne during his Paris exile. He was able to frequent the court and was awarded an annual pension of one hundred pounds (worth several thousand pounds in today's currency), even if there were occasions when the payment did not always materialize. But in the course of the years Hobbes had become so comfortable, financially speaking, that he could afford to live very well without his pension and was in a position to reward his friends and relatives with generous gifts of one kind or another.

By this stage Hobbes was reluctant to become directly involved in political matters, but he continued to pursue his interests in natural science and was even prepared to challenge the views of the important chemist and physicist Robert Boyle (1627–1691), publishing his own *Dialogus Physicus Sive De Natura Aeris* (*On the Nature of Air*) in 1661. Boyle, one of the founding members of the Royal Society, which had been established the year before, responded with *An Examen of Mr. Hobbes his Dialogus Physicus* in 1662. In that year Hobbes published his *Problemata Physica*, dedicated to King Charles II, along with a brief defense of his *Leviathan*. And even in the year before his death he published in London his *Decameron Physiologicum, or Ten Dialogues of Natural Philosophy* (1678).

Hobbes also ventured to prove himself in the field of mathematics, although he must probably be said to have lost his way in this area. His claims provoked the mathematician, logician, and Presbyterian theologian

John Wallis (1616–1703), an important precursor of Newton, to compose his *Elenchus Geometriae Hobbianae* (*A Refutation of Hobbes's Geometry*) in 1655. Hobbes responded in the following year with *Six Lessons to the Professors of Mathematics*. This controversy with Wallis also provides the context for another text that appeared in 1662 under the title *Considerations upon the Reputation, Loyalty, and Manners of Thomas Hobbes of Malmesbury*.

Thus we find Hobbes expending much time and effort attempting to square the circle (*Quadratura Circuli, Breviter Demonstrata*, 1669) and transform spheres into cubes of identical volume (Opera vol. IV, p. 485). In 1671 he published his *Rosetum Geometricum* (*Rose Garden of Geometry*) and *Three Papers Presented to the Royal Society against Dr. Wallis*, and in the following year his *Lux Mathematica* (*The Light of Mathematics*). And in 1674, in a remarkable overestimation of his own mathematical contributions, he also published *Principia et Problemata Aliquot Geometrica*. Even if we merely wished to convict Hobbes of clinging to an obsolete conception of geometry, it has to be admitted that in comparison with Descartes, Leibniz, or Pascal, he was in fact a poor mathematician who can only really be classed as a "curiosity" as far as the history of mathematics is concerned.

Hobbes was far more successful in these years when he turned his attention to questions concerning English law, in *A Dialogue between a Philosopher and a Student of the Common Law of England* (composed around 1670 and published posthumously in 1681), or to the subject of ecclesiastical history, in *An Historical Narration concerning Heresy and the Punishment Thereof* (again published posthumously in 1681).

Although Hobbes himself was certainly very well versed in humanistic learning, he believed that the thorough study of Greek and Latin, one of the central concerns of the Western educational tradition, was something "dearly bought." For it is from Aristotle and Cicero, and many other Greek and Roman authors, Hobbes thinks, that we have inherited a false conception of liberty along with an unjustified hatred of monarchy (cf. L ch. 21: 110–11; ch. 29: 170f.). This evaluation, however, did not prevent him in his final years from translating the two Homeric epics into rhyming iambic verse, the *Iliad* in 1675 and the *Odyssey* in 1676.

More important than these contributions is *Behemoth, or the Long Parliament*, Hobbes's history of the English Civil War, where he attempts to identify the ultimate causes behind the conflict. This work reveals Hobbes as a significant contemporary historian of seventeenth-century

England. Behemoth is the name of the second monster that appears in the Bible, a huge terrestrial creature that serves Hobbes as a symbol of the anarchy unleashed by the Civil War. As for the sea monster Leviathan, it is clear from the engraving and the relevant biblical allusion how it symbolizes a mighty and unconquerable power that is subject only to God. But why the terrestrial monster Behemoth should stand for anarchy is not entirely clear to this day. Perhaps it is intended to symbolize not so much anarchy itself as the Long Parliament, which, like the biblical Behemoth in comparison to the biblical Leviathan, is weaker than all genuine sovereignty (see Watkins 1973[2], p. 2).

Hobbes composed *Behemoth* because he believed that nothing was more instructive as far as loyalty and justice are concerned than the vivid memory of a protracted period of civil war. Like Thucydides' *History of the Peloponnesian War*, Hobbes's *Behemoth* is a work that would be described in the German philosophical tradition as an exercise in "reflective history." It was completed in 1668, but since permission for publication was withheld, it appeared a decade later, in 1679, just before Hobbes's death. And even then it appeared only in a non-authorized edition, effectively a pirated edition, under the title *Behemoth or an Epitome of the Civil Wars of England from 1640 to 1660.*

From 1665 onward, according to his biographer John Aubrey, Hobbes suffered from "the shaking palsy" (E, p. 241). But intellectually he remained as vigorous, disputatious, and unyielding in his views as ever. He basically identified seven groups as responsible for the Civil War. He begins by enumerating three religious groups: the Presbyterians, the Roman Catholics, and the independents such as Anabaptists and Quakers, etc. In the fourth place, he mentions the scholars and educated people who have been seduced by the erroneous conceptions of freedom propounded by leading Greek and Roman writers. Then he mentions the city of London and other great commercial centers, which sought to emulate the flourishing economic life of the Low Countries. He also alludes to some who even wished for war. And finally, he blames the fact that "the people in general were so ignorant of their duty, as that not one perhaps of ten thousand knew what right any man had to command him" (B: Works vol. 3, p. 168).

In 1679, the same year as *Behemoth*, there also appeared, again in a pirated edition, the autobiography Hobbes had composed in Latin verse about seven years before under the title *Vita carmine expressa.* This text raises a number of questions that have still not been entirely resolved in the modern scholarship on Hobbes, questions pertaining to his actual and precise attitude to religion, to antiquity, and to the world of traditional humanistic learning.

Shortly after the completion of the *Vita*, Hobbes died at the age of ninety-one on December 4, 1679, in Hardwick Hall, which belonged to the Cavendish family. Earlier, when he fell very ill in Paris in 1647 and already believed himself on his deathbed, he "declared that he liked the religion of the Church of England best of all other" (E, p. 242). Whatever the truth of this, he was buried in the nearby parish church of Hault Hucknell in accordance with the Anglican rite. His legacy amounted to a thousand pounds sterling, equivalent to ten years of the pension that King Charles II had awarded him, and a very considerable sum of money in contemporary terms.

In spite of his capacity for making enemies, Hobbes also had numerous friends to lament his passing. In the eyes of public opinion, however, he departed this world as a famous defender of absolutism, as a critic of the political pretensions of the Church, and above all as a monstrous advocate of materialism, hedonism, and unbelief.

II

THE ENCYCLOPEDIC
CHARACTER OF HOBBES'S
PHILOSOPHY

In the history of philosophy Hobbes has been principally regarded as a philosopher of law and a political theorist, and also as a moral philosopher who endorsed a naturalistic and hedonistic perspective. If he has also been recognized as something more, then at best it is as a historian of the English Civil War. Yet in fact Hobbes actively engaged with almost all the leading issues and controversies of his time. Even if we discount his not particularly significant contributions to natural science and his rather unfortunate forays into the field of mathematics, we are still confronted with an encyclopedic body of work that also extends to reflections on the art of poetry. It is only music, painting, and the plastic arts that fail to find an appropriate place within this edifice of thought.

The ultimate purpose of Hobbes's encyclopedic philosophy is to serve the cause of peace, and it is to this end that the fundamental appeal to science is made. After presenting his complex conception of scientific knowledge itself (chapter 4), we examine the basic elements of what can be described as his "science of freedom," beginning with his natural philosophy and theory of knowledge, and proceeding to his theory of language, reason, and science (chapters 5–6). Then we investigate his doctrine of the passions, of the state of nature, of absolute sovereignty, and the foundation of the state (chapters 7–9). After discussing his theory of law (chapter 10) and his doctrine regarding religion and the church (chapter 11), we examine his critique of Aristotle (chapter 12) and conclude with an account of his historical writings (chapter 13).

FOUR

Science in the Service of Peace

Although Hobbes wishes to present his argument in strictly scientific terms, he does not regard this scientific character of his work as an end in itself. The idea of knowing simply for its own sake—the ideal of a truly theoretical science and of philosophy—is quite alien to him. He certainly thinks that a genuinely theoretical interest, i.e., a desire to understand the causes of all things, is part of human nature. And on account of this natural desire for knowledge he claims that science is as important to the mind as "food is to the body." But while the body can be "satiated with food," the mind can never be "filled up by knowledge." The human desire for knowledge is thus recognized as limitless. But Hobbes goes on to introduce the idea of "practical sciences," which are expected to be useful to us (H ch. 11, §9, p. 50). He rephrases Bacon's motto "knowledge is power" ("*tantum possumus quantus sciemus*"; SHE VII, 241) as "knowledge for the sake of power" ("*scientia propter potentium*"; Co ch. 1, §6), and argues that "*reason* is the *pace*; increase of *science* the *way*; and the benefit of mankind, the *end*" (L ch. 6: 22). And when it comes to the theory of the state, philosophy even comes to acquire an existential significance, for this bears directly on the life of every individual (see C, the preface to the reader), and this latter can only be secured under conditions of peace.

Nonetheless, the scientific character of knowledge is not a matter of merely secondary importance for Hobbes. It is essential to his overall purpose, for it is only this character of knowledge that helps us to avoid stoking conflict in the realm of human convictions. Indeed, a strictly scientific approach can only promote the condition of peace, if only in the first instance an epistemic peace within the field of knowledge itself. For this reason, the governing methodological goal—namely to secure the strictly scientific character of knowledge—intrinsically belongs to the substantive goal, which is peace itself.

4.1. The Principal Aim of Hobbes's Philosophy

We can identify four normative principles that have played a fundamental role in the history of political philosophy from its very beginnings. They are principles that partly overlap and partly supplement one another, and can rarely be said to compete with each other. They involve (1) the general good or the public interest; (2) happiness in the sense of a good and fulfilled life; (3) the idea of justice; and (4) the idea of peace, and the accompanying warning against civil war.

We encounter all four of these principles in Hobbes's work. In the epistle dedicatory that introduces *The Elements of Law,* Hobbes speaks of an "incomparable benefit to commonwealth" (E, p. 20), which clearly involves the first principle. He also mentions justice, specifically the political justice that concerns the nature of the state, rather than justice in the personal sense. The dedication accompanying *De Cive* alludes to three of the principles. On a cursory examination of *Leviathan,* his most mature work, it may look as though he is only concerned with the last of the four principles, but in fact the other three are also recognized, albeit in a strongly relativized form. The principles are no longer presented in a sequential and unstructured fashion, and thus as if they were somehow all equally justified in their own right. The idea of peace has clearly become the dominant theme.

Either implicitly or explicitly, the first principle, regarding the common good, has now been defined more precisely in terms of peace. For Hobbes refers to the state in Latin as "*civitas,*" and in English as "commonwealth," that is to say, the common weal or good. This now provides the context within which each individual, secure against the threat of violent death, can pursue his own happiness. And finally, according to *Leviathan,* it is only in the condition of peace secured by the state, rather than in the state of nature, that "the notions of right and wrong, justice and injustice" have their place (L ch. 13: 63).

The full significance of the idea of peace in *Leviathan* extends to the heart of the matter and is not confined to a few particular formulas. Here too, Hobbes does not change his original approach to the basic political questions, and certainly introduces no essential qualifications in this regard, but he does achieve much greater clarity. Already in *The Elements of Law* (part I, ch. 14, §§11–14), the fundamental opposition in question is that between war and peace, since human beings find themselves by nature in a "state of war," whereas "reason dictateth peace." *De Cive* endorses the rational demand that we should seek the establishment of peace (C ch. 1, §15), and Hobbes emphasizes this all-important task in the preface to this text when he says he would "show us the highway to peace" (C, p. 98).

The old formula *opus justitiae pax* assures us that peace arises from justice. Where just social relations prevail, we can already see *eo ipso* that a form of peace prevails too. At first sight it looks as though Hobbes contradicts this traditional claim in the most direct possible way, but on closer examination we see that his critical position is more differentiated. For the "laws of nature" that he defends (L, chs. 14–15) are what we would today describe as principles of justice. But the purely individual interpretation of these laws actually creates the conflict that threatens the basic interest that human beings share. The highest evil that confronts us is that of violent death, while the highest good consists in permission to live as much as possible as individuals themselves see fit. Hence we require a position of authority that can interpret the principles of justice in a binding and authoritative fashion. And it is this position of authority—the sovereignty of the state—that establishes the peace that hinders the highest evil, while making the highest good itself possible. It is thus no accident that Hobbes's second law of nature, which is fundamental to the concept of justice, essentially reappears in two of the most significant modern theorists of justice, in Kant as the moral concept of right (*The Doctrine of Right*, § B) and in Rawls as the first principle of justice (*A Theory of Justice*, § 11).

4.2. The Complex Method

It is important not to oversimplify the method that Hobbes adopts in the cause of peace. The mathematical paradigm that Hobbes constantly evokes, along with the notion of reason as a form of calculation, is indispensible to his argument, but it is not decisive in every respect. The extension of this paradigm by appeal to causal-mechanistic explanation, namely the combination of mathematics and mechanics, is not sufficient on its own. In fact at least three specific methodical elements or partial methods play a role throughout his work. And these in turn are supplemented by two further partial methods. In the dedications, prefaces, and introductions that accompany the three political works we can identify the first three partial methods: (1) mathematics (in the first place geometry and later arithmetic too) represents the methodical paradigm; (2) the combination of mathematics and mechanics leads to the metaphor of the state as an "artificial" human being, which is comparable to a machine constructed out of natural human beings; (3) the resoluto-compositive method defines and clarifies the nature of this construction: the artificial human being is decomposed into its smallest constituent parts and then recomposed, i.e., constructed, out of these parts.

With the first part of the resoluto-compositive method (the recourse to absolutely first principles or elements), Hobbes undertakes to provide an ultimate grounding or foundation for all genuine knowledge. A "first philosophy" or "fundamental philosophy" of this kind is precisely what has been known since antiquity as "metaphysics." It is quite true that Hobbes dismisses Aristotelian metaphysics as a senseless enterprise, as "vain philosophy" (L ch. 46: 367), but his own philosophical project, albeit *à contra coeur*, still retains a certain metaphysical character. Hobbes's strictly naturalistic approach does of course repudiate any notion of supernatural objects or realities. Not only in the general formulation of his philosophical program but throughout the actual execution of the project, he avoids appealing to anything beyond nature or our investigation of nature (*meta ta phusika*). But that dimension of metaphysics, which we have described as "fundamental philosophy," is clearly preserved, so that we could perhaps speak of a "non-metaphysical metaphysics" here. Hobbes's philosophy is metaphysical in the sense that it argues for and claims to provide an "ultimate foundation," but with regard to the objects it investigates and the theoretical explanations it offers, this philosophy is radically non-metaphysical. Hobbes represents a special case insofar as he defends a form of thought which is metaphysical with regard its starting point, which relies on absolutely basic elements and principles, and in a sense with regard to the formal object of its inquiry, but is decidedly non-metaphysical or anti-metaphysical with regard to the substantive claims and conclusions it endorses.

But Hobbes also represents a special case in another respect. What we have called "fundamental philosophy" generally consists in a theory of knowledge and a theory of the object of knowledge and culminates in a metaphysical *theory*. Hobbes certainly begins in this way, but his intentions go far beyond this. For he is ultimately concerned with developing a fundamental philosophy of human praxis, in short, a practical metaphysics. Whether we consider his philosophical system itself (the tripartite *Elementa philosophiae*), or *Leviathan*, or even already *The Elements of Law*, we are dealing here with a "fundamental philosophy" whose ultimate goal and destination is a theory of the state. The history of philosophy has Hobbes to thank for furnishing a political metaphysics that emphatically dispenses with metaphysics.

The text of *Leviathan*, and especially the first part and the first few chapters of the second part, is organized in accordance with the three partial methods just described. In one sense the resolutive part of the resoluto-compositive method has already been applied before *Leviathan* begins and lies outside the text itself. In the first half of the first part of *Leviathan*, specifically in chapters 1 to 9, Hobbes proceeds step by step to "compose" the human being as an individual. He begins with the contributions of natural philosophy and the cognitive dimension of experience (chapters 1–5) and proceeds without a break to a discussion of the practical dimension of human motives, inclinations, and passions (chapter 6). After developing his account of the cognitive faculties in further detail (chapters 7–9) he presents an account of power in a transitional section (chapter 10), which concludes the first half of the first part by considering power in relation to the individual and anticipates the second half of the first half (chapters 11–15) by considering power in relation to the social context.

The following reflections on the "Difference of Manners" and on "Religion" thus expressly take up the social perspective (chapters 11–12). At first glance, the discussion of religion might look like a kind of diversion, but in fact in this section Hobbes is interested in this subject from an anthropological point of view, whereas later in the text, in parts three and four, he is principally concerned with questions of religion in relation to church and state.

This chapter on religion leads directly to his theorem of the state of nature (chapter 13), a concept of decisive significance for the anthropological considerations of this first part of *Leviathan*. Then Hobbes discusses the pre-political prerequisites for overcoming the state of nature (chapters 14–15), and this is followed by another transitional section (chapter 16) concerning the idea of an authorized representative. This discussion concludes the first part of the text, which concerns anthropology, and also serves to introduce the second part, which concerns the philosophy of the state. At the beginning of this second part Hobbes presents the theory of absolute sovereignty, which constitutes the core of his conception of the state (chapters 17–19). A number of the chapters that follow are strongly concerned with specific political issues relating to the immediate context of the time.

There is no single place where Hobbes presents the three principal methodical elements we have mentioned in their internal connection with one another. This creates the danger that one of these elements is easily privileged at the expense of the others, so that one is tempted to focus exclusively on the idea of reason as "reckoning" or calculation (L ch. 5: 18), for example, or on the machinelike character of the state (L: 1), or merely on the step-by-step construction of his theory of the state (C, the preface to the reader). But we can only do proper justice to the actual argument that Hobbes presents if we attend to all three elements, expose the internal connection between them, and also, last but not least, are ready to recognize further methodical elements where necessary.

When Hobbes comes to look back over the first two parts of *Leviathan* (L ch. 32: 195) we can see that further methodical perspectives are also in play. In their different ways they are compatible with the three principal methodical elements we have discussed. The first of these perspectives can be integrated directly with those elements: the derivation from the principles of nature recalls the procedure of mathematics and corresponds to the *mos geometrico*. According to a further perspective here, Hobbes tells us that we are not to renounce our natural reason. This is not really a new fourth method in its own right, but a methodical aspect that underlies all three principal methods. By alluding to the "natural" rather than supernatural character of reason, Hobbes is emphasizing the way that his own science of freedom is independent both of metaphysics and of theology and revelation. According to the third perspective he mentions the principles are "found true," or "made so" through consent regarding the use of essential words, on the basis of experience. This introduces a new and fourth method, which philosophy requires in order to supplement the contribution of mathematics (see chapter 4.5, below), and which allows it to counter the exclusive pretensions of any purely rationalistic approach.

Finally, no considered appraisal of Hobbes's method can afford to ignore the role of introspection, which he mentions in the introduction to *Leviathan*: "*nosce te ipsum: read thyself*" (L: 2; see chapter 4.3, below). This again does not introduce a real fifth method but can easily be integrated into the fourth method as a specific type of "experience." The fifth method, or quasi-method, that Hobbes recognizes involves the rhetorical gifts of a persuasive author.

4.3. The Mathematical Paradigm and Its Limits

In *De Cive* Hobbes distinguishes three "sorts of things," and three corresponding branches of philosophy: geometry, which treats of figure; physics, which treats of motion; and morals, which treats of natural right (the dedication, p. 91). One would be mistaken in assuming that at least the first of these branches, that of geometry, is devoid of that external utility that Hobbes usually expects of the sciences. He nowhere expressly denies the possibility of a pure geometry divorced from all considerations of utility, but he does not mention the idea and emphasizes instead the manifold benefits of this science: "For truly whatever assistance doth accrue to the life of man, whether from the observation of the heavens or from the observation of the earth, . . . whatsoever things they are in which this present age doth differ from the rude simpleness of antiquity, we must acknowledge to be a debt we owe merely to geometry" (C, p. 91). Physics too can be said to owe its achievements initially to geometry. And if moral philosophy is to contribute anything to knowledge of the truth, it must know "the nature of human actions" just as certainly and distinctly "as the nature of quantity in geometric figures" (ibid.), so that the entire argument may constitute an unassailable fortress.

The reason why Hobbes admires mathematics here is not due to its (axiomatic-deductive) method. Rather, he esteems it so highly partly on account of its useful applications, from astronomy and geography through to physics, and partly on account of its exemplary certainty, although this could hardly be achieved without recourse to the aforementioned method.

In other passages Hobbes expresses his views on this matter directly (see the dedication in E, the introduction to L, and L ch. 5: 20ff.), emphasizing that ever since his conversion to the cause of method he could only regard philosophy proper as a science, and the only enterprise that qualified as a science was mathematics, or a form of argumentation that employs mathematical method. For only then would we be in a position to reap the desired fruit, namely that "mankind should enjoy such an immortal peace . . . that there would hardly be left any pretense for war" (C, p. 91). In fact, Hobbes does not appeal in the first instance to considerations of political experience, or of political prudence, or of any comprehensive historical reflection. He also avoids appealing to comparative juridical considerations of any kind. Rather, precisely in order to escape "the erroneous opinions of the vulgar as touching the nature of right and wrong" (ibid.), Hobbes appeals to a strictly axiomatic-deductive science, namely the science of geometry.

In the course of his development, it is quite true that we can observe a certain change in his angle of approach here. In the dedications of the two earlier texts (*The Elements of Law* and *De Cive*) Hobbes almost exclusively takes geometry as his paradigm of scientific knowledge, and he speaks of arithmetical "reckoning" only in passing (C, the preface to the reader). Later on, in *Leviathan*, Hobbes clearly privileges arithmetic, as when he claims that reason "is nothing but reckoning" (L ch. 5: 18). But the one thing that does not change is his view that a philosophy of the state does not substantively imitate either geometry (the science of space) or arithmetic (the science of numbers), but simply emulates the paradigmatic method they represent (that of a strict derivation from first principles). It is only in this way, by appeal to a complete and transparent rational structure of argument, that an unassailable certainty may also be established in the realm of morals, law, and the state.

The unassailable character of this approach is however qualified by the fact that philosophical principles, in contrast to mathematics, require that appeal to experience that we have already mentioned (chapter 4.1, above). This is what permits Hobbes to avoid the danger to which an exclusive orientation toward mathematics would have exposed him, namely the idea that his principles could be regarded, like the axioms of mathematics, as being arbitrarily assumed in the first place. But those who wish to know and understand the world itself, the natural and the social world, will indeed have to base their thought upon experience. But in that case Hobbes has to renounce the special advantages that he so prized in mathematics, for no aspect of experience is ever capable of attaining such unassailable certainty.

In methodological terms, experience can itself play different roles, but to simplify matters we can identify the two principal ones here. It can either help to establish the truth of merely partial assumptions and propositions, or that of the entire system of assumptions and propositions in question. Hobbes does not explicitly raise the question in these terms. But if we look at the way in which he pursues his actual argument, we can see these two principal roles at work. On the one hand, Hobbes appeals to experience with regard to numerous partial propositions, as he frequently does in his theorem of the state of nature (C, the preface to the reader; L ch. 13: 60–63). And he also insists on the importance of taking human beings as they are (see E, part I, ch. 1, §2). What is more, in the introduction to *Leviathan* he interprets the notion of introspection that is emphasized there ("read thyself") in an essentially objective rather than subjective fashion. In other words, we are encouraged not to concentrate upon our own personal conditions and circumstances, but rather upon the universal features of human life and recognize the "similitude of the thoughts, and passions, of one man, to the thoughts and passions of another," and "read and know, what are the thoughts, and passions of all other men, upon the like occasions" (L: 2). In observing in the field of actual life how we ourselves "think, opine, reason, hope, fear," and so on, we can develop a philosophical anthropology based upon universal human experience. In this sense the introspection involved here is not, as we have already indicated, a new particular method but simply a dimension of that fourth element, which is experience itself.

Yet this notion of introspection reveals a special feature of Hobbes's understanding of experience, insofar as he tacitly assumes a rather narrow empirical basis for his philosophy. By abstracting from the specific characteristics of one's own experience in this way he hopes to discover the shared and universal aspects of experience, yet he does not recognize the potential danger of extrapolating all too freely here.

On the other hand, methodologically speaking, he seems to regard both the principles that underlie his entire system and the definitions that he introduces at key junctures of this system simply as if they were the corresponding components of geometry: he treats them as arbitrary postulates that have been unanimously agreed upon. Yet he escapes the decisionism that threatens here in two ways. On the one hand, he introduces principles and fundamental definitions that provide the terms of general linguistic use with a precise conceptual meaning, as in his definitions of "good," "evil," "vile," and "inconsiderable" (L ch. 6: 24). On the other hand, these elements are supposed to acquire the character of truths insofar as they concur with the entire system of experience.

In this sense Hobbes offers us a complex account of truth that embraces the three most important theories of truth that are familiar from the history of philosophy. It is true that Hobbes does not explicitly present or defend this complex account, but it certainly informs his actual philosophical practice. In the first place, "true" and "false," which are "attributes of speech, not of things" (L ch. 4: 15), have a conventional character inasmuch as one comes to an agreement regarding the (fundamental) definitions in question, which in turn has the advantage of promoting peaceful relations among us. Insofar as the definitions and terms derived from them are regarded as true if they concur with the entire system, truth also reveals the characteristic of coherence. And since inner coherence of the system alone is not enough, for it also needs to agree with experience, Hobbes also recognizes the third traditional theory, the correspondence theory of truth (as correspondence with experience or reality).

4.4. Ethics and Political Authority

Since Hobbes's philosophy is intended in its entirety to serve human interests, it can be regarded as practical and political philosophy in the emphatic sense formulated by Aristotle, the philosopher who was otherwise the favorite target of Hobbes's criticisms: the aim in question does not consist in (mere) knowledge, but rather in action or practice (*to telos estin ou gnosis alla praxis*, as Aristotle puts it; see *Nicomachean Ethics*, book I. 1, 2095a5f.). This should not of course be interpreted simply as a dubious form of philosophical ideology. As Hobbes sees the matter, he is engaged solely in the pursuit of truth rather than of any partisan objectives. Far from defending a dogmatic conception of science that approaches its subject matter with a host of preconceived opinions, he wishes to proceed like a mathematician dispassionately comparing figures and movements and arguing on the basis of "infallible rules of reason" (E, the epistle dedicatory, p. 19).

According to Aristotle practical philosophy starts and arises from a praxis that is already essentially ethical in character, but a praxis that it seeks to elucidate in its own right and also to improve it in the light of this elucidation (cf. Höffe 2008, part 1). But in the historical context of Hobbes himself, defined as it was by the experience of civil war, one could hardly speak of an already prevailing domain of an intrinsically ethical praxis, or presuppose a community of human beings living more or less peaceably with one another. Hobbes thus sees himself compelled to rethink fundamentally the whole approach to practical philosophy. In order to do justice to the idea of a truly political philosophy, he has to develop a science that in the systematic context of Aristotle's philosophy would be described as a technical or "poetic" body of knowledge, i.e., one essentially concerned with the principles involved in the making or crafting of things (in the original Greek sense of the word *poiēsis*).

According to the introduction to *Leviathan*, the state, which is its central theme, along with the mighty power that belongs to it, must be seen as "an artificial man." (For the resemblance between an "artificial" and a "natural" man, see *Leviathan*: introduction; ch. 23: 124; ch. 24: 130–31, among many other passages.) This artificial man is indeed created and constructed by human beings as the natural creatures they are, and Hobbes's philosophy of the state explicates the relevant instructions for the construction and constitution of the state. But these are not instructions in the usual sense, not a set of directions for the construction of the machine in question. The introduction to *Leviathan* certainly tells us that the state is an artifact, and thus something artificial. The state has thus appeared to many of Hobbes's interpreters as essentially an engine or machine, and thus as something that can be directed and controlled, something whose maker, man as *artifex*, must basically be regarded as a kind of engineer who plans and envisages the machine, then constructs it, and, if necessary, also repairs it. (For the paradigm of the "machine" and its role in early modern philosophy, see Sutter 1988 and Stollberg-Rillinger 1986.)

It is true that Hobbes does not explicitly exclude any of these suggestions. Nevertheless, he does not appeal to the conception of man as machine that would later be defended by La Mettrie for example (in his *L'homme machine* of 1748). For Hobbes it is not that natural living things behave like machines in general, but rather that a certain kind of machine, namely the "automata" that move themselves, are like living things, not indeed natural living things, but artificial living things.

Even in the case of the state, that artificial being that is so crucial for Hobbes, the metaphor of the machine, taken on its own, can lead to certain misunderstandings that can only be avoided if we read him very carefully. In the introduction to *Leviathan*, Hobbes begins by describing man as the "most excellent work of nature." In this regard, he is following and responding to three quite traditional considerations: firstly, man has not produced himself and is thus a creature; secondly, he is a creature who assumes a particular status as the crown of creation; thirdly, the source of this status and specific privilege is his possession of reason.

In the course of *Leviathan*, however, it is clear that all this is by no means reduced to the mere faculty of an engineer or a constructor of machines. It is true that the introduction paints a detailed picture of this image of the "artificial man," in which sovereignty is presented as the artificial soul of the state, the magistrates and officers as its artificial joints, and reward and punishment as the nerves; where counselors are described as its memory, while equity and laws are presented as an artificial reason and an artificial will. Hobbes employs this image late as well, as when he compares trade and the exchange of commodities through gold, silver, and money to the circulation of blood in the state, or the "sanguification of the commonwealth" (ch. 24: 130–31). Yet in the main text, which follows on immediately from the very brief introduction, Hobbes never speaks of the faculty of reason as if it were that of an engineer who first procures the relevant building materials and then uses them to construct the artificial man, the mighty creature known from the Bible as Leviathan.

A clear anti-Aristotelian point is also being made here: the state does not arise by nature, spontaneously as it were, but through agreements and compacts (C ch. 1, §2, p. 110; L: 1, the introduction). In this sense, the state is indeed something that is produced or fabricated, albeit not like a clock that is made out of springs and wheels and finally stands before the maker as an independent product that now functions on its own and can thus be used in principle by anyone, and not just by the one who produced it in the first place.

The artificial man is thus to be regarded not so much an independent machine but rather as a social institution. For while a social institution does indeed possess a certain independence, it is not merely created by those who constitute it, but is also either sustained in its existing form or is changed, or even destroyed, by the way in which its members behave. The most striking feature of the famous engraving on the title page of *Leviathan*—the giant figure embracing the individuals within itself—thus far more effectively captures what Hobbes actually has in mind than the metaphor of the machine.

Another traditional element in Hobbes's image of the artificial man is his understanding of sovereignty as its artificial soul. Insofar as the soul imparts life and movement to the body, it cannot be regarded as

something merely external or secondary in character. We are not dealing with the kind of dualism we find in Descartes, for the soul here is
regarded as the principle of actualization that makes something into a
living being, as in Aristotle (*De Anima*, book II, 2 and 4).

In relation to the state as an artificial man, this means that where the
artificial soul of sovereignty is lacking there may be persons who can be
called judges, or others who could be described as officials or officers of
the state. Yet just as a dead body is not an actual human being, so too a
community without the soul of sovereignty is not actually a genuine, i.e.,
a living, community, and its judges and all other officials of the state do
not realize or fulfill their roles in the full sense of these terms. Even the
frequently defended claim that the Hobbesian state must be intrinsically
controllable illegitimately reduces his idea of the artificial man to the
notion of a machine. Just as human beings must take care of their health
but cannot entirely control it, so too the health of the community cannot
entirely be controlled.

Thus, in spite of the metaphor of the machine, Hobbes is quite right
not to see himself as a kind of social engineer or bio-engineer, as we
would say today, or as an engineer at all, but rather as a philosopher who
demonstrates his calling solely through the thoroughness of his fundamental analysis. If he were simply concerned with devising means for
securing social peace, he could certainly have reduced the range and task
of his philosophical work. In composing *The Elements of Law* he could
simply have omitted the opening two-thirds of the first part on "Human
Nature" (dealing with the faculty of cognition and the faculty of motion)
and started immediately with his discussion of the "state of nature" (in
chapter 14). Similarly, he could simply have dropped the first two parts
(*De Corpore* and *De Homine*) of the three-part *Elementa philosophiae*. And
the first part of *Leviathan* ("Of Man") could then have dispensed with
the first two-thirds of the text and commenced directly with chapter 13
("Of the Natural Condition of Mankind as Concerning their Felicity and
Misery"). A certain modesty also belongs to Hobbes's thorough analysis
here, since in making an artificial animal man is simply imitating nature
or the creation, as he indicates in the very first sentence of *Leviathan* (L:
1, the introduction).

Yet the genuinely philosophical thoroughness of Hobbes's analysis exacts a high price. The parts and chapters of his texts we have just
mentioned also involve views (such as the relentless materialism of his
mechanistic and radically empiricist anthropology) the special discussion

of which creates digressions that are not directly relevant to the theory of the state. As a result Hobbes's theory of the state seems to be vulnerable at points where his two principal theorems (regarding the state of nature and regarding the sovereign as authorized representative of unlimited power) have not even yet been introduced.

On the other hand, these additional elements are not simply irrelevant. In chapter 5 of *Leviathan* ("Of Reason and Science") Hobbes introduces important elements of his method, and explains reason, for example, as a kind of "reckoning." In addition, Hobbes points out, in a move that may be unusual for a mathematician but anticipates certain features of his theory of the state, that even professors of mathematics can err in their calculations, so that even a great many individuals cannot guarantee certainty where arithmetical conclusions are concerned. In the same chapter Hobbes attempts to prepare the way for his contractualist theory of representation (in chapter 16) in terms of mathematical reason: "And therefore, as when there is a controversy in an account, the parties must by their own accord set up for right reason, the reason of some arbitrator or judge" (L ch. 5: 18–19). But on closer inspection this proposal is simply a *deus ex machina*, a solution that is alien to his preceding reflections. It can also be seen that Hobbes also overestimates the potential conflict that can spring from disagreements in the field of science.

According to an influential tradition of interpretation, Hobbes's thought is so rigorously constructed that if one accepts his initial principles then one must also accept the whole system (Watkins 1978), including the absolutist consequences of his theory of the state (cf., for example, Borkenau 1934 and Macpherson 1962). Our previous observations have already cast doubt on the supposed rigor of his general argument. Relevant doubts move in two directions here, involving both the first principles themselves and the conclusions derived from them. It may be that Hobbes's theory of the passions does not strictly follow from his theory of imagination, or again that this latter theory does not necessarily presuppose the former theory. And Hobbes's theory of reason in turn does not follow as a strict conclusion from any of this. Similarly, his thesis regarding the state of nature may be independent of the reflections that precede it. Hobbes himself seems to think so, for in the final section of *Leviathan* he presents a summary of the argument, which, independently of his entire philosophy of the mind and the passions, essentially starts from his theory of the state of nature. Finally, even those parts of the text that must be regarded as the heart of Hobbes's theory of the state (chapters 13

through 18, or arguably through 22) are not entirely rigorous in themselves. For the theory of representation, which serves to support Hobbes's
absolutist conception of sovereignty, does not strictly follow from the
theory of the state of nature.

Hobbes's basic claims are all related with one another, but there is
no direct contradiction between them. At the beginning of chapter 31,
when Hobbes passes from "the kingdom of God by nature" to the idea
of "a Christian commonwealth," he even provides a summary review of
his previous considerations that goes all the way back to the notion of
the state of nature. And at the start of chapter 34 he goes back further
still, returning to his earlier philosophical investigations of language and
nature. In this regard Hobbes seems to make use of almost all of his earlier
claims as he proceeds, so that *Leviathan* inevitably appears as though it is
constructed in a thoroughly encyclopedic and systematic fashion.

Yet it may be that Hobbes's philosophy actually springs from two specific and in part competing interests. On the one hand, the encyclopedic
interest appears to conflict with a theory of the state that, for the sake of
avoiding all unnecessary conflict and superfluous theorems, should proceed without appealing to claims and propositions that are not required
for the development of his central argument. And in that case, the work
would certainly correspond more closely to Hobbes's own remarks, when
he says at the very end of part 2 ("Of Commonwealth"), which contains
his philosophy of the state in the strict sense, that "this writing of mine"
is "short" (L ch. 31: 193). On the other hand, Hobbes's fundamental
materialist interest and perspective runs counter to the social-theoretical
intention of his book, which is precisely to reconcile those aspects of
human beings that generate conflict with the human desire for peaceful
coexistence.

It is only with these qualifications that Hobbes's theory of the state
can be described as a scientific philosophy in the form of a political *technē*.
Like all forms of technology, this philosophy serves the one who constructs it, namely man. From *The Elements of Law* through *De Cive* up
to *Leviathan* itself, Hobbes places his life work entirely in the service of
what he considers to be the most important good: the life of individuals,
and the peace that is the social condition of this life.

Insofar as this "science of peace" is presented as a *technē* for securing
peace, it is also a form of political instruction. Hobbes develops his theory
of the state not as a philosophy that is simply supplemented with political
instruction, but expressly as a political guide for the production of the

"Leviathan," which is its object. And in this sense it is indeed a social technology, or more precisely, a *technē* for the production of the state. Hobbes sees no difference between his general theory and this guide for a particular political praxis that depends upon a specific historical context. In his theory the science of philosophy coincides with this direct guide for action, with the demand to secure in reality the necessary and sufficient means for establishing the peace that is required. It is true, of course, that we must qualify the idea of a "direct" guide to action by describing it as "almost direct." For Hobbes is perfectly well aware that we still need a form of authority that is able to "convert this truth of speculation into the utility of practice" (L ch. 31: 193).

But this involves Hobbes in a circular pragmatic argument: if the theory that justifies absolute sovereignty is to be of any use in practice, this sovereignty must already exist. But then this matter of greatest utility must already be established, or must be accomplished before the work of speculation begins. And if this absolute sovereignty already exists, we must ask why we really require a specific theory for it. Perhaps we need a theory to confirm its nature, but this would remain a purely theoretical question of no particular practical significance. Occasionally Hobbes recognizes the modest value of such a theoretical approach, as when he acknowledges a certain negative rather than positive utility on the part of moral philosophy, including the philosophy of the state (L ch. 46: 367f. and 379f.).

Such a theory of the state appears to reduce the practical political task of philosophy to a cognitive one: those who have read and understood *Leviathan* would immediately possess the knowledge and the readiness to end the civil war and establish the peaceful order that is necessary. One would not require any further practical considerations, like those regarding ethico-political processes of recognition, for example. According to Hobbes, no further considerations of this kind are indeed needed, although the reader, our author assumes, already brings the inclination or desire to overcome the situation of war and see peace established. Hobbes thinks no preaching or exhortation is necessary here, as long as these three passions can be presumed: the fear of violent death, the desire of such things as are necessary for a "commodious" life, and the hope of obtaining them through our own diligence or "industry" (L ch. 13: 63). Over and beyond this, the reader must simply possess the faculty of "reason," theoretically analyzed by Hobbes, which proposes the appropriate principles for peace. But can this be presupposed in regard to human beings as they actually exist, even human beings in a time of civil war?

4.5. Analysis and Composition

In one important respect Hobbes's philosophy deviates from its own methodological model: whereas mathematics does not present its basic propositions or first principles as substantive truth claims, philosophy has to begin with certain true principles, especially where such an existentially decisive issue as the political state is concerned. Here, therefore, philosophy must appeal to experience as the fourth method, which we discussed above.

In the preface to *De Cive* Hobbes tells us that we can derive these principles if the object we are attempting to understand, the state, is first "dissolved" (C, p. 99), that is to say, conceptually resolved into its elements and then recomposed from these elements. We can see how Hobbes has altered his methodological model here. It is not geometry that demonstrates how we can analyze and recompose the object, although Hobbes could have pointed to its procedures of construction in this regard. He appeals instead to the second method, namely that involved in the construction of a machine. Here he adopts a favorite paradigm of the period, invoking the example of the watch as an object whose mode of operation can only be understood when we take the object apart and examine its springs, wheels, and other components (L: 1). Before reconstructing it Hobbes starts by dissolving the state into the components of human nature, which, according to *The Elements of Law*, is "the sum of his natural faculties and powers, as the faculties of nutrition, motion, generation, sense, reason, &." (E, part 1, ch. 1, §4).

In *The Elements of Law* Hobbes identifies a further criterion of the truth of his principles, which we could regard as a sixth methodological element in his theory, although it springs directly from the task he has set himself. He is seeking principles, as he indicates in the epistle dedicatory, that could readily be accepted from an egoistic point of view: "there is no way, but first, to put such principles down for a foundation, as passion not distrusting may not seek to displace" (E, p. 19). One might consider this a highly questionable assumption on his part, both from the moral and social-theoretical point of view, given that Hobbes lays such emphasis on his realistic picture of humanity: "I shall leave men but as they are" (E, part I, ch. 1, §2, p. 21). But there are some convincing reasons to support this assumption: if we ascribe a different kind of nature to human beings, such as a social nature marked by altruistic motives and impulses, the task in question will be unduly simplified. For even if human beings are not pure egotists, their individual interest can always be overpowered, and we must be able to legitimate the state in this more difficult case as well.

The method of breaking something down and reconstituting it in turn is hardly an entirely novel approach in philosophy, as we have already indicated. We already find a version of this approach in the work of the two founding fathers of Western political philosophy. Plato identifies and employs a similar method in his account of the origin of the polis (*Republic*, book II, 367d to book IV, 445e), and Aristotle does the same when he justifies his own account of the political nature of man (*Politics*, book I, 2).

This process of breaking down and putting together again is more technically described in terms derived from Latin and Greek as the resoluto-compositive or analytical-synthetical method (the terminology Hobbes uses in *De Corpore*, ch. 6, §6). This refers to the way in which something is conceptually or actually broken down into its ultimate constituent parts (through "resolution" or "analysis") and then reassembled (through "composition" or "synthesis").

Hobbes begins with the process of resolution, by dissolving the state into its elements, namely the individual human beings that make it up, and breaking these down in turn into their ultimate elements, namely the faculty of knowledge and the human passions, and these again into their ultimate elements, namely "matter in motion." Once this analysis has been accomplished, Hobbes can begin *Leviathan* with matter in motion as the ultimate and primary element. But new elements are then constantly brought in, and without this ongoing but tacit enrichment (which can also be described as a substantive evolution), without this incorporation of new components it would be impossible for Hobbes to move from "bare" motion to processes of sensible, intellectual, and volitional motion, and finally arrive at the anthropology—based on the desire for self-preservation, happiness, and indeed power—that is decisive for his theory of the state.

The resoluto-compositive method was also cultivated during this period by the School of Padua. In Hobbes's lifetime it was Galileo, active in Padua for almost two decades (from 1592 until 1610), who applied it to the field of mechanics. And Hobbes's friend William Harvey, who discovered the primary circulation of the blood, extended the same approach to the field of biology.

In Padua the method was initially employed in the faculty of medicine, where they used "resolution" or "analysis" for the anatomical investigation of the human body. This paradigm actually fits *Leviathan* better than Hobbes himself realized. Thus the mythical symbol of the Leviathan should also be read as an anatomical allegory. For Hobbes resolves the mighty body of this artificial man into its constituents, namely "natural" man, and this again into its anatomical constituents. Once this anatomical "resolution" has been accomplished, he goes on step by step to construct or compose the natural man, and then the artificial man. He begins with the impressions of sense, those sensations of external bodies that finally lead along the pathway of the "nerves" and passages to the heart and brain of the body.

But this anatomical allegory also has its obvious limits. For the anatomist dissects not a living body but a corpse, and no anatomist, however brilliant, can ever re-create a living human being from the constituents of a corpse. In this regard, the image of the watch is better suited to the artificial yet living man that is the state. For its spring is a driving power that keeps the mechanism in motion from within, and stands for the twofold task Hobbes has set himself to solve with regard to the state, namely to discover what drives human beings to organize themselves in the form of the state and what it is that keeps the created state in motion.

As far the ultimate constituents are concerned, Hobbes's position seems to waver. Sometimes he speaks of elements, i.e., first constituents, of the state, and sometimes of first causes (H ch. 10, §4, p. 41). There is not necessarily any contradiction here, as long as these elements involve powers, i.e., causes that generate effects. Hobbes's philosophy of the state is concerned to identify precisely this causal type of power, and understands itself as the scientific investigation of causes of war and peace. Hence this genuine theoretical interest in investigating causes converges with the practical interest in promoting peace. For our ignorance of the causes of war and peace is regarded as the cause of civil war (C ch. 1, §2, p. 110). Hobbes's theoretical concern converges with his practical concern, of course, only because the scientifically identified causes hold both for the past, with its latent or actually acute experience of war, and for the future, for "those things that can be," for a permanent condition of peace (H ch. 11, §10, p. 50).

FIVE

Natural Philosophy
and the Theory of Knowledge

Although *Leviathan* is principally concerned with political philosophy, the work begins by presenting a philosophical anthropology (part I: "Of Man"), and in this anthropological context with a question that barely hints at the problem of the state that is the ultimate theme of the work. The question belongs to the field of natural philosophy, and indeed to what we would now describe as the theory of knowledge and the philosophy of mind. It belongs to natural philosophy since it deals directly with the nature of bodies, and to the theory of knowledge since it also investigates how the properties of material bodies appear to and are represented in human thought, i.e., how they can truly be known. And it belongs to the philosophy of mind since it also concerns the relationship of mind and body.

In this connection Hobbes begins his investigations with a theory of sensation. He thus adopts a classical schema for deriving conceptual definitions in the context of his own anthropology. For he starts with the generic properties that human beings share with animals, with those pre-linguistic cognitive abilities that extend from the capacity for sensation through basic forms of retention up to that more complex form of memory that identifies regularities in the sensible world, and thus represents "experience" in the cumulative sense, and which culminates in "prudence" and comparable capacities (E part I, chs. 1–4; L chs. 1–3).

78 THOMAS HOBBES

It is true that in *De Corpore*, a later text, Hobbes begins with a theory of science and philosophy presented under the title of "reckoning or logic" (*computatio sive logica*). But here too Hobbes refers us back to the two pre-linguistic cognitive abilities of sense perception and memory (C ch. I, §2). And it is only after this that Hobbes introduces what he regards as the characteristically human capacity for "language" or "speech" (C ch. I, §3; L ch. 4). It is the latter that makes reason and science possible, which remarkably enough are initially introduced without reference to language: for Hobbes reason presupposes language, though language does not presuppose reason, and his theory of science follows upon his theory of reason and language.

With his natural philosophy and theory of knowledge, Hobbes clearly stands in the tradition of Bacon's restoration of the sciences in the name of "experience." Hobbes himself was personally acquainted with most of the most important scientific figures of the age, except for Kepler (1571–1639). It was this turn to experience that essentially accounts for the violent contempt with which Hobbes regarded the tradition of scholastic philosophy, believing as he did that it sought refuge in hallowed texts of alleged authority rather than consulting the truly authoritative book of nature itself. The fact that Aristotle, the privileged point of reference for the scholastic tradition, was himself an important natural philosopher and indeed also an outstanding researcher of nature is another question entirely. (Hobbes's specific criticisms of Aristotle are examined in chapter 12, below.)

5.1. Empirical Realism

In accordance with his plan to consider "the thoughts of man . . . first singly, and afterwards in train, or dependence on one another" (L ch. 3: 3), Hobbes begins with those activities of the human mind that are "naturally planted in him, so, as to need no other thing, to the exercise of it, but to be born a man, and live with the use of his five senses" (L ch. 3: 11). These activities are not of course particular to the human species. The range of capacities that extends from sensation through imagination to prudence is also open to the animals, for Hobbes in fact entertains an uncommonly high opinion of animal capacities.

Human action, to put it simply, arises from the interplay of the two faculties of knowledge and will, and thus possesses both a cognitive and a volitional side. By beginning with sensation and imagination Hobbes ascribes a certain priority to the cognitive side. He does not actually think that this is more important than the volitional side, but it forms the basis for the latter. For once the cognitive side, at a certain level of complexity, approaches actual knowledge we encounter the concept of "desire" (L ch. 3: 9), and thus a concept directly connected with willing. Nonetheless, we can see that the priority still lies with the cognitive dimension. For Hobbes now proceeds to discuss language (in chapter 4) and reason and science (in chapter 5) before turning to "voluntary motions," or what he calls "the passions" (in chapter 6). The only reference to the practical significance of the cognitive dimension is a brief allusion to the possibility of error and disagreement even in the basic form of reason that Hobbes calls "reckoning" (L ch. 5: 18f.).

Hobbes's epistemological reflections are clearly informed by the basic ideas expounded in his natural philosophy. From the beginning, since the *Elements*, Hobbes had attempted to ground his theory of knowledge and his philosophy of mind on the basis of his philosophical conception of nature. In *Leviathan* there are two basic and decisive factors, which can be described as a basic concept and a basic principle respectively. The basic concept is this: the entirety of nature, whether external nature or the nature of the human body, is essentially matter in motion. Here "matter" is equivalent to "body" (L ch. 4: 16), and "body" signifies everything that occupies some determinate space and does not depend on the "imagination" (L ch. 34: 207). And the supplementary basic principle is the law of motion "that nothing can change itself," which implies that "when a thing lies still, unless somewhat else stir it, it will lie still for ever." And when "a body is once in motion, it moveth (unless something else hinder it) eternally" (L ch. 2: 4).

This basic principle echoes an axiom of mechanics, namely the principle of inertia or the law of persistence, which toppled the Aristotelian theory of motion that had prevailed for so long. According to Aristotle's teleological perspective, all bodies were believed to strive toward their "natural place," with lighter bodies striving upward and heavier bodies striving downward in pursuit of their natural place of rest (*Physics*, book IV, 4, 210b32). According to the revolutionary new formulation of the law of motion, the law of inertia, by contrast, any given body persists in a state of rest or of uniform linear motion unless it is compelled to change its state by forces acting upon it.

Hobbes ascribes a far-reaching and comprehensive role to this law of motion. He adopts it from the science of mechanics and extends it first to his theory of knowledge and philosophy of mind, then to further elements of his anthropology, and finally to his philosophy of the state. Hobbes's basic formulation of the principle is not inspired by Isaac Newton (1643–1727), who was two generations older than himself, but was almost certainly influenced by Galileo, and perhaps also indirectly by Kepler and Descartes, that is to say, by the three most important figures to formulate the principle of inertia before the subsequent investigations of Newton and Leibniz.

On account of these two fundamental elements (the basic concept and the basic law of motion), Hobbes's theory of knowledge begins from a mechanistic theory of sensation and perception: external bodies exert pressure, directly in the case of taste and touch or indirectly in the case of seeing, hearing, and smelling, on the corresponding sense organs, which thus react passively in turn. By means of the nerves and other bodily channels the pressure is continued further to reach the two central organs of the brain and the heart. But these still predominantly passive processes are not sufficient to produce sensation, which only arises through a counterpressure: in order to relieve themselves of the original pressure to which they are subjected, the brain and the heart exercise a responding pressure through which the object first becomes something that can be touched, tasted, smelled, heard, or seen.

What is interesting here is not merely what Hobbes explicitly says but also what he ignores. Whereas the process of perception itself is described in some detail, we learn nothing at all about the mechanical functioning of the brain and heart. He makes no attempt to explain what it is that generates the counterpressure. And in the case of the imagination, and specifically of memory, Hobbes is also silent in this regard. It remains quite unclear where and how the sensory impressions, which themselves are no longer present, are stored and gathered in such a systematic way that they make experience proper possible.

For Hobbes the real source of knowledge lies outside of human beings themselves. In this regard the original activity proceeds from the external world, to which the sense organs relate passively and to this extent merely form a quasi-inner world. Borrowing an image from the philosophers of antiquity, we could say that human understanding resembles the wax upon which the senses are able to impress their own form (see Plato, *Theaetetus* 191c–d). This image provides the model for a "sensationalist" epistemology that claimed that the understanding furnishes no specific contribution to knowledge that is independent of any sensory input. The notion that human understanding might spontaneously contribute its own concepts or categories, as Kant maintained with regard to the "pure concepts of the understanding," is simply inconceivable to Hobbes, as it is for every strictly empiricist or "sensationalist" account of knowledge.

And the more modest post-Kantian phenomenological notion that consciousness does not consist of bare data simply furnished through causal processes, that the data in question must be interpreted and endowed with "meaning" by consciousness, is entirely alien to Hobbes and the "sensationalist" approach to epistemology in general. From the sensationalist perspective one is merely confronted with a variegated form of sensuous impressions. The phenomenologist, on the other hand, would claim that what we actually perceive are specific objects such as houses, plants, and human beings. And this already means ascribing a certain meaning to the mere impressions of sense, although this meaning does not lie in the sense impressions themselves.

The sensationalist approach does not necessarily have to elevate the image of the impressionable wax into an absolute model. As we have pointed out, Hobbes does not simply reduce knowledge to the passive reception of sensory impressions and nothing else. For the external pressure of objects produces the counterpressure that arises from within the perceiver, which implies that what we have called the quasi-inner world exhibits a certain activity of its own. More than simply a seal impressed on wax, sensation as a whole involves a passive movement, the capacity for receiving an external impression, and an active movement, the counterpressure that is exerted in response. Yet this activity lacks any power of spontaneity, for in the strictly sensationalist model this is a purely reactive activity, which recalls Newton's third axiom of classical mechanics: "for every effect (*actio*) there is always an equal reaction (*reactio*)." If Hobbes had said more in this regard and specified the place and character of the counterpressure he mentions more precisely, he would have presented a weaker but nonetheless more convincing form of sensationalism than the one he offered.

The first aspect of Hobbes's mechanistic sensationalism is actually not so problematic from a contemporary perspective, even if we have now effectively replaced this mechanistic physiology with a biochemical account: the sensory organs are stimulated from without and then pass these stimuli on to the brain. But there are two further aspects of Hobbes's account that are more problematic even in relation to the level of discussion in his own time, namely the straightforward "realism" involved in his naturalistic grounding of the theory of knowledge and the philosophy of mind, and its strict sensationalist character. Hobbes's theory of sensation and the theory of knowledge he constructs on this basis are realist theories insofar as they posit bodies "outside of us," and thus an external world independent of thought. And these theories are strictly sensationalist in character since all knowledge is supposed to originate in, and not simply be occasioned by, our sensory impressions.

In accordance with his Euclidean paradigm Hobbes defends both positions as emphatic theses. He does not offer specific arguments for and against this realist and sensationalist position, in order to assess them and thus acquire the "true" propositions that will furnish the desired starting point. On the contrary, he proceeds directly to his philosophical argument and announces the theme of his inquiry: to take "the thoughts of man" and "consider them first singly, and afterwards in train, or dependence upon one another" (L ch. 1: 3), and immediately proposes, without any further reflection, the fundamental theses of his theory of knowledge and his philosophy of mind.

It is true that in his late work *De Corpore*, at the beginning of chapter 7, Hobbes does offer some relevant preliminary reflections, although he only presents a single argument in favor of realism and a sensationalist epistemology. Where natural philosophy is concerned he claims that we should begin with a kind of "privation" argument or thought experiment that consists in "feigning the world to be annihilated." Then all that we would be left with would be the "memory and imagination" of magnitudes, motions, sounds, and colors, and notions of their various parts and relations. But even here Hobbes does not provide any possible counterarguments or ways of meeting possible objections.

Hobbes does emphasize the advantages of his own theory of sensation, arguing for its superiority over the highly obscure or unintelligible theories of ultimately Aristotelian origin that were defended in the universities of the time. It has to be said, however, that Aristotle's subtle theory of perception (*De anima*, book II, 5) was presented in a distorted or even caricature form by the university teachers and Hobbes alike. But this contrast between his approach and that of the Aristotelian tradition, or indeed that of Aristotle himself, does not take us very far, since a highly critical view of Aristotle was already widespread among other pioneering contemporaries of Hobbes. Thus it might have been helpful if Hobbes had engaged directly with alternative approaches defended at the time, with the work of Descartes, for example, and specifically with his theory of perception and his methodical skepticism regarding the external world. Descartes's theory of perception shares the mechanistic starting point of Hobbes's philosophy, but is not developed and elaborated in exactly the same mechanistic fashion. For the Cartesian theory allows the brain a greater role in its own right than Hobbes's conception of mere reaction to external stimuli. For Descartes the sensory impressions are not themselves the origin of human thought but simply the occasion for what is thus a more creative and independent cognitive process. In this regard Hobbes's assault on the scholastic version of Aristotle that was still defended in the universities is directed against an oversimplified and already obsolete intellectual target.

5.2. Levels of Knowledge

Hobbes presents our innate mental capacities as a hierarchy that advances from the origin of all supposed knowledge in sensation (L, ch. 1: "Of Sense"), through imagination and the cognitive levels of memory and experience (L, ch. 2: "Of Imagination"), to arrive at the series of mental activities that adds the capacity for prudence to the preceding kinds of knowledge (L, ch. 3: "Of the Consequence or Train of Imaginations").

This progressive series of mental capacities and accomplishments differs little from that presented by Aristotle in the introductory chapter of his *Metaphysics*. Indeed the initial phases here are so similar that we could regard this as an expression of a well-established philosophical heritage. Thus the level of sensation or perception is succeeded by that of imagination or mental representation, and the latter for Hobbes is nothing but a decaying form of sensation occasioned by other sensations. When we wish to express the fading, decaying, or evanescence of our sensations we speak of memory; and in the case of accumulated memory or the memory of multiple things we speak of experience.

We can then proceed seamlessly to a further level. Hobbes develops this mechanistic theory of perception into a mechanistic theory of knowledge that encompasses all possible processes of thought or "mental discourse" as he puts it: "All fancies are motions within us, relics of those made in the sense" (L ch. 3: 8). For Hobbes the human mind is nothing but matter in motion, although this material and its movements are far more complex than in the case of more rudimentary nonhuman entities. With this thesis Hobbes naturally runs the risk of committing the empiricist error of moving from the plausible claim that we can think nothing but what is at least in part generated through the senses and falsely concluding from this that sense perception itself is the origin of all knowledge.

5.3. On Dreams

In the context of his theory of knowledge and philosophy of mind, Hobbes also considers the problem of dreams, a theme which is at best rather marginal in contemporary philosophical discussion but which was a prominent issue in his time, above all through the famous *Meditations* (1641) of Descartes. Hobbes had been interested in this question since his very first work on political philosophy, *The Elements of Law*, composed a year before the appearance of Descartes's book, and was still reflecting years later on it in *De Corpore* (ch. 25, §9), the part of the *Elementa philosophiae* that was written in 1655. It is here that his most systematic observations on the subject are to be found.

Unlike Descartes, who addressed the question from the perspective of providing a fundamental grounding for philosophy, Hobbes did not approach it with the same degree of epistemological radicality. Thus he did not think it was necessary in *Leviathan*, composed a decade after the *Elements*, to change his own approach to take account of the *Meditations*, which had appeared in the meantime. Hobbes had engaged with the *Mediations* in the sixteen "Objections" that he had already published, to which Descartes responded point by point, just as he did to the philosophical objections raised by a number of other important contemporaries.

Descartes asks for convincing assurances that allow us to distinguish between the states of dreaming and waking, and raises the resulting epistemological question as to whether we might merely be dreaming what is taken to be an external world (*Meditations*, I, paragraph 6f.; AT VII, 18f.). He answers the first question by proposing the criterion of coherence: "our memory can never connect our dreams one with the other, or with the whole course of our lives, as it unites events which happen to us while we are awake" (*Meditations*, VI, final paragraph; AT VII, 89). Hobbes doubts the force of this argument and asks "whether a dreamer who doubts whether he is dreaming or not, might not dream that his dream were connected with the ideas of past events in a long train" (Opera, vol. V, p. 273f.).

In his own observations on dreams Hobbes is pursuing an obvious strategy of "enlightenment." He does of course wish to trace the natural causes of dreams, but even here he is ultimately concerned with issues that bear on religion and the state. In the third part of *Leviathan*, in his theory of the Christian commonwealth (L ch. 32: 196), Hobbes concedes the possibility that God "can speak to a man by dreams, visions, voice, and inspiration," but he goes on to point out that "he [God] obliges no man to believe he hath so done to him that pretends it." For any human being can err, that is to say, may merely dream "that God hath spoken to him." And of course, "which is more," a man "may lie."

Hobbes does not deny that there may be such things as supernatural dreams or visions (L ch. 34: 209). But those who are unable to distinguish the simple phenomenon of natural dreams from supernatural attributes, from visions sent from God, fall victim to the "superstitious fear of spirits" and "prognostics from dreams, false prophecies, and many other things" with which "crafty ambitious persons abuse the simple people" and turn them away from "civil obedience" (L ch. 2: 7–8).

In the first part of *Leviathan* at any rate, Hobbes is concerned solely with dreams as natural phenomena. In accordance with his mechanistic theory of knowledge he regards them as the "imaginations of them that sleep," which "have been before, either totally or by parcels in the sense," or again, in a quite pre-Freudian sense, as "caused by the distemper of some of the inward parts of the body" so that, for example, "lying cold breedeth dreams of fear" (L ch. 2: 6).

5.4. Prudence

There are obviously strict limits to a purely mechanistic theory of knowledge. It is not easy to see how this approach can do full justice to such sophisticated activities of the mind as mathematics, poetry, painting, and music. Although Hobbes characteristically entertains a particularly high opinion of mathematics, he denies that we can conceive one of its concepts, that of infinity, as an attribute of anything (L ch. 3: 11). In this connection, of course, he is thinking of God. Yet in order to defend the claim that we cannot conceive the infinite, he should also have appealed to mathematics. But Hobbes cannot regard this as a serious option here since in the context of his own strictly materialist perspective he cannot conceive of a mathematical object that is not material in nature (Works VII, 64ff.).

The level of knowledge that succeeds experience, namely thought in the narrower sense ("mental discourse"), consists for Hobbes in a *pre-linguistic* series or train of thoughts. Such thought is either "unguided" and "without design," that is to say, ungoverned and inconstant, or it is governed by desire and design, and thus determined by ends and purposes. In this case, a regular and connected train of thoughts serves to organize our sense impressions. Comparable in this regard to Aristotle's notion of willing (*boulēsis*), it seeks the means to realize the desired end in a starting point or "beginning within our own power."

In this regard Hobbes distinguishes between two kinds of "regulated thoughts." In the first, which is "common to man and beast," we look back over the past and seek the causes for a given effect. In the second and more developed kind, we investigate the utility of a thing by exploring all the possible effects that any given thing is capable of producing. It is only this kind of thinking that is specific to human beings, for it presupposes a "curiosity" that is lacking in living beings that are driven merely by "sensual" passion. Human beings alone possess the requisite capacity for such exploration and invention, and the *sagacitas* that it involves. But once again Hobbes does not explain precisely how such capacities are possible within the sensationalist and mechanistic framework he provides, or, that is to say, how the relevant organs of the heart and the brain are different in the case of human beings and nonhuman animals.

In the context of experience the capacity of "prudence" plays a distinctive role. In the philosophy of Aristotle the concept of prudence (*phronēsis*) is an authentically ethical power of judgment capable of determining a particular line of action in concrete cases, if the requisite ethical dispositions have been cultivated. In Hobbes, by contrast, the notion of prudence has a more emphatically epistemological significance, while the idea of ethical character, which is indispensible in Aristotle's account, is conspicuously absent here. Hobbes's concept of prudence is not connected to specific ethical virtues such as temperance and justice, which necessarily accompany it as in Aristotle. It is not of course normatively neutral, since it is supposed to promote the agent's own good, something that Aristotle and the tradition that began with him also recognized. But with regard to this governing end they defended a far more demanding normative concept, namely a notion of happiness (*eudaimonia*) intrinsically bound up with the ethical virtues. (Here we can ignore the fact that

Aristotle regards the life of *theoria* as the highest form of *eudamionia*.) By contrast, Hobbes's idea of prudence (also glossed as "foresight" and "providence") consists in a "conjecture" or "presumption" regarding the future satisfaction of our interests, which draws on the experience of the past and is independent of considerations of virtue (L ch. 2: 10–11).

In the further course of his reflections, Hobbes discusses the two means that significantly enhance the exercise of prudence, namely speech and quickness of memory. He also says that prudence is a comparative capacity proportional to experience: the more experience one has, the more prudence one is able to exercise. Lastly, this ethically neutralized notion of prudence involves a feature that is relatively independent of experience, namely a "natural judgment" that enables human beings to weigh up and consider all the effects of their own actions and the actions of others in the light of their own interests.

Astonishingly enough, Hobbes mentions only in passing that no amount of experience can make up for the lack of this capacity (L ch. 5: 22). He certainly recognizes the importance of "good judgment," but he connects it with the capacity for distinguishing and discerning differences ("discretion") rather than prudence (L ch. 8: 33). Thus in his discussion of the state of nature, Hobbes says that prudence belongs among those things in which nature has made human beings more or less equal: "For prudence, is but experience; which equal time, equally bestows on all men, in those things they equally apply themselves unto" (L ch. 13: 60–61). Since Aristotle's theory of prudence has not proved very influential in historical terms, but also represents a subtle and differentiated discussion of this subject, one might have expected greater clarification of the precise relationship between prudence and judgment in this regard.

Finally, it should be noted that Hobbes does not regard prudence as a uniquely human capacity. Yet his argument that some animals of only a year old are more prudent than children who may be ten years old overlooks three relevant questions here: whether adult human beings are not generally more prudent than fully grown animals; whether the prudence of human beings regarding their own good may be qualified not merely by a lesser degree of prudence in specific cases but also by ethical considerations that set their own good in a different light; and whether the prudence of animals is often merely an apparent prudence actually based on instinctively regulated behavior or something of this kind.

Questions such as these might give the impression that Hobbes underestimates the quite specific capacities of human beings. But this impression would be wrong, for Hobbes does emphasize the superiority of human beings in comparison with nonhuman animals. This superiority lies in the privileged human capacity we have already mentioned, namely that of inquiring into the consequences and effects that follow from any envisaged thing whatsoever. It is also true that this privilege has its negative side too: the "privilege of absurdity" to which human beings alone are vulnerable (L ch. 5: 20). But Hobbes also introduces a further reason and a further criterion to clarify the prudence exercised by human beings, and in this sense he qualifies his high estimation of the prudence he already ascribes to animals. For the capacity of language, possessed uniquely by human beings, enables them to develop all of their inborn capacities, including prudence, to a height quite unknown to any other living being (L ch. 3: 11). And here it is the range and stock of words that decide the degree of prudence, or of foolishness, in the case of human beings. The more someone is in possession of the right definitions or "significations" of things, the more prudent he is; the more he entertains false definitions, or none at all, the more foolish he is.

SIX

Language, Reason, and Science

The summit of Hobbes's intellectual hierarchy is the process of "imagining" produced by language, and it is this that makes the world of reason and science possible for human beings. While Hobbes regards the elementary data, sensations, and the faculty of memory as something "born with us," and prudence as something "gotten by experience," he claims that reason and science are only "attained by industry" (L ch. 5: 21; see also L ch. 3: 11).

In the course of his reflections he also introduces a distinction between two kinds of "intellectual virtue". The natural virtues of experience and prudence are not something we possess from birth, but are developed only through "use and experience" though "without method, culture, or instruction" (L ch. 8: 32). The intellectual virtues that are "acquired by method and instruction"—what Hobbes describes in short as the "acquired wit" of science and wisdom—simply amount to "reason; which is grounded on the right use of speech" (L ch. 8: 35).

6.1. Language 1: The Pre-communicative Dimension

It is language in the sense of speech (L ch. 4) that is responsible for man's superior abilities in comparison with other animals. But Hobbes has no

purely theoretical interest in language itself. He does specifically consider
the question of language in two respects, on the one hand in relation to
science and on the other in relation to the state. But in both cases he is
principally interested in the dangers that lie in the human capacity for
language, in the first place with the danger that the abuse of language
at the hands of scholastic philosophy poses to the advance of scientific
knowledge, and in the second place with the danger that the strategic,
demagogic, or ideological use of language poses to the sovereignty of the
state.

For both of these reasons Hobbes is less interested in language itself
than in the various kinds of misuse to which it lends itself. In order to
remedy this danger he demands emphatic clarity in the use of language,
while effectively ignoring the almost unlimited creativity that also belongs
to language. He accepts the claim in the Book of Genesis that God,
"the first author of speech," instructed man how the creatures were to be
named. But to be instructed in this manner is not itself to be empowered.
Downplaying human creativity and productivity in this regard, Hobbes
claims that man is not authorized to name things on his account and can
only "add more names" as the experience and usefulness of the creatures
suggest (L ch. 4: 12).

The systematic context in which Hobbes deals with the phenomenon of language furnishes an initial basic thesis. Neither the earlier *The
Elements of Law* nor the later *Leviathan* begins with a theory of science
into which the account of language has already been integrated. Nor do
they begin with a philosophy of language that would furnish a basis for a
philosophical analysis of the language of science or for a theory of science
itself. On the contrary, reason presupposes language, but language does
not presuppose reason. Thus Hobbes's theory of science is only presented
after his theory concerning the nature of language and his theory concerning the nature of reason.

As with many of his other doctrines, Hobbes's views regarding the
philosophy of language remain essentially the same whether we consider
The Elements of Law or his later systematic writings. His most detailed discussions in this regard are to be found in *Leviathan* (principally in chapter
4) and *De Corpore* (chapters 2–5). Following the condensed formulations
provided in *De Homine*, the last of the texts in which he deals with this
question, we learn (1) that language is peculiar to man; (2) that it consists
of words or names; (3) that the latter are constituted arbitrarily by the
will of man; (4) that they are connected with one another in order (5) to

stand for the conceptions of the things about which we think (H, ch. 10, §§ 1–3; cf. the condensed formulations in L ch. 46: 372ff.).

For Hobbes, therefore, there is a pre-linguistic form of thought (or "mental discourse"), which is merely verbalized by language proper. Remarkably enough, Hobbes does not begin with the social function of language, with that of interaction and communication, but with its purely individual function. And here he begins not with its affective or practical side but with the cognitive side, which is concerned with designating our thoughts. In terms of this pre-social function words are primarily signifying marks that serve as an aid and support for memory, and it is only in a secondary sense that they serve as a means of communication, which is the main role that has long been generally ascribed to them. Hobbes argues as follows: "Were there but one man in the world, these [i.e., the signifying marks] would be of use to him as the support of memory, though they could not serve him to communicate if there was no one there to communicate with" (C, ch. 2, §3). The human being therefore needs language even as an individual. And disregarding the alleged divine origin of language, the latter could have been developed on the basis of the single individual alone. In *De Corpore* Hobbes explicitly tells us (Co ch. 2, §4) that the names that constitute language serve "originally as marks in order to produce in our minds thoughts which resemble earlier thoughts."

Even if we would probably reverse this sequence and stress the social dimension of language, the other individual dimension deserves the recognition and significance that Hobbes himself emphasizes: language is also an aid and a support for the processes of memory.

And it is not in fact the case that Hobbes completely downplays the other social function of language. For in his opinion language does enable us to communicate our own ideas and desires to others. Language facilitates the mutual understanding that is based on knowledge ("conceptions") and will ("wishes"). In *De Homine* Hobbes also stresses the importance of "instruction" in this connection: through language we are able to give warning and counsel to others, and are able, as he makes clear in *Leviathan* (L ch. 4: 12–13), to provide assistance to one another.

If we look ahead in this connection to the question of the state, we can see that the latter also reveals a fundamental aspect that we might not have expected in Hobbes. For here in the first instance the state consists not in dominion, commandment, or obedience, but in the mutual assistance of human beings. But the discussion in *De Homine* introduces a further advantage of language that we would rather expect to be explored in the theory of the state, which is provided in *Leviathan*: "that we can command and understand commands is a benefit of speech, and truly the greatest. For without this there would be no society amongst men, no peace, and consequently no disciplines; but first savagery, then solitude, and for dwellings, caves" (H ch. 10, §3). The linguistic modalities of counsel and command certainly play a role in *Leviathan*, but they are treated there not in the context of the theory of the state but only in a subsequent discussion in the chapter that leads into Hobbes's account of civil laws (ch. 25: "Of Counsel").

In terms of all these specific purposes Hobbes sees no reason to extend or supplement the "sensationalist" character of his philosophy of mind by introducing a genuinely non-empiricist element, such as the idea of an intrinsically active or spontaneous cognitive faculty. And it is these purposes that explain why in all of his reflections Hobbes lays such emphasis on the requisite clarity and intelligibility of language.

There are three reasons why this pre-communicative origin of language is so important, indeed indispensible, in Hobbes. Firstly, it is an inevitable consequence of his method of "resolution," which by extracting human beings from their social content leads to an individualistic or solipsistic conception of the human subject; secondly, without this specific focus on the nonsocial side of language Hobbes would find it extremely difficult to maintain his purely naturalistic and mechanistic approach in relation to language; thirdly, and not least, this particular emphasis also serves the individualist character of his theory of the state.

Irrespective of whether they are interpreted as personal marks or as social signs, Hobbes treats the "names" that constitute language as so many labels we affix not to things themselves but to our images or representations of things. In terms of a general theory of knowledge and language this approach may well strike us as problematic, or even naive. In terms of the theory of the state, on the other hand, this approach does seem to have much to recommend it. What at first sight appears to be an entirely nonpolitical distinction between mental and verbal discourse, between pre-linguistic and linguistic thought, allows Hobbes to combine a theory of absolute political sovereignty with a very high degree of individual freedom and thereby "safeguard the free thought of the citizen within the state from any inquisitorial control or intervention on the part of the sovereign" (Kodalle 1996, p. 120f.), or, as Hobbes puts it: "men's belief, and interior cogitations, are not subject to the commands" of the sovereign (here the sovereignty of God: L ch. 26: 149). No one can be obliged to think in any other way than reason persuades one to think (L ch. 32: 196). One is responsible for one's inner thoughts only before God.

This same interest in personal freedom explains why Hobbes makes a distinction between crime and sin, emphasizing that "every crime is a sin; but not every sin a crime." Thus in a strikingly moralizing fashion he says that to "intend to steal, or kill, is a sin, though it never appear in word, or fact . . . but till it appear by something done, or said, . . . it hath not the name of crime" (L ch. 27: 151).

With regard to the fivefold definition of language already cited above, Hobbes's third point regarding the arbitrary constitution of linguistic names is not contradicted even if the divine origin of language is assumed, for he tells us that God established the corresponding names of things and animals as he saw fit. Since these original names were lost and forgotten with the Tower of Babel (C ch. 2, §2; L ch. 4: 12), they had to be reinvented in the context of different cultures.

It is the arbitrary or conventional character of human words that distinguishes them from the sounds or cries produced by other animals, as well as the fact—a sixth feature of language—that the human being possesses a more flexible kind of voice that allows the production of speech sounds. Hobbes explains this in terms of matter and motion, the basic concepts of his natural philosophy: language is generated through the movements of tongue, palate, lips, and other vocal features.

Interested as always in considerations of utility or "commodity," Hobbes begins the chapter on language in *Leviathan* by alluding to a hierarchy of useful inventions. But none of these is concerned with the means or techniques we employ for improving or alleviating the conditions of human life or labor. They all relate to language itself as the meta-technique, so to speak, of almost all other inventions. Thus Hobbes certainly recognizes the preeminent significance of language, but he understands this in wholly instrumental terms. In this regard language serves neither the cause of pure knowledge nor that of moral improvement. It is based rather upon an interest in power, though not simply power over other human beings.

Hobbes sees the superiority of human beings over animals in our capacity to envisage or project universal rules. In this sense man alone is capable of attaining a universal perspective on things. There is also a reverse side to this capacity: man is also the only being capable of falling into error and nonsense. Thus man possesses the dubious privilege of producing "absurdity" or "senseless speech" (L ch. 5: 19). Human beings can also fall victim to a "kind of madness" where they completely lose track of their thought for "lack of steadiness, or direction to some end" (L ch. 8: 33). Furthermore, seduced by the very facility of speech, human beings can talk even when they are thinking of nothing at all, and deceive themselves by taking such talk for truth. Lastly, since a human being can also deceive others, Hobbes can say that through language "man is not made better, but only given greater possibilities," that is, becomes more powerful (H ch. 10, §3, p. 41). In spite of all this, however, he does not underestimate the original and positive aspect of language, namely that abundance of wisdom that, along with folly and error, is only to be found among human beings (Co ch. 3, §8).

In the hierarchy of inventions that Hobbes begins by discussing, the invention of printing, though recognized as "ingenious," occupies the lowest place (L ch. 4: 12). A higher place is ascribed to the invention of written characters or letters, but the highest place belongs to the "most noble and profitable invention of all," namely speech, which consists of "names, or appellations, and their connexion." The hierarchy Hobbes construes is convincing enough, for without letters there would be no art of printing, and without speech there would be no letters, so that the more fundamental level of significance in fact belongs to language itself.

Although Hobbes does ascribe great significance to language, it is nonetheless surprising to note that he does not regard it as a constitutive element of human beings after all. He might indeed have done so by appealing to his own thesis that necessity is generally the mother of all invention. In this regard he could have pointed to the specific disadvantages that are peculiar to man in comparison with other animals, something already recognized in antiquity (see Plato, *Protagoras* 321c–d). Hobbes could then have derived the human prerogative of language precisely from the characteristic defects of a being that is inadequately equipped as a natural organism and lacks the requisite instincts that would immediately enable it to survive. But Hobbes makes no attempt to account for language in this way. Indeed he treats God rather than man as the original creator of language, thus forgoing the possibility of explaining language as the result of a constitutive lack or need intrinsic to the human creature.

Since Hobbes claims that language made certain forms of cooperation possible "amongst men" (L ch. 4: 12), it seems as though we can say that human beings existed before language. And in that case language would simply be a particular rather than a constitutive feature of man. It would be true that human beings alone possess language, but we could not claim that they have utilized it from the beginning of history. It seems therefore that human beings could have lived without language even in the earliest times. But Hobbes nonetheless ascribes a certain fundamental anthropological significance to language insofar as he already ascribes the capacity for language to Adam as the forefather of the human race.

6.2. Language 2: The Political Dimension

If we ask why Hobbes should incorporate a philosophy of language expressly into his philosophy of the state, and why he should accord so much space to this issue, the relevant chapter of *Leviathan* provides a very clear answer to this question. For the detailed investigation he offers here is not an end in itself for Hobbes. On the contrary, language is examined essentially as an indispensible condition for the political state itself, for without language, as Hobbes says, "there had been amongst men, neither commonwealth, nor society, nor contract, nor peace, no more than amongst lions, bears, and wolves" (L ch. 4: 12).

The comparison here is not particularly apposite. For the animal species he mentions, the so-called predatory animals, do not live off or prey on their own kind but on other species. And wolves live in packs, social groups within which individuals may fight to establish dominant status but rarely engage in a life-and-death struggle for victory. We must nonetheless admit that in large part Hobbes pursues his philosophy of language with a genuinely political rather than ideological intent. Indeed, his ultimate purpose is precisely to overcome any purely strategic and ideological calculations of utility. Thus for Hobbes it is a perfect example of ideological language to describe a king as a tyrant, or to describe regicide as tyrannicide in order to justify the act (L ch. 29: 170–71). And we simply conceal our own ambitions for power when we obstinately persist in maintaining opinions however absurd they may be under "the reverenced name of conscience" (L ch. 7: 31).

Fully recognizing its strategic, demagogical, and ideological possibilities, Hobbes regards language as the most useful of inventions, but also as a rather ambivalent one. Like every other means or technique, this meta-technique, as we have called it, can be used legitimately, but can also be abused, so that a "copious" store of words, as we have pointed out, can render human beings either wiser or more foolish. Animals, by contrast, possess an entirely innocent capacity for communicating with each other. For they are capable of "making known to one another their desires, and other affections," yet they lack that sophistical "art of words, by which some men can represent to others, that which is good, in the likeness of evil; and evil, in the likeness of good," thus creating discontent among human beings and disturbing the peace (L ch. 17: 87).

The ambivalent character of language affects the state on two levels. On the lesser level, the conflation of normatively saturated words derives from our passions, so that "one man calleth wisdom, what another called fear, and one cruelty, what another justice" (L ch. 4: 17). On the more serious and existentially crucial level, language offers greater security to the state—for it is language "by which we, having been drawn together and agreeing to covenants, live securely, happily, and elegantly" (H ch. 10, §3, p. 40)—while also posing a greater threat to it inasmuch as language makes war possible in the first place.

Alongside the "sophistical" art of words that we have already mentioned, Hobbes also includes our conflicts and arguments with regard to words among the ideological causes of civil war (a thought clearly expressed in B, part 2). We may counter these dangers in two complementary ways, which provide the linguistic basis for a rational politics: we can purify our language and encourage the unambiguous use of words. We must therefore keep to the settled definitions of terms if we are not simply to get "entangled in words, as a bird in lime twigs" (L ch. 4: 15).

In the fourth part of *Leviathan* ("Of the Kingdom of Darkness") Hobbes trenchantly and eloquently explores the abuse of language and presents his own strategy for countering such abuse. Once the state has been established, the sovereign's monopoly over the proper definition and interpretation of words inhibits the emergence of those subversive terminologies that undermine the stability and legitimation of the state. It is thus one of the essential tasks of the sovereign to maintain the required clarity in the language through which we communicate, and to keep this language free of disturbing conflict.

6.3. Realism and Nominalism

Although its origins can be traced back to classical thought, a fundamental philosophical controversy regarding the nature and status of universals had come to dominate the theory of knowledge, the philosophy of language, and the theory of reality (ontology) in Western philosophy since the eleventh century. The argument as to whether or how universal concepts (*universalia*) indicating genera (such as "living being") and species (such as "man") can properly be said to exist bears directly on the relationship between thought, language, and external reality. Since for Hobbes there is "nothing in the world universal but names" (*nomina* in Latin) for "the things named are every one of them individual and singular" (L ch. 4: 13), he is clearly a nominalist who denies any real validity to the universal. His conventionalist philosophy of language is equally nominalist in emphasizing the arbitrary ascription of names to things.

But since the first names (the names of the animals) are taught us by God, they do seem in a certain sense to be demanded by the created things themselves. It is true that on the basis of experience, and of the possibility of using living things for their own purposes, human beings can "augment" the world of names. But the fact that general names are supposed to arise from observing similar properties and features means that names are connected back to the "nature" of things. In this sense Hobbes overcomes a more traditional nominalism with what could be called an "objective conventionalism" and a "realist-oriented nominalism." Names are not indeed signs for the things themselves, as we have seen (C ch. 2, §3), but labels attached to our conceptions and representations of things.

Hobbes recognizes two hierarchies within the world of language, one regarding the names themselves (L ch. 4: 12) and one regarding the way we use them (L ch. 4: 16). With respect to the first hierarchy, the lowest level consists of the names of natural things and creatures. The next level comprises the manifold and relatively heterogeneous world of *abstracta,* which identify figures, numbers, and measures, as well as colors, sounds, imaginary representations ("fancies"), and relations. The next and highly variegated level in turn comprises other useful words such as universal ("general"), particular ("special"), affirmative, negative, interrogative, and optative. Remarkably enough, Hobbes also includes the word "infinite" here, although he had earlier claimed that we cannot form any idea or conception of the infinite.

Lastly, in the fourth place, Hobbes mentions those senseless and redundant words such as "entity," "intentionality," and "quiddity," which have been invented by the scholastic tradition of philosophy. Hobbes already rejects this vocabulary in advance of any further substantive considerations simply on the basis of his own philosophy of language, which is so strictly focused on the issue of utility. Hobbes only recognizes the significance of language to the extent that it serves this cause. Thus the idea of a language that is developed and extended for the purposes of mere knowledge as such is expressly excluded. There is clearly also a certain anti-elitist and democratic moment at work here. In his dispute with Bishop Bramhall we can see why Hobbes demanded that the scholar as well as the cleric should use only those words that any ordinary person can understand (Works, vol. V, p. 268). Hobbes also makes the anti-elitist point that any scholastic distinction must first be examined to see if it can be translated "into any of the modern tongues, so as to make the same intelligible; or into any tolerable Latin" (L ch. 8: 39).

6.4. The Framework of Language and Reason

Hobbes's conception of language as a connection of names is not itself revolutionary in any way. Yet his notion of the "reckoning" that is involved in language is certainly anything but traditional (L ch. 4: 14). We can see this from the second hierarchy, which he identifies in language. For here we use names to consider things in different perspectives and "reckon" with them accordingly. On the lowest level we consider "a thing" with respect to "matter" or "body," and then describe it, for example, as "living," "moved," or "hot" (L ch. 4: 16). On the next level we proceed to accidents or qualities, speaking now of "life" instead of "living," or of "motion" instead of "moved." On the third level we move on to consider subjective perceptions, that is to say, not the things themselves, but the sight or color of these things in our "fancy or conception." Lastly, in the fourth place, we "reckon" with names themselves, with the names of names such as "universal," "special" (particular), or "equivocal," or again with specific forms of language ("speeches") such as "affirmation," "interrogation," "commandment," "narration," "syllogism" or "sermon." Any names that cannot be accommodated within one of these four legitimate classes are repudiated by Hobbes as "insignificant sounds" produced "by Schoolmen, and puzzled philosophers" (L ch. 4: 16–17).

As far as the source of truth and falsity is concerned, Hobbes assures us that this is language, and dismisses the alternative view that truth resides in things themselves: "For *true* and *false* are attributes of speech, not of things" (L ch. 4: 14–15; cf. C ch. 3, §2). In contrast to the widespread view that the senses can deceive us, Hobbes roundly claims that neither the senses nor indeed our conceptions or representations are themselves the source of error. Nor are the names that furnish the building blocks of language capable of being true or false. It is only the connections between them that can be true or false. Names may, however, be assigned wrong definitions or no proper definitions at all (L ch. 4: 15). For Hobbes there is a corresponding name or sequence of names for every conception, although not every name has a corresponding conception. Truth consists in an affirmation or assertion in which the names are correctly ordered and connected. And the "reckoning" that belongs to language is responsible in this regard. It is through such reckoning that our assertions are capable of truth in spite of the arbitrary character of name-giving. Once one names one class of objects "man," and a more extensive class "living beings," the assertion that "men are living beings" is necessarily true. The arbitrary origin of names does not affect the truth-capacity of language.

In interpreting language as reckoning, Hobbes underestimates the process of synthesis or connection expressed in the copula "is." This is already required by reckoning ("two and two is four") and must be recognized as a specific accomplishment in its own right. Hobbes does not claim that language is already propositionally structured (essentially "asserts something as something"), nor does he recognize a "pre-logical," perhaps even pre-linguistic or purely affective, stratum of language, which would manifest itself, for example, in sounds expressing pleasure or pain. As far as the intrinsic character of assertion is concerned, the limitation of Hobbes's approach here is not surprising. For his naturalistic empiricism leaves no room for any specific or independent contribution on the part of understanding or "reason" as Hobbes calls it.

In claiming that human beings employ language to designate their thoughts Hobbes defends a "copy theory" of knowledge. In this view, there is such a thing as pre-linguistic thought that arises in a mind not yet structured in linguistic terms, which then simply transfers its thoughts into words by means of language. In this sense there is a structural identity between cognition and language, although the substantive and ultimately also temporal priority here lies with cognition: the already existing relations of our representations or "conceptions" with one another are then taken over by language.

Since Hobbes minimizes any specific contribution on the part of the mind, he defends a certain parallelism here, with an emphasis on the preexisting thoughts. Language possesses no real structure or structural principles of its own, for the structure of language ("verbal discourse") follows or reflects the structure of thoughts ("mental discourse"). This is also why it is so important to characterize these thoughts, and the names that designate them, correctly. The principal task of (scientific) speech consists in the correct definition of names. And one must also keep to these established meanings or "significations" as Hobbes calls them.

Apart from the two general uses of language Hobbes recognizes four other specific ones. These again begin with pre-social and cognitive-utilitarian considerations and, with the exception of the fourth, are built up on one another in a series of stages. In its primarily personal function, language serves for the acquisition of knowledge. In the context of its social function it serves, in what is basically a secondary sense, for the communication of this acquired knowledge, for mutual counsel and instruction. It is only the third use of language that reveals its practical dimension, although this is concerned with the expression of one's own will and purpose rather than with the world of feelings and passions. But this use of language is not concerned with what we would typically expect of Hobbes, the allegedly pessimist philosopher who so strongly emphasized the idea of *homo homini lupus*. In fact he is not principally concerned with rivalry or competition between human beings, but rather with the possibility of mutual human support and assistance, already indeed evoked by the significance he accords to mutual counsel.

The fourth use of language concerns the more playful level of delight and decoration (which suggests a relatively positive estimation of the dimension of rhetoric). There are two particular aspects that are absent here: the rivalry or competition between our desires—the struggle for recognition or "glory" (cf. L ch. 13: 61)—and the disinterested use of language in a theoretical or contemplative sense not directed to any practical interests or considerations.

Hobbes contrasts each of these four legitimate uses of language with a corresponding abuse of language. He begins with self-deception based on the false description or identification of one's own thoughts, and goes on to discuss the metaphorical use of words that are capable of deceiving others, and also the (mendacious) concealment of our true will and intentions. The fourth kind of abuse, the absolute opposite of the harmless delight in language, consists in offending or insulting someone through speech, something that is only permitted for the purpose of instruction and correction (L ch. 4: 12).

There are several critical questions one would naturally want to ask with regard to Hobbes's account of language. How, for example, would we accommodate the experience of the deaf and dumb in a theory of language that is based on names, and in the theory of reason, which is constructed on this basis? Do such individuals possess no language at all? And do they have no share in reason either? Can we not interpret the use of sign language, supplemented by imitative and other gestures, as a functional equivalent of spoken or written language? Hobbes's assumption that linguistic signs must primarily consist in vocal sounds is not particularly convincing, and in any case does not necessarily follow from his other fundamental assumptions.

One could broadly accept four of the five basic aspects of language that have already been mentioned: language as a distinctive capacity of human beings; the arbitrary or conventional character of names; language as a means of connecting our thoughts; and its role in designating our conceptions or representations. It is only the second aspect ("words in the sense of names") that would need to be defined more formally, as "unequivocal signs" for example, although words might well represent the most prominent, even the most important, form of signs in this regard.

For Hobbes reason has two basic tasks to fulfill: the "apt imposing of names" and securing "a good and orderly method" that permits us to make assertions and connect these assertions with one other (L ch. 5: 21). In his *Dialogue between a Philosopher and a Student* Hobbes says that all study is "either in accordance with reason or it is worthless" (D ch. 1). If we take the great mathematicians as our model, therefore, we are less likely to go astray than are the great experts on law.

In fact Hobbes goes even further and claims, with considerable exaggeration, that reason is "nothing but reckoning" (L ch. 5: 18; cf. the dedication in *The Elements of Law* and the preface to *De Cive*). Hobbes thankfully restricts this conception of reckoning—an essentially dispassionate and disinterested activity—to the first two fundamental kinds of reasoning that are identified as "adding and subtracting." But elsewhere he adds that "if any one would include multiplication and division here, I should have no complaint, for multiplication is the same as the addition of equal items" (C ch. 1, §3; see also L ch. 5: 18).

Charged with the two principal tasks of ordering one's own thoughts and presenting these thoughts to others, the function of reason is to add and subtract "the consequences of general names." Indeed the character of reckoning already belongs to the pre-linguistic thinking that is performed by the human mind (L ch. 4: 14; see also C ch. 1, §3). For through language "we turn the reckoning of the consequences of things imagined in the mind, into a reckoning of the consequences of appellations."

Reckoning on its own of course is not enough. If thought actually consisted in nothing but this, then general names would also arise through the process of addition and subtraction. But Hobbes merely appeals to similarity ("similitude"), so that the corresponding names arise through comparison rather than reckoning. Insofar as reckoning is accomplished in language it only commences once we are already in possession of names. This is why in the course of his chapter on reason (L ch. 5) Hobbes specifically defines reason in terms of two tasks, proper name-giving and methodical inference.

The correct definition of words, the atomic building blocks of reckoning, precedes this process of philosophical arithmetic. But those thinkers, like the "schoolmen" who would rather rely upon established philosophical authorities such as Aristotle, Cicero, or Aquinas, and offer only false definitions or none at all, are merely abusing the name and task of science.

6.5. Science

Hobbes defines science as a syllogistic connection of propositions ("assertions") concerning the causal relations obtaining between facts. It is pursued to the point where we "come to a knowledge of all the consequences of names appertaining to the subject in hand" (L ch. 5: 21). Science in the proper sense thus exhibits four distinctive features: it is the investigation of causes; it reasons strictly on the basis of sure and reliable rules (this recalls Descartes's *Treatise on Method* of 1637); it aims at complete knowledge, an attainable and indeed constitutive feature for Hobbes since this relates to the names that belong to things rather than to the domain of objects itself; and lastly, it maintains the clear and stable meaning of words or names, an essential condition of all true inference.

As we have pointed out, it is the investigation of causal relations that allows science in Hobbes's sense to serve humanity: "reason is the pace, increase of science, the way; and the benefit of mankind, the end." The strictness of its reasoning preserves it from subjective errors and thereby renders it objectively reliable. And once we are in a position to "teach" science, that is, to "demonstrate the truth thereof perspicuously to another," we can even describe it as "certain and infallible" (L ch. 5: 22).

Some of Hobbes's claims are particularly problematic. He regards geometry as the ultimate model for all the sciences, but he defines science, just as he defines reason and language, in essentially arithmetical terms: as a form of "reckoning" based on operations of addition and subtraction. There are two reasons for this. On the one hand, what he takes from geometry is simply the method: the idea that we must start from precise definitions and derive our conclusions strictly from these definitions and these alone. It would certainly have been more accurate to understand "reckoning" merely on analogy with geometry, avoiding this talk of addition and subtraction and referring instead to affirmation and negation as a means of presenting our own thoughts and wishes to ourselves and to others. On the other hand, he understands geometry not in geometrical terms, as the spatial construction of figures, but rather in arithmetical terms. He supposes that the geometer approaches lines, figures, angles, and proportions in the same way that the arithmetician approaches numbers, namely in terms of addition and subtraction.

It is also astonishing to note that Hobbes extends the list of objects supposedly treated by geometry to include time, velocity, force, and power, concepts that belong to the domain of physics (L ch. 5: 18), and thus fails to distinguish geometry from physics. Yet in his own schema of the sciences Hobbes does clearly separate these two sciences. In the context of his natural philosophy as a whole Hobbes contrasts two fundamental domains: that of physics, which is concerned with the "consequences from qualities," and that of mathematics, which is concerned with the "consequences from quantity, and motion determined." Here geometry is specifically concerned with "figure" and arithmetic with "number" (L ch. 9: 40).

It is not easy to interpret what Hobbes means when he says that geometry is "the only science that it hath pleased God hitherto to bestow on man" (L ch. 4: 15). This might mean that mankind has possessed geometry from the very beginning, namely that it is in some sense innate in man. Yet this would contradict Hobbes's repeated claim that reason is not inborn but is subsequently acquired "by study and industry" (L ch. 3: 11).

Since the time of the pre-Socratics, philosophers have often seen their own activity as a kind of knowledge or "science," indeed as the highest science. But they have also tended to contest this claim to science on the part of their predecessors. A scant regard for the achievements of others, and a correspondingly high regard for their own, is eminently characteristic of Hobbes. In his chapter on "science," philosophy proper does not appear at all, though he alludes in wholly negative terms to those "that profess" philosophy. Indeed they are especially exposed to what he calls "the privilege of absurdity" (L ch. 4: 20). In the chapter on language Hobbes does refer to Aristotle, Cicero, and Aquinas, but only to imply that all those who appeal to such authorities are "fools" (L, ch. 4: 15).

As well as elegantly omitting any mention of his other contemporaries or predecessors, such as Mersenne, Descartes, Galileo, or Gassendi, Hobbes simply dismisses the earlier contributions of two thousand years of intellectual history as irrelevant or even pernicious. He thus indirectly presents himself as the first truly "scientific" thinker. It is only in his late text *De Corpore* ("To the Reader") that he observes more modestly that thanks to the natural reason that "belongs to every man," philosophy dwells "within you," though not yet developed in a clear form. Although Hobbes wishes to employ his method precisely to accomplish this, he says that he does not want to "press upon you what is mine, but to offer everything merely as a proposal." (This more modest suggestion is at least hinted at in the maxim cited in the introduction to *Leviathan*: "*nosce teipsum*," or "read thyself.")

Francis Bacon had already tried to show the fundamental errors to which the human understanding was prone. In his *Novum Organon* (*New Method*) he systematically identified the roots of these errors in his famous discussion of the "four idols." After his own analysis of the four "abuses" to which language is subject (L ch. 4), Hobbes goes on to distinguish less harmful errors, to which even the wisest may fall victim, from the more serious danger of producing "absurd" propositions. The causes of the latter (L ch. 5: 20) start with "want of method," namely with the failure to proceed from settled definitions. This leads to category mistakes that arise by confusing "bodies" with properties or "accidents" (as when we describe "extension" as a body).

Hobbes's extensive list ends with a discussion of two particular snares of thought: the use of metaphors and figurative forms of speech, and the use of meaningless names. With derogatory hyperbole Hobbes equates metaphors with contradictory expressions. Thus to speak of "in-poured virtue" is as meaningless as to refer to a "round square." Later on Hobbes says that in "demonstration, in counsel, and all rigorous search of truth" metaphors must be "utterly excluded," for they "openly profess deceit" and it would be "manifest folly" to admit them (L ch. 8: 34). In spite of these severe criticisms Hobbes toward the end of *Leviathan* does permit certain images and metaphors after all: an "earthly sovereign" can be described as "the image of God" and an "inferior magistrate" as "the image of an earthly sovereign" (L ch. 45: 359).

Here Hobbes contradicts his own professed method for constructing a scientific philosophy of the state. In the *Leviathan* itself he makes use of a number of images and metaphors, including of course the conspicuous figure of the Leviathan that adorns the title page, the comparison of man with an artificial animal and of the state with an artificial man in the introduction, and such a striking comparison as the following, to name but one of many: "For the thoughts, are to the desires, as scouts, and spies, to range abroad, and find the way to the things desired" (L ch. 8: 35).

Even in a strictly systematic work such as the three-part *Elements,* Hobbes does not approach his philosophical ideal of an argument cleansed of all metaphor. In the first part of *De Corpore* (ch. 3, §8) alone we are presented with two striking metaphors. He says that human language is like "a spider's web; weak spirits hang therein and entangle themselves, while stronger spirits break out with ease." And to emphasize how "rules are less necessary than practice" when it comes to deriving rational conclusions, he points to the way that "little children learn to run, that is, not through precepts but through practising" (Co ch. 4, §13).

The other snare of thought, the use of meaningless names, appears self-explanatory. But Hobbes's examples, the use of terms like "hypostatical" and "transubstantiate," prompt the question whether he is not avoiding a substantive engagement with the issue. The neo-platonic tradition employed the term "hypostases" to designate the individual levels of being that spring from divine being; and in scholastic Christian theology the term "transubstantiation" refers to the alleged transformation of the "substance" of bread and wine into the body and blood of Christ. Both expressions therefore stand for claims that may be false, but this cannot be decided solely by reference to the words or names themselves. It would thus be more appropriate to speak of false theses or erroneous doctrines in this connection.

6.6. Hobbes's Division of the Sciences

Hobbes regarded the overall structure and division of the sciences as so important that he dedicated a specific chapter to the subject. As had been customary since the time of classical philosophy, Hobbes begins by distinguishing the knowledge of facts from the knowledge of grounds, in Hobbes's language "consequences." He restricts the "knowledge of fact" to the first two levels of knowledge, which are based on sensation ("sense") and memory respectively.

In accordance with his own sensationalist position, and in contrast to a long philosophical tradition, Hobbes ascribes the status of "absolute knowledge" to sensation rather than to science itself. He points out that this knowledge of fact is what, for example, we demand of a witness in court. The second kind of knowledge, or the "knowledge of consequences," which constitutes "science," is essentially conditional: "as when we know, that, if the figure shown be a circle, then any straight line through the centre shall divide it into two equal parts" (L ch. 9: 40). And this is the kind of knowledge that we require of the philosopher, though we cannot expect it from the "schoolmen." A true philosopher, by contrast, is one that properly "pretends to reasoning" (ibid).

Following traditional usage, Hobbes describes the "register of knowledge of fact" as "history," where the word is used in its older comprehensive sense (the gathering of empirical facts or information of any kind). In this connection he distinguishes the history of facts that are not dependent on the human will, or "natural history," from the history of facts that are dependent on the human will, or "civil history."

In accordance with the broad understanding of the term "philosophy," which was then common, Hobbes describes the "registers" of all the sciences as "philosophical books." The twofold division he applies to the knowledge of fact is here also applied to scientific knowledge, yielding the twofold division between the science of natural bodies, or "natural philosophy," and the science of political bodies, or "politics and civil philosophy."

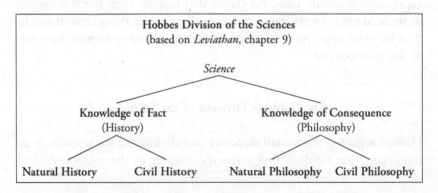

Hobbes Division of the Sciences
(based on *Leviathan*, chapter 9)

Science

Knowledge of Fact
(History)

Knowledge of Consequence
(Philosophy)

Natural History   Civil History   Natural Philosophy   Civil Philosophy

It is worth drawing attention to certain peculiarities of Hobbes's elaborate schema of the sciences. Thus it is rather surprising here that Hobbes does not follow the threefold division of his philosophical system propounded elsewhere. Instead of a philosophy of bodies, a philosophy of man, and a philosophy of the citizen, we now have a twofold schema, as was already the case in *The Elements of Law*. There the twofold schema was presented under the titles "Human Nature" and "De Corpore Politico," or as we might say, "Anthropology" and "Political Philosophy," although this anthropology already includes and indeed begins with natural philosophy. The schema Hobbes adopts in *Leviathan*, on the other hand, distinguishes between natural philosophy, which here includes anthropology, and political or civil philosophy.

As another characteristic feature of Hobbes's schema, we should note that "first philosophy" (*philosophia prima*) is not something that precedes or stands above the distinction between natural philosophy and civil philosophy. In Hobbes's "sensationalist" perspective there is no room for a preliminary ontology of objectivity itself. His "first philosophy" is concerned with natural bodies from the first, that is to say, with matter. Hobbes is a materialist in the fundamental philosophical sense: the only thing that exists is matter. Since "first philosophy" essentially investigates bodies with regard to their (admittedly indeterminate) quantity and motion, it belongs to the domain of natural philosophy, although it occupies the highest place here. Thus it belongs to the first part of Hobbes's philosophical system, under the title *De Corpore*, which is surprising only at first sight. For "first philosophy," which is in effect metaphysics, here falls within Hobbes's philosophy of bodies.

Hobbes's philosophy of language is not actually worked out in detail, but its most fundamental part would belong to this "first philosophy." On the other hand, what could be called a kind of applied philosophy of language would fall under the sciences concerned with the "consequences from speech." For Hobbes these constitute four disciplines, although the order in which he presents them is astonishing: firstly, we have poetry, which he says, remarkably enough, is concerned with the language of "magnifying, vilifying, etc." (L ch. 9: 40). In spite of this, Hobbes, who would himself subsequently translate both the Homeric epics, sometimes shows a broader and more perceptive understanding of this subject. For he also tells us that "judgment," and more especially "fancy," is what we desire and expect of a good poem (L ch. 8: 33). The former encourages due discrimination, while the latter, which is more important here, provides for originality ("extravagancy").

After poetry Hobbes goes on to list rhetoric ("persuading"), logic ("reasoning"), and the science of what is just and unjust ("contracting"). It is another peculiarity that this latter science appears under the rubric of natural philosophy, rather than that of civil or political philosophy, which both corresponds to and contradicts the presentation of the argument in *Leviathan*. It corresponds to the text of *Leviathan* insofar as Hobbes does present his reflection on natural laws in the first part of the text. But it also contradicts it insofar as he says that notions of right and wrong, of justice and injustice, have no place where there is no "common power" or established authority (L ch. 13: 63). But it is only in the second part of the text, which deals with political philosophy ("Of Commonwealth"), that this common power is analyzed and discussed.

In everyday language, terms like "just" and "unjust" are normative concepts. But in the presentation of his argument Hobbes relates them directly to the concept of "pact" or "contract," which evokes the non-normative or wholly "positive" conception of law that *Leviathan* actually endorses, albeit in part 2 of the work, especially in chapter 26 ("Of Civil Laws").

Moreover, the "science of just and unjust" does not belong to the domain of ethics. For the latter is a science in its own right, one that is concerned with the human passions, and is decidedly nonnormative. Remarkably enough, in the Latin version of *Leviathan*, in the last section of chapter 9 on "Ethics, Logic, and Rhetoric," these are discussed one after another in a way that suggests an equal relationship between them. Last but not least, we notice that the schema presented in *Leviathan* includes no mention of religion, either Christian or non-Christian, or of the Church, themes which were of crucial importance to Hobbes.

We may also note that *De Corpore* offers a different division in one respect. Although Hobbes here retains the twofold division of philosophy into natural philosophy and civil or political philosophy (*Philosophia Civilis* in the Latin version of *Leviathan*), the latter in turn is divided into ethics and politics, so that ethics is transposed from natural philosophy to civil philosophy.

SEVEN

An Anthropology of the Individual

The Passions

In his theory of the passions Hobbes adopts a strictly individualistic approach. Just as *Leviathan* begins with an asocial epistemology and philosophy of mind, and originally ascribes a pre-communicative function to language, so too its analysis of the moving forces of human action, namely the "passions," is focused on the individual. This approach may not be entirely satisfactory but seems highly plausible nonetheless. For with respect to our particular sensations and passions, we are certainly directly, if not exclusively, concerned with ourselves and our own existence.

7.1. A Naturalistic Hedonism

It had been recognized since antiquity that the possession of reason and language was a distinctive and fundamental feature of man, and Hobbes accepts this as self-evident. In the first five chapters of *Leviathan* he concentrates on the theoretical side in this regard: the fact that external bodies produce images and sensations that lead to connected trains of thought, that these trains of thought become capable of bearing truth through the verbalization afforded by language, and become truly scientific once they trace and identify the causes and consequences of things. It is only in chapter 6, and here alone, that Hobbes addresses the practical side under the name of the "passions," the "interior beginnings of voluntary motions" or the motivating forces that provide energy and direction to human behavior. These are the motions of "appetite" and "aversion" (the positive desire for a thing or the negative desire to avoid it) through which things, conditions, and persons are evaluated as good or evil respectively.

While Hobbes's political philosophy is clearly directed against Aristotle, the theory of passions that introduces it reveals some significant similarities with Aristotle's thought. Like Aristotle, Hobbes connects the theory of action, of the desires that motivate human behavior, with a theory of the good, and its opposite, and in that sense with an "ethics." Like Aristotle, Hobbes's account of action employs the concept of striving or "endeavor" and also expounds a relational concept of "the Good." What is more, Hobbes's method similarly appeals to the way we ordinarily speak (what is "commonly called," "that we call," "the forms of speech by which the passions are expressed," etc.). But unlike Aristotle, he ascribes no importance to the distinction between two kinds of striving, one that involves making or producing something (*poiēsis*) and one that finds satisfaction or fulfillment within itself (*praxis*).

Above all, however, Hobbes understands his fundamental ethical concepts of good, bad ("evil"), and happiness ("felicity") in descriptive rather than normative terms, in a purely subjectivist and naturalistic sense. To put it paradoxically: Hobbes's naturalistic anthropology compels him to defend, as a basic normative thesis, a literally nonmoral concept of "the Good" that has been released from any normativity. And the concept of what is bad is nonmoral too. For this negative evaluation Hobbes uses the word "evil" (equivalent to the Latin *malum*). While the word can sometimes signify evil in a strong moral or spiritual sense, such overtones are alien to Hobbes's nonmoral understanding of the term. This spiritual sense of the word is absent from *Leviathan*, as it was absent from *The Elements of Law* (part I, ch. 7, §3) and will be absent in *De Homine* (ch. 11, §4). It is rather misleading to translate it with a more moral or religious term (as Walter Euchner does in his translation of *Leviathan* when he uses the German word *böse* instead of *schlecht* in this connection).

Hobbes certainly recognizes the ambiguities that attach to the expression "good." Referring back to the Latin (L ch. 6: 24), he specifically distinguishes things that promise good or are good in contemplation (*pulchrum* or beautiful) and things that exercise a good effect (*jucundum* or delightful), and which are therefore desired for their own sake (H ch. 11, §5), and again things that are good as a means (*utile* or useful). But he denies that anything can be intrinsically good in itself, thus repudiating anything resembling the Platonic Idea of the Good. Nor does he recognize the functional concept of good that would apply to the objective fitness or reliability of a tool or instrument, for example. Although he offers no real justification for this claim, Hobbes asserts that all human beings agree in calling that which they desire good and that which they hate or avoid bad (L ch. 6: 24). For Hobbes, "good" is at the least a two-term predicate: something is "good for someone," or, according to *De Homine* (ch. 11, §4), even a four-term predicate: "good is said to be relative to person, place, and time."

Like the basic positive concept of good, happiness ("felicity") as the sum of the good is also defined in nonnormative terms: "since life is but a motion" (L: 1), human desire, whether in the positive sense of appetite or in the negative sense of aversion, can never be extinguished, so that the Stoic ideal of "perpetual tranquillity of mind" (L ch. 6: 29) is ruled out in principle. Being driven from one object of desire to the next, we seek to procure "a contented life" for ourselves, and indeed to assure it for the future as well (L ch. 11: 47). The greatest good, or happiness in this life, lies in "always progressing towards ever further ends with the least hindrance" (H ch. 11, §15, p. 54), or the "continual success in obtaining those things which a man from time to time desireth, that is to say, in continual prospering" (L ch. 6: 29).

In his division of the sciences in *Leviathan*, Hobbes assigns the theory of the passions to the domain of ethics, but assigns ethics to the domain of natural philosophy (L ch. 9: 40). For Hobbes does not understand ethics in the usual sense of the word, as the theory of morality or of "the good life," that is to say, as a normative theory of the right or the good; nor again as "meta-ethics," as a nonnormative theory of basic normative concepts. For when he discusses concepts such as good, bad, happiness, etc., he introduces them, as we have seen, in a way that runs quite counter to the common understanding of such terms. Thus one might speak of a new and provocatively nonmoral theory of morality here. Yet it is more appropriate to interpret the ethics expounded in chapter 6 of *Leviathan* as a theory of action, and more specifically a theory of affects or emotions, which has been expanded through evaluative but nonmoral concepts. This theory follows on quite logically from the fundamental concept of Hobbes's natural philosophy, that of matter in motion.

Hobbes includes man among the animals, but he also distinguishes between "vital motions" or processes that transpire independently of thought or representation (imagination), such as the circulation of the blood, respiration, digestion, etc., from animal or "voluntary motions" such as walking or speaking. Since these latter motions "depend always on a precedent thought of *whither, which way*, and *what*," it is evident that imagination in this sense is "the first internal beginning of all voluntary motion" (L ch. 6: 23). Hobbes has thus indicated the basic concept that is decisive for human action, and was already mentioned in a preliminary way in his discussion of the "train of thoughts" (L ch. 3: 9), namely that of desire, which is now identified as "endeavor" and differentiated, as we saw, according to its two basic forms as appetite and aversion.

Hobbes's nonnormative definition of good and bad, in its individualistic and hedonistic aspects, fits perfectly into this naturalistic and mechanistic anthropology. On account of the individualist aspect the expressions "good" and "bad" are both always defined in relation to the particular person involved, while on account of the hedonistic aspect they are both defined in terms of pleasure or displeasure, in terms of the satisfaction of needs and interests: "enjoyment applies to something proposed as an end" (H ch. 11, §5, p. 48). Hobbes does not focus exclusively on the pleasures of the senses, for he also recognizes pleasures of the mind, although what he understands by such pleasures are not the intellectual ones of the mathematician, the historian, or the philosopher, but those released by the expectation of sensible pleasures to come.

Hobbes's approach anticipates that of Jeremy Bentham (1748–1832), the father of classical utilitarianism, but also recalls one aspect of Plato (*Protagoras*, 355eff.), when he suggests a kind of hedonistic calculus capable of comparing and even quantifying various goods and evils: "If good and evil be compared, other things being equal, the greater is that which lasts longer. . . . And, other things being equal, that which is stronger." Hobbes also says, surprisingly given his individualism, though not for the logician who regards the universal as greater than the particular, that "what is good for more is greater than what is good for fewer" (H ch. 11, §14, p. 53).

There are two other basic concepts that sit very well with Hobbes's sensationalist-hedonistic perspective. He obviously recognizes that a person may entertain both hopes and fears with regard to one and the same thing This results in the process he calls "deliberation." But this is interpreted not as a reflective assessment or evaluation of the situation but as an exclusively affective or emotional process that finally leads to "doing or omitting" (L ch. 6: 28). It is true that "experience or reason" can play a role in this affective process, for they help us to foresee longer chains of consequences (L ch. 6: 29). Reflective assessment, on the other hand, is described by Hobbes as "discourse," which refers only to the realm of "opinion," which can claim the status of truth.

The result of this affective process of deliberation, the last appetite or aversion, is what is called "the will," understood not as a faculty but as an act of willing. Hobbes rejects the scholastic notion of the will as "rational appetite," arguing that if this were right there could be no such thing as a voluntary act against reason. Consequently, he is quite prepared to ascribe will to "beasts" insofar as they are capable of deliberation in his sense (L ch. 6: 28). Since Hobbes maintains a strict separation between the theoretical and the practical domain here, he has no place for the notion of anything like practical reason, let alone pure practical reason.

7.2. A Topography of the Passions

A subjectivist and hedonistic conception of the good does not necessarily commit human beings to egoism, self-love, or asocial priorities in any normative sense. Hobbes is perfectly capable of recognizing the varied and many-sided character of human life in an unprejudiced manner, and although he discusses such antisocial passions as envy or vengefulness, he also investigates socially neutral passions such as hope, fear, and trust, and indeed above all obviously social ones such as benevolence, goodwill, charity, and liberality.

The free self-interest that basically governs human behavior includes all those appetites and aversions that arise naturally and spontaneously in human beings, irrespective of whether they involve social considerations or not. But Hobbes has no room here for genuinely moral demands, which may oblige us to curb or restrict such spontaneous desires and inclinations. It is only in the context of his theory of the state, and the natural laws involved here, that Hobbes establishes various moral principles that while not eliminating the human passions serve at least to domesticate them.

The tacit assumption that human beings are ultimately determined only by their self-interest does not mean that all motives, intentions, affects, and passions merely represent so many open or covert forms of self-interest. Unselfish impulses such as compassion or charity are by no means dismissed or unmasked by Hobbes as rationalizations of human self-preservation or of the desire for happiness, and thus as impulses that are only apparently social. Among other things, Hobbes's theory of the passions does seek to instruct and enlighten us with regard to our ultimate intentions, and perhaps even involves a moral critique of hidden intentions that run counter to our conscious beliefs and convictions. But this moral critique is not intrinsically directed against everything that we would ordinarily describe as moral in character.

Rather than adopting a moralizing or an anti-moralizing posture, Hobbes assumes the role of a morally neutral cartographer of the rich domain of the human passions. He does not judge, still less condemn, these passions, although he does subsequently concede that "the understanding is by the flame of the passions, never enlightened, but dazzled" (L ch. 19: 96). In a sober and dispassionate spirit Hobbes simply asks what the principal human passions are. And with a pedantic concern for completeness he enumerates and defines each of them in somewhat wearying detail. Nonetheless, his discussion also reveals an often subtle appreciation of the variegated world of the passions, of the phenomena themselves, and of the linguistic forms and other signs through which we express our feelings and passions, so that Hobbes is able to provide some very striking and perceptive observations in this regard.

Hobbes's map of the passions begins with the appetites and aversions, which he says are "born with men," the first one he mentions being the appetite for food that serves the immediate preservation of life. He identifies the "simple passions" in terms of four basic factors (L ch. 6: 25): the likelihood of our attaining what we desire (with hope in the positive case, or despair in the negative case); the object itself that is loved or hated (with fear when hurt is expected, or courage at the prospect of avoiding hurt); the consideration of several objects (with constant hope or "confidence" in ourselves, or constant despair or "diffidence" in ourselves); lastly, the alteration or succession of the relevant objects (with indignation in the negative case or benevolence, goodwill, or charity in the positive case). Hobbes goes on to discuss many other passions, always in the same normatively neutral fashion, such as covetousness, ambition, pusillanimity, magnanimity, kindness, luxury, and natural lust.

The basis for this whole cartography is the act of introspection that Hobbes mentions in the introduction to *Leviathan*. If we "read" within ourselves, each individual can discover the same passions at work in everyone. Of course, a certain process of abstraction is required here, to which Hobbes indirectly alludes when he clarifies the fact that it is the passions themselves that are the same in all human beings, rather than the objects of the passions, or the things that are desired or avoided in each case. The last paragraph of the introduction also indicates a further process of abstraction, which in addition to the individual and particular features also sets aside any specific and particular cultural conditions involved. For Hobbes says that what we must "read" here is "not this, or that particular man," but rather mankind as such (L: 2).

As far as the passions are concerned Hobbes thinks the abstraction required is not so difficult insofar as it is already implicit in the careful analysis of our actual language and linguistic behavior itself. This position seems on the one hand to look back to Aristotle's investigation of the ambiguities harbored in ordinary thought (*pollachōs legomena*) and to anticipate the Oxford school of "ordinary language philosophy" that was inspired by Wittgenstein's *Philosophical Investigations*. Hobbes's approach can be captured by the motto: To examine ordinary language, is to examine mankind. It is quite true that certain culturally specific features enter into ordinary or everyday language, but Hobbes attempts to reduce if not eliminate these wherever possible. For he is not satisfied with simply appealing to English language and usage, but constantly appeals to Latin and Greek terms as well in order to buttress his claims.

In only one regard does Hobbes exchange his morally neutral or reticent "enlightened" critique of the philosophical tradition for a more engaged and acerbic form of moral criticism, and this concerns the human propensity to wage war on one another. He attempts to unmask this propensity for war as a kind of "false consciousness," a dysfunctional urge for self-preservation that actually undermines human self-interest.

7.3. Freedom, Self-Preservation, and Determinism

If we consider Hobbes's second partial method, the resoluto-compositive method, in this context, we can read his theory of the passions in two directions. The resolving or analytical aspect, looking backwards, returns to the systematic beginning of the overall philosophical argument, and in this sense the theory connects seamlessly, as we already suggested, with Hobbes's mechanistic natural philosophy and his sensationalist theory of knowledge. From the compositive or synthetic perspective, looking forwards, the question is this: Does this theory of the passions constitute an appropriate basis for a philosophical justification of the state? As it turns out, we can only conclude that it does.

Although Hobbes's theory of the passions operates with the concepts of good and bad, which are normally deployed in a normative sense, his theory is not intended to provide a philosophical ethics in the usual sense. And offered as such it would hardly be convincing, but it is certainly convincing as foundation for the justification of the state. For since political authority is entitled to coercion where necessary, every individual person must be convinced of the advantage derived from this power, irrespective of whether the individual in question is willing or unwilling to cooperate with others in society. Even for the pure egoist the existence of public authority and its sanctions must be more advantageous than the absence of such authority. We must also recognize here the methodological and political reason for Hobbes's desire to avoid an ideological civil war waged through language. For if we define "good" and "bad" in a strictly nonnormative fashion, solely by reference to the individual subject in each case, we are less likely to fall into the sophistical snare of describing as good what others regard as bad, which only results in "discontenting men, and troubling their peace at their pleasure" (L ch. 17: 87).

The ultimate normative criterion of free self-interest involves more than mere survival. In *De Homine* (H ch. 11, §6, p. 48) Hobbes grounds the idea of self-preservation in these words: "For nature is so arranged that all desire good for themselves" (cf. L ch. 17: 85 and ch. 30: 175). Nor does he simply reduce the notion of self-interest to an unsocial principle of self-love, to some form of egoism in contrast to any social form of interest. Hobbes is basically concerned with two things here. On the one hand, he distinguishes the human subject from the lower nonhuman beings in terms of language and the way in which the latter makes reason and science possible. On the other hand, the human self or subject is not submitted to any normative restrictions. What precisely the self strives to attain or tries to avoid is, apart from self-preservation, entirely down to the self in question. Self-interest *may* include eminently social impulses, but it does not have to. The social inclinations or impulses do not possess the character of natural endowments that are more or less reliably directed of themselves toward cooperative behavior and the state as the public framework of such behavior. Nor do they signify demands that would on occasion oblige us to limit our spontaneous inclinations.

It may seem problematic that Hobbes describes the self-interest that is understood in this way as "free." For his assumption that the world is entirely subject to the principle of mechanical motion involves an emphatically deterministic position. Indeed he regards determinism as so self-evident that he does not even discuss it in his theoretical account of the passions. Nor does he offer there any explicit argument against the freedom of the will as this is usually understood. If various desires or aversions arise in relation to the same object, then we certainly engage in deliberation, but this process is not essentially cognitive but rather affective in character, or "voluntary" in Hobbes's specific sense of the term, even if reason or experience may also play a role here.

For Hobbes the dominant and all-inclusive impulse, namely the urge for self-preservation, is free not because it consists in a will that is independent of inner restrictions, nor because it can exercise sovereign choice when confronted by a range of options, nor even in the sense that it can inwardly consent to the inclinations that present themselves. On Hobbes's purely negative conception of freedom, or "liberty," it consists in "the absence of external impediments" (L ch. 14: 64; see also L ch. 21: 107f.). Internal hindrances or impediments such as uncontrollable impulses or paralyzing fear are not regarded by Hobbes as restrictions or limitations of freedom.

Free self-preservation thus consists in "the liberty each man hath, to use his own power, as he will himself, for the preservation of his own nature; that is to say, of his own life" (L ch. 14: 64). This freedom is regarded as a natural right (*jus naturale*), to which however the natural right of every other human being is opposed, and this produces the hostile and insecure state of nature (see chapter 8, below). Once the state of nature is overcome in the civil state, the subjects of the state retain this freedom, although it is now limited to "those things, which in regulating their actions, the sovereign hath praetermitted" (L ch. 21: 109). It is striking that it is only when he comes to address this theme in chapter 21 ("Of the Liberty of Subjects") that Hobbes expressly discusses his determinism and maintains that freedom and necessity are quite compatible ("consistent"). For all that is required for freedom is that an action springs from one's own will, although "every act of man's will . . . proceedeth from some cause," which in turn is caused, so that we are confronted with a "continual chain" of causality here (L ch. 21: 108).

7.4. Power

Hobbes's discussion of the intellectual virtues already revealed the enormous significance he ascribes to power. In that context he had clearly subordinated the other factors of wealth, knowledge, and honor to that of power.

In the modern debate regarding the nature of power, Max Weber's definition has proved particularly influential: "'Power' [*Macht*] is the probability that one actor within a social relationship will be in a position to carry out his own will despite resistance, regardless of the basis on which this probability rests" (*Economy and Society*, §16, p. 53). Weber the sociologist limits power here to a social phenomenon. But Hobbes, along with the philosophical tradition, is reluctant to begin with any such limitation. Hobbes will introduce the social perspective when he presents his theory of the state, but he rightly refuses to start with this. He defines his starting point more universally as follows: "The power of a man . . . is his present means, to obtain some future apparent good" (L ch. 10: 41).

In his usual confident and forceful way Hobbes is here implicitly contrasting this approach with other comparable concepts: with the idea of power or dominion acquired through contract, that is to say, through consent, with the authority of the sovereign, with the force to which we subject ourselves, for example, through "fear of death, or bonds [i.e., bondage]" (L ch. 20: 100). But Hobbes regards power not as a contrary or opposed concept here, but as the all-embracing one. For the greatest human power is composed out of many human beings who are united as a single person as the power of the state (L ch. 10: 41). In Hobbes's interpretation, power is not an end in itself but simply a means. Furthermore, it must be regarded as a subjective concept in a twofold sense: (1) as the sum of the means that are dependent on the subject in question; (2) with regard to what the subject takes to be its good.

If we look more closely at the way Hobbes applies the concept of power, we would have to distinguish three domains here: power in relation to nature, in relation to one's fellow human beings, and in relation to oneself. Hobbes himself, it is true, specifically distinguishes two principal kinds of power, while going into rather tedious detail about its numerous subordinate kinds. The common denominator here is the social framework in which they are considered. Although a truly comprehensive analysis would require all three domains we have indicated to be addressed, Hobbes ignores two of them. But the bodily and mental capacities he mentions mean we do not have to exclude technology as the sum of our power in relation to nature or medicine as the sum of our power in relation to the human body. And this corresponds to the first domain. Nor would we have to neglect the third domain, and virtues such as circumspection, which Hobbes could regard as a second-order passion, virtues that afford us power over our usual first-order passions. Or without wishing to eliminate these primary passions we could certainly attempt to domesticate them in the interest of one's own well-being.

When he introduces the first kind of power (described as "original" or "natural" power) Hobbes already emphasizes its eminence in expressly social terms (L ch. 10: 41). The social perspective informs all the sorts of power and assumes a clearly political coloring in what follows, for Hobbes speaks explicitly about the titles, offices, and functions with which the sovereign honors his subjects (L ch. 10: 43).

The second kind of power (described by Hobbes as "instrumental") appears with respect both to its origin and purpose as a second-order power. For it is itself acquired through "natural power" or through "fortune," and serves to increase power even further.

In the wealth of his particular observations Hobbes once again reveals his considerable insight into politics and human life in general. Thus he acknowledges the significance of "riches" as a form of power, but only when combined with that "liberality" that "procureth friends and servants," for otherwise riches simply "expose men to envy, as a prey." He goes on: "Also, what quality soever maketh a man beloved, or feared of many; or the reputation of such quality, is power" (L ch. 10: 41). In many of the subordinate forms of power Hobbes shows just how it is not only actual power but also reputed power that counts, the reputation of power that is skillfully produced in the eyes of others. It may seem very surprising that Hobbes ascribes so little power to the sciences, even though he is himself dedicated to scientific knowledge and hopes to further "the benefit of mankind" by doing so (L ch. 5: 20). Even in the case of mathematics he lauds its practical and not just its methodological utility (see the dedication of *De Cive*). Is Hobbes not simply contradicting himself here, as well as contradicting Bacon's famous motto that greater knowledge implies greater power (*tantum possumus, quantum scimus*)? Hobbes mentions two kinds of ignorance as a not wholly implausible reason for the slight power that science possesses: on the one hand, the sciences are understood only by the few, and, on the other hand, it is not recognized that in many cases, as in the construction of fortifications, it is the underlying mathematics rather than the builder himself that is responsible for the achievement in question. Hobbes does not even consider the possible alternative suggestion that scientists enjoy a special intellectual privilege on account of their greater knowledge. In the last analysis it remains true that Hobbes sees power as something available principally to those directly engaged in politics, for the scientist exercises only an advisory role here.

An important feature of power as far as human beings are concerned, in Hobbes's eyes, is the restless desire to increase it wherever possible (L ch. 11: 47), and this is not only discussed in the context of the state of nature. Since happiness (felicity), which is the governing end for human beings, is "a continual progress of desire, from one to another," which can never finally or definitively be secured, the individual as such cannot help seeking constantly to extend and increase it.

Once again the method Hobbes actually pursues in his reflections on power owes less to his conception of reason as reckoning than to the notion of introspection we have already discussed. But this process of introspection is not free of assumptions. Although the two objects of introspection mentioned in Hobbes's introduction, namely thoughts and passions, can both be discovered directly and immediately within ourselves, the means of securing and increasing power can only be discovered indirectly. For one must also consult the great book of the social world in order to see what kind of phenomena present themselves as forms of power. A process of selection is also required, in which the social dimension acts as a further filter in this regard. Only what remains after this process can confer or assure power in the social field. Hobbes himself does not actually present this methodologically complex process as such. He presents the direct result, inquiring only after the means that effectively realize power. But he offers a brief but perceptive account of each of these means.

EIGHT

An Anthropology of the Social

The Possibility of Peace in a Condition of War

8.1. The Conditions of Peace

It is in chapter 11 of *Leviathan*, in the midst of the exposition of his anthropology, that Hobbes decisively and explicitly takes up the social perspective, and begins to present his political philosophy under the title "Of the Difference of Manners." What Hobbes means by manners here concerns neither the rules of decent or fitting personal behavior ("small morals"), nor the matter of morality in the emphatically "moral" sense. Hobbes's ambitious but purely functional concept of manners is concerned rather with "those qualities of mankind, that concern their living together in peace, and in unity" (L ch. 11: 47).

Remarkably enough, Hobbes does not define the principal aim, namely that of peace, more precisely here. And when he does identify this aim as the purpose of the state or commonwealth (L ch. 17: 87) he provides no further substantive clarification of the question. It is quite true that in this discussion of "manners" in chapter 11 Hobbes's talk of unity already furnishes some idea of his aim, but it still lacks sufficient clarity. In his doctrine of the state of nature, on the other hand, it appears almost too ambitious, being presented as the counter-concept to the condition of latent war: peace prevails if we can be sure that human beings are not prepared to resort to war. But as Hobbes concedes, this is hardly the case even in the civil state, for although "there be laws, and public officers, armed, to revenge all injuries shall be done to him," every individual still arms himself when taking a journey, and "when going to sleep, he locks his doors" and "even in his house he locks his chests" (L ch. 13: 62). Must we say therefore that the state or commonwealth that is erected precisely to overcome the state of war has failed in its purpose?

In the chapter on manners, which offers a condensed version of his argument for the necessity of the state, Hobbes introduces a number of those key concepts that he undertakes to justify and elucidate at a later point of the text. Referring emphatically back to his analysis of the motivating forces of human action, Hobbes here presents a range of different options. But astonishingly enough he does not even mention the uncompromising demand that the state establish a condition of peace.

Hobbes explains that human beings strive after ever-greater power, although he does not yet attempt to justify this claim in a social context. He begins from the individual's interest in creating a satisfactory life and securing it for the future. It is only from the social perspective that this restless striving for power leads to competition, which is intensified in the form of "contention, enmity, and war." But anyone who seeks a pleasant and enjoyable life, anyone who also fears harm, injury, or death, anyone who further desires knowledge and the cultivation of peaceful arts and skills, is already prepared to obey a "common power" or authority.

With his sober analysis Hobbes sees more than a wish for peace at work here. He does not even claim that the desire for peace always wins out in a conflict between competing inclinations. On the contrary, Hobbes says, needy and hardy individuals, who are "not contented with their present situation," or those "ambitious of military command" are "inclined to continue the causes of war; and to stir up trouble and sedition" (L ch. 11: 48). Three key notions of Hobbes's subsequent argument are certainly absent from this discussion: the role of reason in promoting peace, the natural laws that reason identifies, and the doctrine of the sovereign representative. But none of these will actually guarantee the ultimate victory of the desire for peace. So that, in fact, chapter 11 (on manners) preserves an openness on certain substantive issues that chapter 13 (on the natural condition) abandons in a way that seems implausible from the perspective of this chapter.

8.2. "Man Is a Wolf to Man"

Every state, even an entirely just state, possesses laws and prohibitions, along with regulations of various kinds, which may be directed against the explicit will of an individual in certain cases. Consequently these laws and prohibitions must reveal and maintain their binding character through coercion or the threat of sanctions where required (we only have to think of fiscal and penal law or the regulations of civil law). A state consists of public powers or structures of authority that promulgate or enforce the relevant laws and provide binding decisions where conflicts arise. Every political community involves some form of rule or "dominion," although not necessarily, as radical social critics often suppose, a system of domination or exploitation.

Since no human being ever willingly accepts an infringement of his or her own freedom, the emergence of utopian social projects that repudiate the idea of authority or dominion is in a sense quite natural. The theory of the state that Hobbes adumbrates in chapter 13 thus responds to the still topical question whether such utopian conceptions of a condition without dominion or government, of anarchy in the original sense of the word, can really stand up on closer examination. Hobbes's theory takes the defenders of just such a utopian absence of government at their word and thinks all the consequences through to the end: what would result if we assume a condition in which there were no institutionalized political order at all, so that all individuals and social forces could unfold completely without any hindrance whatsoever?

Such a condition, devoid of any legal or political order, is described by Hobbes as a "natural condition" (L ch. 13) or "state of nature" (*status naturalis* in C ch. 1, §4, p. 114, and in other places). From the methodological point of view, this notion does not imply or refer to any actual historical or pre-historical time. It is a rational construction, a philosophical thought experiment that explores the internal dynamics of a hypothetical coexistence of sensuous beings who possess reason and language, but a coexistence not subject to any rules or norms. If one fails to appreciate this, as Hume does in his essay "Of the Original Contract," one already misses the basic point, whatever clever counterarguments are raised against the notion. It is true, however, that the hypothetical character of this thought experiment is not entirely obvious in Hobbes's discussion in *Leviathan*. In the preface to *De Cive*, on the other hand, Hobbes tells us that the state or "the matter of civil government" should be "so considered . . . as if dissolved" (C, pp. 98–99), and in chapter 8 of the same work he writes: "Let us return again to the state of nature, and consider men as if but even now sprung out of the earth, and suddenly, like mushrooms, come to full maturity" (C ch. 8, §1, p. 205). In *Leviathan*, by contrast, Hobbes refers again and again to empirical circumstances and states of affairs. Yet experience is only supposed to confirm his earlier "inference made from the passions" (L ch. 13: 62).

In the state of nature envisaged in this thought experiment human beings are understood exclusively in terms of their natural right (or "right of nature") to free self-preservation (L ch. 14: 64) and to a contented life (L ch. 17: 85), which includes all the "contentments of life" that an individual can acquire by "lawful industry" (L ch. 20: 175). The right of nature, to be precise, consists in "the liberty each man hath, to use his own power, as he will himself, for the preservation of his own nature; that is to say, of his own life" (L ch. 14: 64). The reference to "right" here has various senses; the meaning of "nature" requires further clarification; and the concept of freedom or "liberty," although it is a modest and purely negative one, is problematic.

The first key element here, the notion of "right," does not involve an idea of right in a normative or juridical sense. It does not raise a claim or make a demand since it is not directed at anyone, nor does it express the kind of permission someone may extend or withhold. It does not represent any form of social or political or religious authority that might issue a command, express a prohibition, or grant permission.

The second key element, the nature invoked in this "right of nature," is quite different from the "law of nature" (*lex naturalis*) that Hobbes goes on to mention in the third paragraph of chapter 14. What is common to both concepts is indeed the absence of any instituted political authority, but in the case of natural right "nature" consists in the natural passions, and the (supposedly) principal passion, which is that of self-preservation, while in the case of the law of nature the issue concerns reason as the faculty that is complementary and at the same time subsidiary to the passions.

Once again it is consistent that freedom or "liberty" is determined in negative rather than positive terms, although its characterization as "the absence of external impediments" (L ch. 14: 64) is redundant or even false. For according to Hobbes's preceding reflections the human being may (is permitted to) do or omit to do what he wishes ("as he will"), where the will is understood as the passion that ultimately wins out in that interaction of appetite and aversion that Hobbes calls "deliberation." The question whether there are any external impediments or not is initially irrelevant here. For if such impediments do exist, the human being "may" always seek to overcome them and use all his power to do so.

This negative freedom assumes concrete form in the needs and desires we seek to satisfy. If different human beings desire the same thing—a circumstance that is possible not only in a competitive capitalist society or under conditions of scarcity, but even in social conditions of abundance—they come into mutual conflict. In striving together for the means of self-preservation and happiness or a contented life they become opponents. Hobbes also recognizes two further causes of conflict, namely mutual distrust ("diffidence of one another") and desire for fame and reputation ("glory"). One human being mistrusts his fellow human beings, and thus fears interference or violence at their hands, and also seeks to be recognized or valued by his fellow human beings, which is not always forthcoming. Of these "principle causes of quarrel" (namely competition, diffidence, and glory) the first "maketh man invade for gain; the second, for safety; and the third, for reputation" (L ch. 13: 61–62).

Insofar as the opponents regard the same thing as indispensible for securing their own life or individual happiness, their opposition is intensified into enmity, i.e., it becomes a struggle for life and death. Such an intensification of conflict can never objectively be excluded by some neutral observer. And it becomes all the more likely if there is no recognized authority or rational criterion to adjudicate, and each individual therefore has to decide according to his own passion in each case. Thus in the state of nature man lives in constant fear of violent death, and every individual is exposed to this fear.

This consideration proceeds, like almost every other form of legal and political philosophy, from the assumption that human beings are in some sense basically equal (as Hobbes had already argued in E part I, ch. 14, §2 and C ch. 1, §3). But Hobbes's thought experiment only reveals its specific character when we recognize the nature of this equality. For it is not a question of equal dignity, for example, and only secondarily is it a question of equal physical or mental strength or worthiness, a point in which Hobbes distances himself from Aristotle (L ch. 15: 77). The decisive thing for Hobbes is rather the equal weakness and vulnerability of human beings, which makes all other differences entirely relative, for the weaker individuals who certainly do exist are quite capable through cunning or in conjunction with others of killing even the strongest human being (L ch. 13: 60). No one is so strong that he can never fall victim to violence at the hands of another. Every individual should therefore be fully aware of his own lack of power in certain respects, and also of the vulnerability of other individuals. With his ninth "law of nature" Hobbes even turns natural equality into a (quasi-moral) "precept." Against the Aristotelian thesis that some individuals are more worthy by nature, Hobbes writes: "I put this, *that every man acknowledge another for his equal by nature. The* breach of this precept is pride" (L ch. 15: 77).

In the state of nature, however, the individual cannot rely on the maintenance of this or of any other precept. That is why Hobbes takes up the ancient formula ultimately derived from the classical comic writer Plautus (*Asinaria* II, 4, 88): *homo homini lupus* ("man to man is an arrant wolf"), which had already been cited by Francis Bacon (*De Augmentis Scientarium*, book VI, ch. 3). It is true that this formula should not simply be endorsed in an absolute sense, for like Bacon before him Hobbes also cites the equally ancient counter-formula *homo homini deus* ("man to man is a kind of God") (C, the dedication, p. 89). It is only in the absence of the state that man is a wolf to man; in a state or commonwealth, on the other hand, we are talking about the artificial rather than the natural man, namely the state or "Leviathan" that stands in relation to the individual human beings like a God. As distinct from the true God, the Leviathan is indeed only "a Mortal God" (L ch. 17: 87). It looks as if Hobbes directly adopted both of these formulas from a collection of epigrams by John Owens (1564–1622): *Humano generi lupus et Deus est homo quae nam Deus est homini Adamque lupus* (*Epigrammata*, 3. 23f.; see the discussion in Pagallo 1998). This comparison of stateless human beings with wolves is a typical example of Hobbes's rhetoric. Firstly, the image does not originate with Hobbes himself but is drawn from his stock of humanist learning; and secondly, it has a manifold significance, and in many cases has led to rather problematic or misleading interpretations of Hobbes's work. But if we make the effort to uncover its appropriate meaning, we find a fertile and many-sided thought that is independent of the particular image.

If we consider the way in which wolves live and associate with one another, the image does not indeed seem that well chosen. Behavioral biology has shown that these animals are not as a rule solitary creatures, but live in packs typically made up of an original alpha pair and their various offspring. The wolf pack thus exhibits a hierarchical structure, and may consist of eight or occasionally even as many as twelve members depending on the size and strength of the principal prey. But the struggle *among equals,* which is decisive in Hobbes's eyes, does hold at least for the wolf cubs. But the latter can rely on something that is absent in the thought experiment of the state of nature: a common power, as Hobbes would say, which is exercised by the dominant alpha pair.

Hobbes's image may allude either to the struggle that transpires between the wolves and their prey, or to the open struggle for dominant status within the group, which occurs when the power of an existing alpha male begins to wane. Both of these interpretations allow two possibilities, only one of which is relevant. The struggle between the wolves and their respective prey does not make that much sense of the image insofar as in Hobbes's state of nature human beings threaten their fellow humans rather than some other species.

The situation is different, in the second possibility, when we consider that the predatory wolf may even take human beings as its prey. That "man is a wolf to man" would then simply mean that a human being can suffer violence at the hands of his fellow human beings, and thereby often fall victim, as is usually the case with wolves, not to the violent attack of an individual but of a group of individuals.

If we turn from the animal as predator to animal as member of the pack and consider the wolf in this context, the struggle between the established alpha male and an emerging younger rival—the third possibility—is not so frequent that it represents the kind of everyday danger envisaged in Hobbes's notion of the state of nature as a state of constant war. It is only when we assume, as the fourth possibility, that the alpha male is constantly threatened by an aspiring younger member of the pack, when we ignore the hierarchical order that usually prevails, that we are in fact presented with a danger that cannot be overcome. Here the comparison of the stateless human being with the wolf once again proves relevant: with living creatures like wolves and their packs there is no such thing as a permanent state of peace.

To return from the image to the underlying thought: for Hobbes the state of nature is characterized by a *bellum omnium contra omnes* (L ch. 13, in the Latin version; see also C, the preface, p. 101 and ch. 1, §3, p. 114). In the English version of *Leviathan* he speaks of a "war of every man against every man" (L ch. 13: 62, and also ch. 14: 64). It is true that this idea of a war of all against all is not new, and we can certainly find a precedent for it in ancient philosophy (see Plato, *Laws*, book I, 626d). But like the wolf metaphor, this idea has typically been associated with Hobbes ever since he elaborated it. Apart from one or two other scholars, this notion and other related ideas have been ascribed more or less exclusively to the work of Hobbes.

What Hobbes understands by the notion of war is not so much the kind of constant cut and thrust or the immediate violent confrontation of an endlessly perpetuated civil war as the condition in which the individual can never in principle be secure with regard to his or her own life in a situation of equal weakness and vulnerability and in the absence of any political authority or "civil power." Hobbes thus furnishes the historical circumstances of the English Civil War with a more probing and fundamental exposition and explanation. For the analysis that results from Hobbes's thought experiment does not merely relate to the situation prevailing in England in the middle of the seventeenth century or merely, in an expanded sense, to the entire period of civil and religious wars in Europe as a whole.

There is another misunderstanding that should be avoided here: the fact that man in the state of nature is always at least a potential source of violence does not mean that man, for Hobbes, is simply aggressive and destructive by nature. It is certainly true that he regards the human passions as value-neutral drivers of behavior that must realistically be acknowledged as they are. Man is not antisocial in some moral sense, i.e., morally bad or evil; nor is man bad or evil in some inevitable or blameless way. It is not that the fundamental human passions simply consist of envy and hatred, or of violence and hostility. They consist rather in that striving for free self-preservation and happiness that we have already discussed. But these primary drives or impulses themselves necessarily lead to the other asocial tendencies, which, while secondary, are nonetheless unavoidable: as long as human beings, unrestricted by any political power or authority, exclusively follow their own unhindered self-interest, they incline toward violence. The thought experiment of the unhindered pursuit of individual self-interest thus leads, from the social perspective, to that condition of a latent war of all against all which threatens the human desire for free self-preservation and happiness so strongly that human life becomes "solitary, poor, nasty, brutish, and short" (L ch. 13: 62).

8.3. A Prevailing Inclination for Peace?

The crucial issue of Hobbes's theory of the state consists in this insight that the rigorous pursuit of self-interest is counterproductive in a social context. The state or commonwealth ultimately proves to be necessary on account of the immanent "contradiction" of the state of nature. The insistence upon one's free self-interest and desire for happiness radically threatens the fulfillment of this fundamental intention itself: "In such condition, there is . . . consequently no culture of the earth; no navigation, . . . no commodious building . . . no knowledge of the face of the earth; no account of time; no arts; no letters; no society" (L ch. 13: 62). The liberty that holds in the state of nature—the unhindered freedom to pursue one's interest in the light of self-preservation and happiness—turns out on closer analysis to be self-destructive. The "right of nature," which is a "right to every thing" (L ch. 14: 64; cf. also E part I, ch. 14, §10) is thus revealed as a right to nothing. Human self-interest here proves dysfunctional, and the condition of peace that eliminates that of latent war thus lies in the self-interest, properly understood, of each. In accordance with the logic of calculated self-interest, therefore, Hobbes's "first, and fundamental law of nature" is "*to seek peace, and follow it*" (L ch. 14: 64).

One might initially think that Hobbes is here attempting to derive peace as a universal or "communicative" interest from its opposite, from an exclusively particular or solipsistic self-interest. But he is actually showing that particular interest, once it negates mere particularity within the social perspective, cancels itself as such. Thus he demonstrates, *e contrario*, through determinate negation, that enlightened self-interest "always already" contains a communicative or universal aspect, namely the interest in overcoming the condition of war.

With regard to this interest, Hobbes introduces two mutually supporting factors: the threefold character of human motivation and the capacity for reason. In accordance with his method of "reading" the nature of mankind (L: 2), Hobbes presents his readers with the following picture: a human being who (1) is moved by his or her passions; (2) is mindful of his or her future; (3) lives under conditions of a shared environment; (4) is as weak and vulnerable as anyone else; and (5) is driven by the three principal causes of conflict into that highly unsatisfactory condition of latent war that hinders the principle human aim of free self-preservation and a contented life.

If this condition of war is to be overcome, it is necessary for three human passions that promote peace to cooperate with the human reason, which is capable of identifying the path that leads to the accomplishment of this aim. Many interpreters of Hobbes have ignored or overlooked the fact that human nature involves more than the "three principal causes of quarrel. First, competition; secondly, diffidence; thirdly, glory" (L ch. 13:

61). The condition of war that springs from these is only half the story for Hobbes. The other half lies in "the passions that incline men to peace." And there are also three of these: "fear of death; desire of such things as are necessary to commodious living; and a hope by their industry [their own efforts] to obtain them" (L ch. 13: 63).

The other factor involved here, our human capacity for reason, shows the way in which this threefold human motivation can be realized. Although reason sets up certain universal principles, and especially the principle that the condition of latent war must under all circumstances be overcome, reason is conceived here as purely instrumental rather than as autonomous in character. Reason stands in the service of a heteronomous albeit not primarily arbitrary principle, namely in the service of the peace that for its part serves human self-interest. Reason as Hobbes understands it thus possesses an individual-pragmatic character, if not a simply technical one. Yet even in this respect, reason is conceived as a merely theoretical rather than as a practical form of reason. For it simply guides a human insight or understanding that is not capable of acting in its own right, namely the insight that on closer examination the right to everything proves to be a right to nothing. For one cannot rely on or be sure of anything, whether it is one's own particular possessions or one's own life or physical safety. But since this insight on its own has no motivating power, it requires the other active and motivating factor that is also directed toward the ultimate human aim.

It is plausible enough to claim that these three passions encourage a genuine interest in peace, but it is not plausible to argue that they must always enjoy an absolute priority for every individual. Hobbes himself has already mentioned certain competing passions in this regard in chapter 11 (see chapter 8.1, above). Even in terms of the text of *Leviathan* itself, the claim for the absolute status of these passions is not sufficiently grounded. One can also argue that Hobbes constantly reduces this claim to universal validity to a more modest one of "considerable empirical probability."

The objection that this claim is insufficiently grounded is also supported by an argument that is not tied to Hobbes's own assumptions in *Leviathan* but arises directly from the issue discussed there. In discussing the principal human aim of self-preservation, Hobbes rather neglects or obscures the manifold senses that attach to the "self" in question. Simplifying the point here, we can say there is a sensationalist or hedonistic "natural self" that is ultimately oriented to nothing but its own life in a biological sense, to nothing but survival and a satisfying life; and there is a "moral self" that sees, for example, its own religious, political, linguistic, or other forms of cultural self-determination or freedom as more important. This self may take as its end or aim something it prizes more highly than mere survival. In renouncing its natural self-interest in this way we might argue that the moral self reveals its own sublime vocation.

Remarkably enough, Hobbes does not address these questions, which arise internally or externally in relation to *Leviathan* itself. Thus it is difficult to avoid the impression that he shifts the weight of the argument when he moves from the "manners" that promote peace in chapter 11 to the discussion of the state of nature in chapter 13. For whereas in his discussion of manners we find passions that encourage peace as well as those that hinder it, in his discussion of the state of nature the passions that are inimical to peace are initially accorded such weight that the final paragraph of this chapter proves rather surprising: firstly, that there are passions that incline human beings to peace; and secondly, that these passions are able to overcome those that are inimical to peace. One might indeed refer to reason here, but the latter only suggests the appropriate "laws of nature" (L ch. 13: 63). It does not say that one should will peace rather than war. Only in his earlier text *The Elements of Law* do we explicitly read that, "reason therefore dictateth to every man for his own good, to seek after peace" (E, part 1, ch. 14, §14, p. 81).

In a subsequent chapter of *Leviathan*, in connection with "the wills of them all, to peace" (L ch. 13: 88), Hobbes does not specifically indicate whether this is the dominant, even absolutely dominant, human wish or merely one human motivation among others. If the latter is the case, one can only hope that human beings "become at last weary of irregular jostling, and hewing one another" (L ch. 29: 168), and that the interest in peace is thus ultimately accomplished. A possible basis for this might be the calculation of advantages and disadvantages Hobbes offers in *De Cive*: "out of the state of civil government" there is only "a dominion of passions, war, fear, poverty, slovenliness, solitude, barbarism, ignorance, cruelty; in it, the dominion of reason, peace, security, riches, decency, society, elegancy, sciences, and benevolence" (C ch. 10, §1, p. 222). Yet one must still ask how reason is supposed to overcome the passions if it has no motivating power of its own.

We can imagine how Hobbes might respond to this criticism: of course, it is true there are some human beings who occasionally or generally regard certain things as more important than their simply "biological self." The civil wars of the period furnish numerous examples of this, and sayings such as "better dead than red" certainly have their equivalents in other periods and cultural contexts. Nonetheless, it would be unwise, even foolish, not to bestow absolute priority upon life itself. But in employing this argument Hobbes would be appealing to the empirically normative perspective that "death is the greatest of all evils (especially when accompanied by torture)" (H ch. 11, §6, p. 48). Yet this perspective is ruled out by two elements of Hobbes's general argument: by his expressly non-normative interpretation of the passions, including the deliberation that is wholly internal to the passions themselves, and by his rejection of any genuine notion of practical reason.

It would seem more promising to adopt a kind of transcendental approach here. Thus we could argue that biological life is a condition of the possibility of having passions at all and pursuing their ends in the first place (see Höffe 1991, p. 26). Even someone who aspires to military command, in Hobbes's example (L ch. 13: 48), or someone who is prepared to die for his religious, political, or cultural freedom must first be alive and maintain that life before he can risk it on behalf of his freedom. One might also argue that Hobbes tacitly presupposes an interpretation of this kind, although there are no obvious indications in the texts to this effect.

If we adopt this transcendental interpretation, then Hobbes's argumentation is convincing, even independently of his own premises. For we can modify the elements of the state of nature as he specifically conceives it and effectively reach the same result: as long as human beings influence and impact on one another by inhabiting the same space and environment, and as long as they are determined here solely by their own free self-interest in the absence of any political structure and authority, acting therefore entirely in accordance with their own notion of what is right or good for them, then neither individuals nor groups of individuals can be secure from mutual conflicts or acts of violence. In these conditions there is ultimately no protection not only for one's property or possessions, but more fundamentally, even for one's own bodily life, and there is no room for one's personal existence itself.

Hobbes's thought experiment thus allows us to draw a conclusion that holds beyond the specific historical circumstances of his time: the limits to free self-preservation do not arise from purely external considerations. These limits do not derive solely from a shortage of goods or resources, nor from the perilous limits that have been revealed by ceaseless economic growth, nor from a degeneration of human nature, like that envisaged in Rousseau's *Second Discourse*, which might be caused or encouraged by particular socioeconomic conditions, namely those of early capitalist market society, and which could be remedied by transforming the social order. The limits in question derive from free self-preservation itself, or, to be more precise, from the free self-preservation of our fellow human beings.

In chapter 4 ("The Truth of Self-Certainty") of his *Phenomenology of Spirit* Hegel argues that human self-consciousness is constituted in a process of mutual recognition that gives rise to an initial and provisional form of social relationship. Hobbes, on the other hand, is interested in a self-consciousness that has already been constituted and in the state as a form of social organization that is no longer provisional in character. Thus the state is not legitimated as the condition of the possibility of a subjectivity that would otherwise fail or collapse. The state is supposed not to make human life itself possible, but to make our shared human life possible. It is meant to serve the coexistence of several "selves" rather than the existence of the individual subject in relation to itself.

The difference from Hegel is evident from the structure of the argument in Hobbes: in *Leviathan* the state is not derived from the anthropological investigation of the individual human being (in chapter 5), but from the theorem of the state of nature that is presented later (in chapter 13). The state is not meant to facilitate the free self-preservation of every individual under internal threat from himself, nor to facilitate property and possessions in the face of the threat posed by outer nature. It is not meant to grant or vouchsafe property and possessions or an internal relationship to oneself in the first place, but rather to guarantee them, i.e., to make them safe. Our self-preservation is to be protected not against inner or outer nature, but solely against the threat posed by the equally free desire for self-preservation on the part of our fellow human beings. While the dangers the subject poses to itself must be countered through the cultivation of inner nature (by recourse to instinctual renunciation and sublimation, to the virtues of self-reflection and self-control), the state is only called into being through the threats and dangers that arise on the essentially intersubjective level.

There is another element in Hobbes, though in this case a deeply problematic one, which transcends his particular historical context. Although the condition of nature that is such a threat to human life furnishes the decisive argument in Hobbes's theory of the state, this condition still prevails as far as the relations between states are concerned (L ch. 21: 110; and see already E part 2, ch. 10, §10, the final paragraph). Yet in spite of this, from the early text *The Elements of Law* through *De Cive* right up to *Leviathan*, Hobbes has nothing at all to say about the idea of an international order of peace.

NINE

Legitimating the State

$\mathbf{W}$ ar cannot be prevented, let alone permanently brought to an end, simply by a well-meaning philanthropic decision. It is necessary to uncover the underlying mechanism that gives rise to war in the first place. It is the activity of reason that clarifies this mechanism by identifying what Hobbes calls the fundamental "laws of nature." But an original "contract" is required if we are not only to recognize these laws but also to ensure their efficacy. According to Hobbes, it is this contract that grants absolute authority to the sovereign power.

9.1. The Laws of Nature

Today we understand "natural laws" or "laws of nature" simply as those laws that govern natural events and processes, laws that can often be formulated in mathematical terms, like Galileo's law of falling bodies or Kepler's laws of planetary motion. But in the seventeenth century these expressions can also refer to moral laws, which were considered to be just as "immutable and eternal" (L ch. 15: 79; see also L ch. 33: 205) as the laws of nature generally are today. If such laws refer, as in Hobbes, to the life that human beings have to share with one another, they belong to the domain of the theory of law or right.

135

The core of this theoretical domain today is concerned with natural rights in the specific sense of human rights. But Hobbes's notion of "laws of nature" as moral laws cannot be interpreted as an anticipation of our modern notion of natural rights as human rights. Indeed, whether his laws of nature can truly be described as moral laws or principles at all is something we shall have to examine in the next section. But we can already see here that they can no more be described as "categorical imperatives of right" than Hobbes's notion of dignity (L ch. 10: 42) can be regarded as an anticipation of Kant's concept of human dignity. What Hobbes understands by the dignity of a human being, as in ancient Rome, refers to the value that the state visibly accords those who bear certain titles or perform certain offices. There are undoubtedly differences where such value is concerned, but they play no role in Hobbes's state of nature or the task of overcoming it.

We might be tempted to see Hobbes's ninth law of nature, which enjoins us to acknowledge our fellow human beings as "equal by nature" (L ch. 15: 77), as a first step toward the idea of an inviolable dignity that belongs to all human beings without distinction. When Hobbes says "by nature" here, this suggests something that transcends any merely positive or empirical feature, something which approaches the notion of inviolability; and when he describes our fellow human beings as "equal," this suggests that one is not simply born as either master or servant, but that one enjoys the same status as one's fellow human beings. But Hobbes appeals merely to considerations of prudence here, and introduces no moral argument of any kind. A man who proudly imagines himself superior to his fellow human beings must reckon with the possibility of defeat in the event of some conflict arising. Hobbes certainly recognizes something like an inalienable right of the individual. But it is conceived in wholly naturalistic terms, and cannot be included among human rights as we now understand them. For Hobbes it is the individual's right to resist all those, even including the sovereign, who would "assault him by force, to take away his life" (L ch. 14: 66).

Hobbes expounds his laws of nature immediately after he has presented his strictly nonnormative "right of nature," namely the entirely natural and principal human end of self-preservation. Reason merely explains how to achieve this end. But through its "reckoning" of general or universal names reason is able to establish universally valid propositions. These begin with the principle that one is forbidden to do anything that is destructive of one's life or that removes the means of preserving that life. And they continue with the rather generalized injunction to undertake whatever measures one thinks will best preserve it (L ch. 14: 64). This injunction does not rule out the principle that no one may be judge or "arbitrator" in his own cause (the seventeenth law of nature; cf. L ch. 15: 78). These first two generalized obligations are expounded and developed in a more precise and detailed manner in what follows until Hobbes has presented us with nineteen laws of nature in all. His complete list of the laws of nature begins with that which commands every individual to seek or to "endeavour peace." Ultimately speaking, all of these laws serve the cause of self-preservation, but once this initial command to seek peace is established, it is clear that they all serve the cause of peace. (It is interesting to note that two and a half centuries earlier, around 1400, long before the age of religious wars, Johann von Saaz's great work *Der Ackermann aus Böhmen* had already, in chapter 32, formulated Hobbes's first law of nature: "seek peace, and follow it.")

Hobbes proceeds to the second law of nature, which enjoins the mutual and equal limitation of our freedom, and then in chapter 15 offers a particularly extensive discussion of the third law, which enjoins us to keep the contracts and agreements ("covenants") we have made. The other remaining laws of nature can be classed thematically in three groups. The first group (laws 4 through 10) exhibits what we would normally describe as a moral character. These laws concern (4) gratitude; (5) mutual accommodation; (6) forgiveness or pardon; (7) punishment as a means of future deterrence rather than as retribution for past wrong; (8) forbidding the expression of hatred or contempt for others; (9) acknowledging others as our equals by nature; and finally (10) forbidding arrogance.

The second group (laws 12 through 14) concerns questions of property, and the third group involves rules for the administration of justice. Thus one who adjudicates between two parties must treat both equally (law 11), and, as we indicated earlier, no one may act as judge in his own cause (law 17). Interestingly enough, toward the end of chapter 15, Hobbes evokes something like the distinction between legality (action in conformity with duty or obligation) and morality (action done from duty or obligation), and seems to anticipate Kant by limiting obligation to morality, for "these laws oblige only to a desire, and endeavour" (L ch. 15: 79). And whoever endeavors to fulfill these laws is rightly regarded as "just."

In the state of nature, Hobbes says toward the end of his specific discussion of the subject, the "notions of right and wrong, justice and

injustice have there no place" (L ch. 13: 63). Yet his talk of laws of nature
seems to contradict this. But this apparent contradiction can be resolved
once we explicitly draw a distinction, which Hobbes tacitly makes. In his
reflections on the state of nature we must distinguish two distinct phases
(in an argumentational rather than historical sense). In the first phase
of the argument, conducted solely from the perspective of the conflicts
generated by the passions (ch. 13, apart from the final paragraph), all we
find is a condition of war where there is hardly place for notions of right
and wrong. (There is no room in Hobbes's argument for the kind of international law regarding war that was initially adumbrated by Grotius and
which was in principle recognized in Europe after the Paris declaration
on the law of the seas in 1856, the Geneva Convention of 1864, and the
Hague Treaties of 1899 and 1907).

The second phase of the argument, which begins in the final paragraph of chapter 13, goes further and takes account of the "passions that
incline men to peace" and of reason's role in serving those passions. The
combined effect of these factors leads to laws of right, and we can interpret Hobbes to mean that we are just when we fulfill these laws and
unjust when we violate them. Thus Hobbes can write that only the "fool
hath said in his heart, there is no such thing as justice" (L ch. 15: 72).
It is only when we reach the third phase of the argument, with regard to
the civil state or the commonwealth, that there is such a thing as right or
justice in Hobbes's full and positive sense. The amoral condition of war
without right or justice is thus succeeded first by a condition of reason
with its laws of right and finally by the civil state or condition, which is
decisive for Hobbes, and which is characterized by positive concepts of
right and justice.

9.2. A Moral Philosophy?

The way in which Hobbes presents his laws of nature at least suggests a
certain moral character. For he tells us that "they oblige in conscience"
or in *foro interno*, that they are "immutable and eternal" (ch. 15: 79),
and that they derive from God (L ch. 15: 80; see also L ch. 43: 322).
Although Hobbes even describes them exclusively as "moral laws" (L ch.
26: 147–48; also C, ch. 3, §31, p. 150), they are not grounded in a universally binding moral law that obliges us categorically, and in that sense
we cannot say they exhibit a genuinely moral character. From a strictly

normative point of view, Hobbes's laws of nature are merely pragmatic imperatives (of right). They are not valid or binding absolutely, but only under two conditions. The fundamental impulse of human action means that every individual wishes to preserve his or her life, and consequently wishes for peace; and reason recognizes that "it can never be that war shall preserve life, and peace destroy it" (L ch. 15: 79).

In this sense it remains unclear from Hobbes's argument how the laws are supposed to possess that binding power over conscience, which a purely personal interest like the passion for peace does not possess. In this connection Hobbes could have availed himself of the so-called Golden Rule, some form of which is encountered in almost all cultures and can also be found in the Scriptures. In fact he does appeal to the Golden Rule, although only in relation to the second law of nature (L ch. 14: 65), and not in the context of the first fundamental law of nature (concerning right). There is a later passage, however, that suggests a more basic or at least more comprehensive understanding of the laws of nature in relation to the Golden Rule (L ch. 16: 79f.).

Where Hobbes does present the Golden Rule as a criterion of the laws of nature, he does not appear to regard the distinction between the positive and negative formulation of the principle as significant. For in chapter 14 of the English version of *Leviathan* Hobbes first cites the Golden Rule directly in its positive formulation ("whatsoever you require that others should do to you, that do ye to them"), and then immediately cites it in its negative Latin formulation (*"quod tibi fieri non vis, alteri ne feceris"*: do not do to others what you would not wish to be done to you). In chapter 26 of the English version of *Leviathan* Hobbes cites it in the negative formulation (L ch. 26: 140), whereas in the Latin version of the work he offers its positive formulation. Yet the difference between the positive and negative formulations of the Golden Rule is considerable. The more modest negative version roughly corresponds to the duties that human beings recognize that they owe one another (duties of right), whereas the more demanding positive version also involves duties of virtue, such as the active readiness to offer assistance to others.

Some interpreters have contested the notion that Hobbes's laws of nature have no genuinely categorical character, and are therefore not truly moral laws at all (cf. Taylor 1938; Warrender 1957; Kodalle 1972). These interpreters regard Hobbes's ethics as a doctrine of genuine moral duties, for these are commandments of God, and they claim that this doctrine can be detached from Hobbes's egoistic psychology since the former has no necessary logical connection with the latter. According to Taylor, Hobbes's moral doctrine turns out to be "a very strict deontology, curiously suggestive, though with interesting differences, of some of the characteristic theses of Kant" (Taylor 1938, p. 408).

It is quite true that Hobbes straightforwardly claims that the laws of nature are the laws of God. And with a pathos we would hardly expect of him he even says: "Princes succeed one another; and one judge passeth, another cometh; nay, heaven and earth shall pass; but not one tittle of the law of nature shall pass; for it is the eternal law of God" (L ch. 26: 144). It is also true that Hobbes's second law of nature, which commands that one shall "be contented with so much liberty against other men, as he would allow other men against himself," implies a strictly reciprocal limitation of one's freedom that seems to anticipate Kant's categorical principle of right, namely, "the sum of the conditions under which the choice of one can be united with the choice of another in accordance with a universal law of freedom" (*Metaphysics of Morals*, "Introduction to the Doctrine of Right," §B). But in Hobbes this reciprocal limitation is qualified by the condition insofar "as for peace, and in defence of himself he shall think it necessary." This command is therefore merely a pragmatic and hypothetical rule of prudence, and it is only with Kant, who omits such a qualification, that the command first acquires its truly moral or categorical character.

In most of Hobbes's laws of nature the qualification is directly suggested. Only occasionally does it seem to disappear, with particular clarity for example in the ninth law of nature, which demands "that every man acknowledge another for his equal by nature." But when Hobbes explains that the "breach of this precept is pride" (L ch. 15: 77), this reflection only seems to exhibit a moral character, for the "pride" in question simply stands for an ill-advised overestimation of oneself. Hobbes makes a further observation that seems genuinely moral only at first sight, namely: "for injustice, ingratitude, arrogance, pride, iniquity, acception of persons [i.e., preferment], and the rest, can never be made lawful" (L ch. 15: 79). But the reason Hobbes then provides—"it can never be that war shall preserve life, and peace destroy it"—qualifies the observation by binding it to the need for peace, which again serves self-interest, so that we cannot speak of a genuine deontological form of morality in this connection. The best one could point to is a considerable degree of coincidence here: the prudential demands that serve one's own interest coincide in large measure with moral considerations that are independent of this interest.

It is precisely on account of this substantial coincidence that Kant lays so much emphasis upon the distinction between duty and inclination. For it is only when these fail to coincide that true morality is clearly revealed as such.

Nowhere does Hobbes claim that the laws of nature are already binding as rights on account of their divine origin. The reason they are binding lies rather in the notion of self-preservation and the peace that serves self-preservation, for which the laws of nature are regarded as the necessary conditions.

In spite of all this, there are still some interpreters who hold that Hobbes does defend a genuine moral philosophy or authentic ethics (for an overview of the older literature see Willms 1987, pp. 240–50; for the more recent discussion see Boonin-Vail 1994, pp. 58–123 and Rhodes 2002). And it is true that Hobbes himself even speaks in this way, defining moral philosophy as the "science of virtue and vice," and citing "justice, gratitude, modesty, equity, mercy" as examples of virtue and identifying the "true moral philosophy" with "the laws of nature" (L ch 15: 80).

But we should not overlook the adjective "true" here. For in the context it refers us to Hobbes's own philosophical doctrine, which already implies the rejection of all other theories and doctrines, and thus the whole tradition of moral philosophy as well. Hobbes does not indeed introduce new virtues, and the examples we have just cited, along with those of valor and generosity, are all traditional ones. But Hobbes does undertake a radical "revaluation of values." Alluding to a well-known and influential doctrine of Aristotle's, he complains that moral theorists have attempted to define virtues as a mean or "mediocrity of passions." Thus in the case of "fortitude" we would be dealing with "degree of daring," in the case of "liberality" with the "quantity of a gift," and so on. But in truth what is decisive is always the "cause" of human action. The virtues are commendable merely as "the means of peaceable, sociable, and comfortable living."

Hobbes explains that the aforementioned virtues and all the other laws of nature are (instrumental) "dictates of reason" improperly described as laws. For in fact they are only "conclusions or theorems" concerning what conduces to the preservation and defense of human life (L ch. 15: 80).

This perspective is clearly incompatible with a strictly deontological ethics. The virtues we have mentioned are not regarded as binding in their own right, but simply in instrumental or teleological terms. And the *telos* in question, the governing aim that serves freedom, remains the idea of peace, here supplemented by that of a "sociable and comfortable" life. It would also be difficult to speak of virtue ethics in this connection, since this is usually understood as an Aristotelian alternative to deontological ethics of the Kantian type. For in contrast to both of these approaches Hobbes defends a radically different individualist-pragmatic position, which he specifically identifies as the "true moral philosophy." But in Hobbes this expression does not imply a genuine theory of morality in the usual sense, whether a eudaemonistic theory of the Aristotelian kind or a theory of moral autonomy of the Kantian kind. The novel meaning that Hobbes ascribes to "moral philosophy" also explains why he empha-sizes the distinction between the dictates of reason and a veritable law. A Kantian theory requires categorical-deontological imperatives that an Aristotelian theory does not recognize. A third option, namely the kind of theological ethics that Taylor (1938) and Warrender (1964), and par-ticularly Hood (1964) and Martinich (1992), have ascribed to Hobbes, surely mistake Hobbes's intentions. The two arguments we have already mentioned—that the natural laws derive from God and that they are binding on conscience (L ch. 15: 79–80)—would indeed seem to sup-port this theological approach. Yet here too Hobbes deviates considerably from established and traditional notions. Without underestimating the more metaphysical meaning of "conscience," which he immediately goes on to mention—as knowledge of our "own secret facts, and thoughts"—Hobbes initially defines it in relation to the word "conscious" and in its literal sense as con-science: in the sense of several individuals who know something together (L ch. 7: 31). The laws of nature are thus binding on the *forum internum*, or conscience, insofar as many, and in principle even all, know that it serves peace and freedom, i.e., that it is wise and prudent to recognize these laws.

These same laws of nature, or, more exactly, these commandments of reason, can indeed be understood as divine commandments. But the reason for this does not lie in their supposedly categorical and thus more than merely "positive" character, but rather precisely in their purely posi-tive character: they are revealed in Holy Scripture expressly as the word of God.

There is no doubt that Hobbes sees a very close connection between his philosophy of the state and the Judeo-Christian theological tradi-tion. Otherwise he would hardly have supplemented the first two parts of *Leviathan* with two further and almost equally substantial parts. Yet this connection is not really internal in nature since for Hobbes ethics remains a part of philosophy itself, whereas the knowledge that springs from divine inspiration or revelation, and thus theology along with it, is excluded from the realm of philosophy (see C ch. I, §§8–9 and B part I). It is true that Hobbes actually modifies this claim somewhat, insofar as he does present a certain theology in parts three and four of *Leviathan*, albeit a radically secularized and naturalistic one. The theologians of his time were certainly hard put to recognize anything of their own understanding of Judeo-Christian theology in Hobbes's text.

As to the question whether Hobbes presents a genuine ethical theory, we can only furnish an unambiguously negative answer. Although the laws of nature are described as "moral" laws, and although they are eternally binding, and thus also binding in the state of nature, so that the latter is not in fact marked by "a complete absence of universal moral standards" as Sprute claims (2002, p. 834), these laws possess a hypothetical, or, more precisely, an individualist-pragmatic character, but certainly not a categorical one. And they can only be identified as divine commandments if we already recognize the Holy Scriptures as the revealed word of God, that is to say, on the basis of an act of faith.

9.3. The Original Contract

According to Hobbes there is only one way in which the state of nature that threatens human life and freedom can be overcome, a way that is valid not merely under the favorable circumstances of a contingent parity of power among human beings, but which is essentially valid in itself. Every human being must step back from the conditions that characterize the state of war, that is to say, from the unrestrained drive for self-preservation. In place of this, every human being must be content with the same degree of freedom that one is also prepared to concede to every other human being. This insight is implied by Hobbes's second law of nature, the essence of which lies in the idea of reciprocity (the mutual limiting and securing of freedom).

Hobbes does not regard this idea of reciprocity as his own discovery. It is already found in the Golden Rule that is acknowledged in many cultures, and which Hobbes himself cites in the formulation provided in the New Testament (L ch. 14: 65; also L ch. 15: 79). With this appeal to the "law of the Gospel" he manages in passing to establish a common point of reference in relation to contending religious factions and positions.

This reciprocity that the second law of nature involves corresponds to the legal notion of a reciprocal transfer of rights, i.e., a contract. If one party to the contract fulfills his part at some later time, and must be "trusted" in the meantime by the other party, then the contract in question is called a "pact" or "covenant."

Since the contracting parties in the state of nature must trust their representative or "sovereign," Hobbes always describes the contract that establishes the state as a "covenant." He thus employs the same word used to translate Yahweh's pact (*berith* in Hebrew) with the Jewish people. But the decisive question as to how far this trust is reasonable plays no role in Hobbes's doctrine of sovereign representation. A covenant involves trust that the party that has not yet fulfilled its part will, in fact, do so. Hobbes often explains that we should trust the representative or sovereign—in this connection he speaks of "confidence" (L ch. 17: 88) as well as "trust" (L ch. 14: 66)—but he does not explain why this is supposed to be rational.

The third law of nature, which Hobbes calls "the fountain and original of JUSTICE," declares that contracts once entered into must be fulfilled: "that men perform their covenants made" (L ch. 15: 71). According to Hobbes, the state or commonwealth arises from an original and fundamental contract between free human beings. Since the condition of war is comprehensive ("a war of everyone against everyone"), the contract must be equally comprehensive, and must therefore be entered into by each and every individual (L ch. 17: 87–88; see also L ch. 18: 88–89; L ch. 21: 111–12; L ch. 43: 322–23).

In grounding the state in the concept of contract Hobbes's account takes its place among the broader family of consensus theories of political legitimation. Since one can only be bound by one's own actions, and all human beings are equally free by nature, the state arises from the agreement of every individual, from a distributively universal consensus. Although Hobbes himself favors the institution of monarchy (L ch. 19), his account of the state, in its origin, does contain a consensus-theoretical and thereby democratic element that ultimately derives a sense of binding obligation solely out of the manner in which we may be said to bind ourselves. The idea of a universal agreement or consensus provides the starting point of his systematic approach (see L ch. 20: 101–03). It is only once the state is established that majority decisions of any kind are permitted. The prior or original decision to ground a state in the first place forbids such majoritarian reflections or considerations. Unanimity must therefore constitute the systematic starting point here.

This original contract is no more to be regarded as a historical event than is the state of nature. We are dealing not with some voluntary act but rather with a rational constriction: the condition for the possibility of entering into a peaceful human coexistence. But the original contract is not yet sufficient on its own to overcome the condition of war. For the mere conclusion of the contract does not guarantee that it will be observed. Since one can also merely pretend to enter into a contract, there is an uncertainty that attaches to the contract in principle. Thus at first the contract only enjoys the same status as all the laws of nature: it is binding solely *in foro interno*, before the inner voice of conscience. There is still no external authority that can secure and maintain the historical and political realities of life: "covenants, without the sword [i.e., without a recognized power for enforcing them], are but words, and of no strength to secure a man at all" (L ch. 17: 85). As we can show with mathematical precision by applying modern game-theoretical procedures, the most advantageously placed actor is one who can conclude a contract and convince the other party that he will fulfill his own part of the agreement, although he has no intention of actually doing so. With the aid of game theory we can also show that the mere repetition of interactive behavior suffices in order to make cooperation possible. Anyone who regards justice as nonexistent is indeed therefore a fool.

Since for Hobbes every individual acts on the basis of self-interest, one must reckon with the possibility that a contract has not been entered into with good faith. Then it simply becomes a worthless document that obscures the latent violation of the contract, and thus also the condition of war that was meant to be overcome. Thus everyone not only wishes to conclude the contract, but also to overcome the persisting uncertainty that attaches to it. If the one who faithfully fulfills the contract is not to fear being cheated or taken advantage of by others, we require some authority that stands over the different parties to the contract, which is also more powerful than they are, and can guarantee fulfillment of the contract, or can punish the violation of the contract in such a way that such violation is not worth the effort according to the calculated logic of self-preservation.

Since such an authority, conceptually speaking, is nothing but a public or "civil" power endowed with sufficient force, the content of this original contract for Hobbes is just this: the lasting establishment of a sufficiently strong political or civil power. This is embodied in the possessor of the highest power, the sovereign, in relation to which all other individuals are "subjects." Thus the state (*civitas*) is "a real unity of them all, in one and the same person, made by covenant of every man with every man, in such manner, as if every man should say to every man, *I authorize and give up my right of governing myself, to this man, or to this assembly of men, on this condition, that thou give up thy right to him, and authorize all his actions in like manner*" (L ch. 17: 87).

According to Hobbes, the establishment of a general or civil power is not some kind of sinful fall from grace, as the utopian visions of peaceful coexistence in the absence of all government or dominion tend to suggest. On the contrary, it represents a kind of "salvation" accomplished by human beings themselves. For the enlightened self-interest of every individual demands that we overcome the natural condition of life-threatening anarchy through a civil power that guarantees peace and with it the free self-preservation of every individual. And here we find a radical transformation of the situation. The human being who is a predator, "an arrant wolf," to his fellows in the state of nature, here becomes a citizen who, as citizen, relates to his fellow citizens as "a kind of God": since it is the virtues of peace, justice, and love that prevail in the civil state, we thereby enjoy a certain "similitude with the Deity" (C, the dedication, p. 89).

This transformation, though at first sight rather surprising, does not contradict Hobbes's highly realistic anthropology, which insists on taking human beings as they are. The human being who is a kind of wolf and the human being who is a kind of God is the same person, one who is ultimately interested in free self-preservation. This human being is capable of yielding to all the better aspects of humanity, though it is only prudent to do so in conditions of peace, whereas in the state of nature one must always lie in wait as a predator (and hide as the potential prey of another).

9.4. Absolute Authority

Hobbes does not try and ground just any form of public authority over and above the potentially conflicting parties. He claims that only an absolute and undivided civil power (cf. L ch. 17: 86–88; L ch. 22: 115) is capable of guaranteeing internal peace and with it the free self-preservation and happiness of all citizens. This particularly strong claim arises from a difficulty that is connected with the establishment of civil power itself: on the one hand this power is supposed to guarantee the upholding of the contract, while on the other hand the civil power is supposed to be established through the original contract in the first place. In this sense Hobbes's justification of the state appears circular: civil power is supposed to arise from the contract but at the same time must already exist in order to guarantee the fulfillment of the contract.

Hobbes attempts to overcome the circularity of the argument through the notion of the "representative." The concept of "representation," with its core idea of "presence," literally signifies a process of presenting something, bringing something before one's eyes. The Latin word *praesentatio* initially denoted an image that represents someone in concrete visible form, and in the commercial context it signified the ability to pay for something directly in cash. Later on, in the specifically judicial context, it came to mean representing someone in court, i.e., legitimately speaking on someone's behalf. In the case of the original contract the authorized representative may be an individual person (in monarchy), a group (in aristocracy), or the people as a whole (in democracy).

Hobbes's analysis appeals to the concept of the "person," which derives from the Latin *persona,* signifying a mask or role. The one who legally represents someone in court may be said to assume the mask of that individual. He or she "impersonates" the latter and plays that role all the more effectively by recourse to the relevant professional expertise. Hobbes's account in *Leviathan* intensifies this sense of impersonation. Here the representative becomes the fully authorized figure to whom all individuals unreservedly subject themselves by transferring all their rights to him. And since the original contract consists in a reciprocal renunciation, in conjunction with the transfer of power to the sovereign as representative, Hobbes's grounding of the state is not circular after all. In Hobbes the representative becomes the personification of those he represents in a twofold sense. As the engraving on the title page of *Leviathan* symbolically illustrates, the sovereign becomes the representative of every individual and of all individuals taken together. For it is only through this representative that they become a united whole or a people, a people constituted through the state or commonwealth.

The contract that constitutes the political state creates a legal person out of the multitude of individual human beings, a person who in absolute sovereignty makes these individuals into both citizens and subjects who, in the condition of peace, are now able to act "in the foresight of their own preservation, and of a more contented life" (L ch. 17: 85). The representative of all parties to the original contract embodies the common will of all, namely the desire for peace. At the same time, conceptually speaking, the representative stands over and above the parties to the contract, for the representative acquires a temporally and materially unlimited authority in this regard. The representative becomes the sovereign in the literal sense, or the bearer of the highest unlimited and undivided civil power. The original contract thus amounts to a contract of subjection. From his earliest political work, *The Elements of Law* (part I, ch. 19; part II, chs. 1, 2, and 5), through *De Cive* (chs. 6, 7, and 10) down to the text of *Leviathan* (ch. 19), Hobbes does not simply attempt to ground the notion of absolute political power on the basis of rational reflections alone. He also appeals to historical and pragmatic considerations, which he uses to try and show that the monarchical system is superior in many respects to other possible political arrangements. But the strongest argument for his view that a single person, namely the monarch, should bear the "mask" of the people is only convincing if this person is less corruptible than the common multitude. Yet why should this be so? It seems to ignore the possibility that a plurality of private individuals may serve as a moderating brake upon one another.

It is true that Hobbes recognizes certain disadvantages in the monarchical system, such as the possibility that sovereignty may actually devolve upon an immature and unsuitable royal successor. Nor does he overlook the possibility that the monarch may fall victim to flatterers or rash and inexperienced advisors, although the same fate may also befall a council or assembly. But Hobbes thinks the advantages of monarchy are more evident, inasmuch as private interest (of the king) coincides with the public interest, for the "riches, power, and honour of a monarch arise only from the riches, strength, and reputation of his subjects" (L ch. 19: 96).

There are two reservations one might have regarding this particular claim. In the first place, it is remarkable that Hobbes's reference to riches, power, and reputation invokes the secondary interests of the subjects of the state, rather than what Hobbes himself takes to be their primary interest in peace, an interest which, as historical experience shows, can itself be endangered by the monarch in two ways: he may reduce or suspend the established rights (of parliament), or he may intervene in religious conflicts instead of staying out of them and allowing religious freedom to his subjects. And in the second place, it is true that a genuinely wise monarch may concern himself from self-interest not merely with peace but also with riches, power, and reputation. But there are plenty of unwise monarchs who may seek to restrict the corresponding freedoms and possibilities of their subjects.

What is more, the sovereign is indeed obliged by his office to serve the "common interest." But personally he is just as much concerned with his "private good," including that of his family, kindred, and friends (L ch. 19: 96). Hobbes himself recognizes that the sovereign, since he is also a "natural person," can come into conflict with the office of sovereignty itself. One might consider various ways of preventing or reducing this danger. Plato, for example, suggested in his *Republic* (416d–417b; 460b–461d) that the ruling elite should be denied the possibility of private property and of a particular family life in order to remove two typical temptations to favor one's own private interest. Hobbes does not engage in any considerations of this kind.

In support of monarchy Hobbes also claims that a monarch is able to make better use of well-versed advisors and counselors. But in fact a democracy certainly has no difficulty in calling on the requisite expertise, from the level of ministerial bureaucracy right down to the innumerable advisory bodies and committees, etc. Generally speaking, Hobbes's argument for the relative superiority of monarchy (L ch. 9) is surely one of the least convincing aspects of his philosophy of the state. There are certain empirical assumptions in play here that are so unconvincing that they can only strike us as ideological. Hobbes rightly points out that everyone who assumes a political role is also potentially corruptible as a natural person, and is thus exposed to the danger of favoring their own interest over the public interest where these conflict. One hardly needs to read Shakespeare's history plays in order to doubt whether public and private interests necessarily coincide in the case of monarchy. Kings tend to have their "privy purse," to which they like to add, if possible. And, as we already said, they also have family and friends for whom they would gladly "do good."

What is expected of a contract is a reciprocal transfer of rights: one renounces one right and receives another back. Thus one gives up the right to a certain item of property and gets paid in return. Contrary to some interpretations of Hobbes, the original contract does not amount to a juridical "self-alienation of the person" (Kersting 2008, p. 179). Even if an almost unqualified subjection to the sovereign results from the original contract, there is still a reciprocal transfer of rights here. The transfer even involves a fundamental principle of justice: an equivalence (or approximate equivalence) in giving and taking. For in return each individual finds that his most important good is secured: the peace that safeguards freedom. In this sense the subjection to the sovereign derives from a process of estimating goods, in which the secondary good is sacrificed where necessary to the primary one: for the sake of the end which is ultimately at stake—the indispensible principle of self-preservation—the human being dispenses with what is more dispensable.

The way in which Hobbes estimates these goods has far-ranging theoretical and practical implications for our understanding of the state. If the civil power is directly identified with absolute and undivided sovereignty, then any alternative does not simply appear as a possible but less satisfactory form of political state. The liberal constitutional state, for example, with its commitment to fundamental human rights and the separation of powers, can then no longer be regarded as a state at all, but only as another version of anarchy or the state of nature.

It is not the idea of an authorized representative itself but the almost unlimited power ascribed to the latter that accounts for the potential illiberal and absolutist character of Hobbes's state. Yet from the systematic perspective, the theory of the representative only appears at a relatively late stage of the text, where it is then linked back to his theory of the human individual, of the state of nature, and the laws of nature. But the fact that it appears at this late stage of the argument also makes it easier to separate, in conceptual terms, Hobbes's justification of the state in general from the notion of the omnipotent and absolutistic state. We can acknowledge his observations on the state of nature, the overcoming of the latter through the reciprocal limitation of freedom, and that part of his theory of the representative that shows why the requisite transfer of power to an authority figure creates the sovereign. But it is not obvious why the sovereign, in addition to his power as ruler, should also exercise legislative and even judicial power, nor is it obvious why the sovereign should exercise more or less unlimited power in all three respects.

Does the concept of sovereignty itself imply that there cannot really be a separation of powers, or a principled commitment to fundamental human rights? Hobbes is right to insist that laws, covenants, and contracts on their own are but words which inspire no fear, and that a coercive legal power is required if we are to overcome the condition of war. Nor is it problematic to claim that all individuals concerned, and not merely some of them, must transfer their own power to the representative of civil power (L ch. 17: 87–88). But what needs to be determined is whether all power must indeed be ceded to the sovereign, so that the latter can employ this power "as he shall think it expedient" (*arbitrio suo* in the Latin version) (L ch. 17: 88). Must we simply speak of unlimited power and authority, rather than of a clearly limited and defined mandate here?

According to Hobbes, sovereignty can be attained in either of two ways: by "acquisition" or by "institution." Both involve the same basic motive of fear. In the first case it is fear of some superior external power (L ch. 17: 88), and in the second case it is fear of each other (L ch. 20: 101–02). And the basic idea of legitimation, involving agreement and covenant, is also the same in both cases. It is not victory itself that first bestows "right of dominion" over the vanquished, but rather the unconditional submission of the vanquished to the victor (L ch. 20: 104). Thus what Hobbes says with regard to sovereignty by institution also holds for every sovereign: "there can happen no breach of covenant on the part of the sovereign" (L ch. 18: 89). A sovereign who can do "no injury to any of his subjects" (L ch. 18: 90), even if he puts an innocent to death (L ch. 21: 109), is not subject to any self-imposed laws (L ch. 29: 169).

A large number of the tasks and rights here are almost self-evident: the sovereign has the right to promulgate laws of property and other civil laws, and thus possesses legislative power. The sovereign has the right to decide in cases of conflicting claims, and thus possesses judicial power. Lastly, the sovereign has the right to direct foreign policy and matters relating to the security of the state, namely the right to declare war and conclude peace treaties, and to act as military commander in chief, and thus also possesses a particularly significant executive power. But these rights do not necessarily have to be exercised, as Hobbes insists, without separation or "division" of powers (L ch. 29: 170), and transferred to a single authority, let alone, as he prefers, to a single "natural person" (L ch. 18: 93f.).

The original contract involves the complete and irrevocable alienation of all our natural rights, apart from the single right to self-preservation that Hobbes himself regards as inalienable. Hobbes's theory of the state is thus a continuation of a conception of natural law that reaches back more than two thousand years and at the same time marks a radical break with that tradition: the rational justification of the state as such (by appeal to natural law) culminates in the legitimation of a sovereign who is "absolute" in the strictest sense, not indeed from a religious, moral, or individual perspective (in terms of "conscience"), but from the political perspective of one who stands entirely above all positive and natural laws.

9.5. A Right to Rebellion?

Since the civil power is subject to one normative restriction or qualification, namely the individual's inalienable right to self-preservation, the accusation that Hobbes essentially deifies the state is inaccurate. Absolutism for Hobbes is not an end in itself. It is not based on a theory of political genius or charisma, or on the notion of a political elite conscious of its own abilities and sustained by a sense of responsibility. This absolutism is merely the necessary and also sufficient condition for the condition of peace, an indispensible element in the calculated logic of self-preservation. But how the state is to discharge this task remains completely open for it to determine.

Since the sovereign does not possess the highest and most far-reaching power in a wholly unconditional sense, therefore, Hobbes is not claiming, as a categorical imperative, that an absolute state power ought to exist. In normative terms, his justification of the state remains a pragmatic one: absolute sovereignty is legitimate and indeed required only as long as it is capable of protecting the life of the citizens both internally and externally. Insofar as it fails to fulfill the task of securing the peace and protecting the citizens, it follows that the basis of the original contract is dissolved.

The literature on Hobbes has been divided on the question of whether he ultimately defends an absolutist or a liberal theory of the state (see Ottmann 2006, p. 294 and Strauss 1956, p. 188, respectively), but we must recognize that in a sense he endorses both positions (although one has to say that Hobbes shows little interest in this question as such). In substantive terms, Hobbes's state is liberal insofar as it is not expected to intervene in the free self-preservation of the citizens any more than is required in order to secure such self-preservation in the social context. Thus the state is meant to protect the institution of property and the fulfillment of contracts and agreements, and to punish infringements of the rights in question. But Hobbes's state is absolutist as far as the effective maintenance of this substantive dimension is concerned. Thus the liberal content is sacrificed to the absolutist form in which it is realized.

One might object to this interpretation by pointing out that in the case of a real threat to life and limb the individual is released from the obligation of obedience, and that resistance or rebellion is permitted. Hobbes even seems to regard rebellion as an inalienable right (L ch. 14: 65–66), which explains why Hampton (1986, ch. 7.2) can echo Bramhall's verdict and describe *Leviathan* as a "rebel's catechism." One could extend the objection still further: since rebellion endangers the position of the sovereign, and even threatens the sovereign's life, the wise sovereign will also be an enlightened one who, from self-interest, will therefore try and promote the free self-preservation of his subjects as far as possible.

This attempt to render Hobbes's view less extreme does not take us very far, since an absolute sovereign does not always act wisely. Subject to human passions as he is, the sovereign may fall victim to their preponderant momentary influence and thus lose sight of his own long-term interest. In contrast to absolute sovereignty, human wisdom is not a constitutional concept, for it depends on personal characteristics that, for Hobbes, belong to that private sphere from which the political domain is meant to be independent. What is more, the possession of absolute power has the potential to corrupt the character of any human being. The trust that, according to Hobbes, we should show toward the sovereign, once again a nonconstitutional concept, is thus negligent or incautious from the political point of view.

A right of rebellion against an absolute sovereign therefore appears little more than a farce. For the anticipation of potential rebellion will only drive the sovereign to increase and strengthen his power. The "wise" sovereign is by no means necessarily an enlightened ruler who promotes the interests of the citizens. In accordance with Hobbes's thesis of the restless human striving for ever greater power (L ch. 13: 61), the sovereign is capable of gradually and secretly building up a whole apparatus of power that would make any future act of resistance or rebellion pointless.

This objection may be formulated in even more fundamental terms: *either* the sovereign possesses the preponderant power to fulfill his proper task, which is at all times to deter or punish all threats to life from whatever quarter they come, in which case he can at any time misuse that power; *or* a rebellion may enjoy a good chance of success, in which case state power is insufficient to compel everyone to show reciprocal respect for life and limb. Thus one cannot will both positions at the same time: an absolute and sufficiently powerful sovereign and a genuine right to rebellion on the part of his subjects. An omnipotent state and a right to rebellion are mutually exclusive.

In any case a right to rebellion is not a matter of positive legal permission, something that would also be absurd in relation to the sovereign. For the permission itself would have to proceed from the sovereign. The notion that the sovereign could expressly allow rebellion against himself and his laws contradicts firstly, the concept of his absolute sovereignty; secondly, the concept of rebellion; and thirdly, the concept of a positive law. For a power that can be limited or opposed by a legally sanctioned power, i.e., the positive right to rebellion, does not possess absolute and undivided sovereignty. Furthermore, the talk of rebellion only makes sense if there is a contrary positive legal order, which in the case of a positive right to rebellion no longer applies, for laws could only hold on the condition that no one challenges them, and that they are thus willingly acknowledged. Finally, the binding character of positive laws would be dissolved if commands and prohibitions were promulgated on the one hand, while a general reservation regarding their validity, namely the right to act counter to these commands and prohibitions, were to be acknowledged on the other.

Hobbes was so concerned with the question, which he raised with such inexorable clarity, namely *quis iudicabit?* (Who will decide?), that he underestimated the two other fundamental questions of all political theory and praxis: (1) Where are the normative limits to any form of political power?; and (2) Who or what controls the ruler who exercises this power? As far as the first fundamental and essentially normative question is concerned, Hobbes lacks a conception of natural rights in the sense of human rights that the state is responsible for upholding.

As far as the second fundamental and empirical-pragmatic question is concerned, it is true that the sovereign is responsible only to God, being his subject (L ch. 21: 109). This religious answer to the question is perfectly logical inasmuch as there is no political power that stands over and above the absolute sovereign. For such a higher power would then *eo ipso* be the real sovereign. On the other hand, this merely religious answer is unsatisfactory on Hobbes's own assumptions. For his construction of the state is based on skepticism toward the idea of any political power attached to some nonpolitical form of authority. In this regard Hobbes's theory contains a fundamental contradiction: the merely religious dimension that is supposed to possess validity solely in the private sphere, but is excluded from the political sphere, nonetheless acquires political significance in the decisive person of the absolute sovereign. The sovereign's violation of a natural law is allegedly an injustice against God rather than against the one who is directly affected (loc. cit.).

Contrary to the much praised and supposedly rigorous and uncompromising character of Hobbes's construction of the state—so far as one simply accepts the extremely one-sided anthropological basis of his account—it seems that the opposite is true: whereas there are good arguments in support of the anthropological basis, the political absolutism contradicts this very basis, i.e., contradicts the principle of free self-preservation. Hence one cannot accept the interpretative approach, which claims that radical individualism is only feasible under extreme relations of domination. On the contrary, Hobbes's political absolutism turns out to be incompatible with his anthropological individualism.

Politically speaking, in comparison with the dangers posed by anarchy, Hobbes has underestimated the complementary dangers posed by tyranny (cf. L ch. 19: 95: "For they that are discontented under *monarchy*, call it *tyranny*"; in the Latin version of *Leviathan*, however, the last paragraph here refers to a "single tyrant who subjugated all three realms"). Since any satisfactory account of the state must avoid the twin dangers of civil war on the one hand and arbitrary despotic rule on the other, Hobbes's construction of the state has to be regarded as a failure in this regard. But this assessment by no means simply identifies political absolutism with (modern) totalitarianism. For Hobbes's state, although it exercises absolute power, is not a totalitarian state, such as those defined by some radically nationalistic or religious factions and ideologies. On the other hand, it is also implausible to present *Leviathan* as an anticipation of political liberalism, as Leo Strauss attempted to do.

What appears as a contradiction from the philosophical point of view reveals itself as a fundamentally mistaken assessment from the historical and political point of view. The conflict between king and Parliament that led to the civil war could have taught Hobbes that the king, apostrophised as the absolute sovereign, is by no means an impartial judge standing over and above all political disputes and particular interests. The king himself represents one party among others, and given his violation of traditional parliamentary rights, and specifically the right to participate significantly in the shaping of legislation and the levying of taxes, he has to be recognized as one of the sources of the resulting conflict. Since the sovereign, even if conceived as a representative of the people standing above all parties, is also, as a natural person, one of them too, and what is true of the parties is equally true of the king, the claim to universal validity on the part of particular interests is a latent form of violence. Reflection on recent historical experience, such as the brutal massacres of Saint Bartholomew's Eve instigated by Catherine de Medici (more than twenty thousand Huguenots were murdered on August 24, 1592), could have shown Hobbes how latent violence can all too quickly be unleashed as open and immediate violence at the appropriate opportunity.

Later on, in *Behemoth*, Hobbes does not deny that the king himself is a party in his own right. But he does not draw the necessary conclusions from this: whether from greed, envy, brutality, or from corruption and capriciousness, whether it is because he is provoked by criticism or opposition, or even from simple foolishness, no absolute sovereign lacks for reasons to threaten his citizens in life or limb. As populist movements and their leaders manifestly show, when unlimited power is transferred to the people as a totality, majority decisions can easily lead to the disadvantaging, the oppression, and even the possible destruction of entire groups of people.

Unless and until the sovereign fulfills Rousseau's demand that the legislator must "behold all the passions of men without experiencing any of them" (*The Social Contract*, book II, ch. 7, p. 194), he will be a threat to his subjects. But since a "superior intelligence" of this kind, as Rousseau says, is "wholly unrelated to our nature," Hobbes's concept of sovereignty only seems convincing in the abstract, that is to say, when this circumstance is ignored.

In view of the Petition of Right, which belongs to the same period, and given earlier English constitutional developments, Hobbes could also have recognized that peace depends on the observance of fundamental rights that have been handed down over time, and that wars arise among other things from the infringement of such rights. Far too often Hobbes is prepared to support the Crown and its increasingly absolutist demands instead of developing the systematic implications of the path already traced by constitutional history, and thinking them through to the end. And this path leads to the recognition of fundamental rights and of the separation of powers (between the Crown, the Upper House, the Lower House, and the judiciary), with the accompanying notion of state power as normatively limited in relevant ways and as a system of relatively independent, mutually regulating agencies.

Where there is no separation of powers, and especially where there is no separation between the executive and the judiciary, Kant speaks of despotism, where the regent "handles the public will [i.e., the legislature] as his private will" (*Toward Perpetual Peace*, First Definitive Article). The solution to the problem that Hobbes raised with such inexorable clarity, the problem of how peace and freedom can effectively be secured, lies

neither in the position of an absolute sovereign nor in its simple opposite, in a condition with no civil power, a condition without "dominion"
(i.e., anarchy). The solution lies in the progressive realization of a liberal
democratic order committed to fundamental human rights.

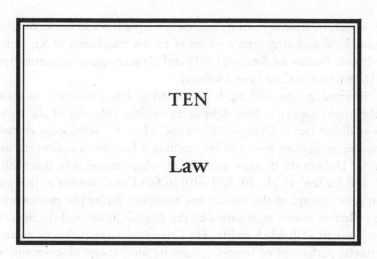

TEN

Law

10.1. "Not Truth but Authority"

Every legal and political order must face the fundamental question as to how fundamental rights can best be secured and protected, and there are basically two sharply contrasting responses in this regard. Hobbes's critics appeal to the wisdom they find embodied in a tradition of established rights, whereas Hobbes himself appeals to the natural reason of each individual person. The latter approach draws on a notion of natural law (in the service of peace), which can readily be understood by all human beings. The former approach draws on the common law, which emerged after the Norman invasion of England (1066) as itinerant judges acting for the Crown gradually succeeded in eliminating regional peculiarities. This common law later came to be administered by an established body of judges who acquired the skill to interpret and apply it appropriately.

Among those who had tried to theorize the nature and status of rights before Hobbes, the name of the great jurist Sir Edward Coke (1552–1634) stands out in particular. It was Coke who rediscovered the significance of the Magna Carta (1215) with its codification of important liberties, and who drew up the Petition of Right (1628), a document hardly less significant from the legal and constitutional point of view. This petition, which Charles I was compelled by Parliament to accept, made it illegal to introduce new taxes without the consent of Parliament and to subject any citizen to arbitrary arrest. But Coke's reputation in Great Britain as a great legal authority rests even more on his translation of Sir Thomas Littleton's *Treatise on Tenures* (1481) and his accompanying commentary of 1628 (cited as *Coke upon Littleton*).

In arguing that nothing is permitted which is contrary to reason, Coke might appear at first sight as an evident defender of the natural law tradition (see *A Dialogue*, *Works* vol. VI, p. 4: "*nihil, quod est contra rationem, est licitum*; that is to say, nothing is law that is against reason"). But for Hobbes the decisive question is "whose reason it is, that shall be received for law" (L ch. 26: 139–40). In fact Coke's answer to this question runs counter to the natural law tradition, for he places his trust in the collective reason represented by the English jurists and the historical development of English rights. For Coke understands this to mean an "artificial perfection of reason, gotten by long study, observation, and experience" (cited by Hobbes: L ch. 26: 140), which he believes has found expression and been refined over many generations in the practices of English law (*Coke upon Littleton*, book III, ch. 6). Hobbes vehemently rejects this approach.

In one of his letters Francis Bacon had already invoked Seneca's remark: "*Lex iubeat, non disputet*" ("The law commands but does not contend"). For law arises from an order or command: "*Lex incipiat a iussione*," as Bacon puts it in *De augmentis scientiarium* of 1623 (book VIII, ch. 3, aphorism 69). Without explicitly appealing to either Seneca or Bacon, Hobbes adopts this position in chapter 26 of *Leviathan*, decisive for his theory of law, where he defends a thesis that is also pursued in his polemical response to Coke in *A Dialogue between a Philosopher and a Student of the Common Laws of England*.

The thesis is expressed in a particularly forceful manner in the Latin version of *Leviathan*: "*sed auctoritas, non veritas, facit legem*" (It is not truth but authority that makes a law.). Precisely in order to accentuate his opposition to Coke, here Hobbes speaks of wisdom rather than truth, both in the English version of *Leviathan* and in the *Dialogue*. As he puts it in the latter text: "It is not wisdom but authority that makes a law." Thus for Hobbes it is not a question of recognizing the wisdom supposedly embodied in English common law or the established legal profession that administers it, but of recognizing the authority of the sovereign power. Hobbes does not ascribe any higher sanctity to this power, either in a religious sense ("by the Grace of God") or in a moral sense. As a secular and soberly realistic philosopher, Hobbes is concerned solely with the ability of sovereign power to secure peace and social order.

He agrees with his opponents, the "lawyers," in claiming that "law can never be against reason" (L ch. 26: 139). But with respect to whose reason is at issue here, Hobbes rejects two specific options for reasons internal to the notion of law. For neither of these options can guarantee the security and stability required by the idea of law. The first option, which appeals to "private reason," cannot be what is meant here, for "then there would be as much contradiction in the laws, as there is in the Schools" (loc. cit.). But remarkably enough Hobbes does not adduce the significant argument that is directly relevant to the security and stability of law, namely that a supposed right to rebellion based on an appeal to the private reason of the individual would permit one to withhold obedience to any law, so that once again civil war could only be the eventual result. The second option seeks an alternative to the private reason of the individual in the collective reason allegedly embodied in the legal profession itself, but this overlooks the possibility that "long study" is also capable of generating erroneous judgments of one kind or another. And contradictions arise among the "reasons and resolutions" of "those that study, and observe with equal time, and diligence." Thus it is not "the wisdom of subordinate judges" but "the reason of this our artificial man the commonwealth, and his command, that maketh law" (loc. cit.). If this were not the case, one would again have to add, we should always be confronted with the threat of disobedience and ultimately that of civil war.

Hobbes's penchant for striking aphoristic expression is not merely evident in the Latin version of his own thesis, *sed auctoritas, non veritas, fecit legem,* even if this formulation can already be found in the Roman poet Juvenal (*Satires*, VI, line 223). This alternative of authority versus truth also evokes the typical opposition between legal positivism and the tradition of natural law, so that Hobbes, with his rejection of *veritas* as a criterion here, easily appears as a proponent, or even as the father, of modern legal positivism. Yet Hobbes himself ascribes a constitutive role to natural law, and thus defends an alternative to this particular approach. If Hobbes is not simply to be convicted of straightforward contradiction here, it is necessary to recognize that the basic thesis of his theory of law cannot be interpreted in purely positivist terms.

10.2. The Division of Laws

In the chapter entitled "Of Civil Laws," which is the longest chapter in the first two parts of *Leviathan*, Hobbes furnishes the fundamental out-lines of what is often later described as a general theory of law, something which is then relegated to the professional domain of legal study. Yet in this regard Hobbes reveals a democratic mentality, for he holds that every individual already possesses the relevant knowledge here, knowledge that helps us to avoid the errors that lead in turn to false courses of action.

The structure of the argument in chapter 26 reflects Hobbes's rationalistic conception of language and science (see chapter 6, above). Since the first task is "the right definition of names" (L ch. 4: 15), his discussion begins with a concise definition of "civil law." In fact, Hobbes's attempt to conceptualize simply what every individual can allegedly discover for himself with due reflection results in the command theory of law that has proved so influential in Great Britain in particular.

In accordance with the thesis that reason is "nothing but reckoning" (L ch. 5: 18), Hobbes calculates that eight conclusions can be derived "by necessary consequence" from this definition of civil law (L ch. 26: 137). Since a "sufficient sign of the will" on the part of the commonwealth is included in the definition, Hobbes now inquires after the sufficient indications of the will of the sovereign (L ch. 26: 140–43). Only after this, once he addresses the question concerning the authoritative interpretation of laws, does Hobbes's principal thesis clearly emerge. The chapter then concludes with a discussion of various "divisions of law," although in this regard only two kinds of law, namely "divine positive laws" and what Hobbes calls a "fundamental law," are investigated in detail.

The notion of "civil law," as the name suggests, points to a specific domain of law distinct from that of public law, namely to the domain of matrimonial, family, inheritance, contract law, etc., which regulates the relations of private individuals. But originally, in ancient Rome, the expression referred to the whole field of law that concerns the Roman citizens as members of the state. Foreigners or aliens, on the other hand, are subject to a law which is common to all human beings (*ius omnium commune*), and which is the province of natural reason. But Hobbes effaces this distinction; for him, civil laws correspond simply to the laws of the state or commonwealth.

Hobbes's own "division" or articulation of the realm of law is not revolutionary in character. It is quite traditional in adopting the distinction between civil and natural law, which derives from the medieval tradition and which can ultimately be traced back to antiquity. Thus in the particularly terse formulation of the Latin version of *Leviathan*, Hobbes writes: "As human beings we must show obedience to *natural laws*, as citizens to *civil laws*." But whereas this distinction had often been interpreted

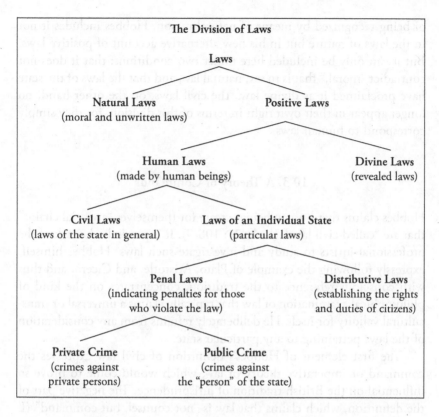

The Division of Laws

Laws

Natural Laws
(moral and unwritten laws)

Positive Laws

Human Laws
(made by human beings)

Divine Laws
(revealed laws)

Civil Laws
(laws of the state in general)

Laws of an Individual State
(particular laws)

Penal Laws
(indicating penalties for those
who violate the law)

Distributive Laws
(establishing the rights
and duties of citizens)

Private Crime
(crimes against
private persons)

Public Crime
(crimes against
the "person" of the state)

as an opposition, Hobbes expressly denies this: "The law of nature, and
the civil law, contain each other, and are of equal extent." For the natural
laws, which in the pure state of nature are "not properly laws, but qualities
that dispose men to peace, and to obedience" (L ch. 26: 138), become
actual laws in the political state, for then they are "the commands of the
commonwealth; and therefore also civil laws" (loc. cit.). But the distinction between laws that hold for the citizens of the state and those that
hold for others disappears, so that civil laws are to be understood as laws
of the state.

Although it is not immediately evident from Hobbes's initial discussion of the fundamental distinctions here, it soon emerges that he
accepts a notion of divinely revealed laws, which was quite unknown
in ancient Rome and derives specifically from Judeo-Christian thought.
Thus Hobbes distinguishes three forms of law: natural laws, divine laws,
and civil laws or laws of the state. Since the intermediate form of law
here, namely revealed law, neither enjoys eternal validity nor is capable

of being recognized by means of natural reason, Hobbes includes it not in the laws of nature but in his new alternative account of positive laws. But it can only be included here under two conditions: that it does not contradict "moral," that is to say, natural law, and that the laws of the state have proclaimed it as divine law. The civil laws, on the other hand, no longer appear in their own right in terms of this division, for they simply correspond to human laws.

10.3. A Theory of Commands

Hobbes claims that human beings create for themselves "artificial chains" that are "called civil laws" (L ch. 21: 108-9). It is precisely the task of the professional jurists to study and investigate such laws. Hobbes himself, expressly following the example of Plato, Aristotle, and Cicero, and thus with conscious reference to the tradition, concentrates on the kind of philosophical examination of law that typically claims a universal or trans-cultural validity for itself. He deliberately refrains from any consideration of the laws pertaining to any particular state.

The first element of Hobbes's definition of civil law expresses the command or imperative theory of law, which would come to prove so influential on the British tradition of jurisprudence. The negative part of the definition, which claims that law is "not counsel, but command" (L ch. 26: 137), is certainly true. But his positive claim that law is a com-mand in the sense of an order is problematic in several respects. For an order has three characteristic elements: it is a purely voluntaristic act; it need not be formulated in linguistic form but could also be expressed, for example, by a high-pitched whistle; and it can be addressed not only to human beings but also to animals.

Laws are certainly not orders or commands in this sense. Although for Hobbes too laws are expressed in linguistic form and are directed exclusively to human beings, he endorses the first element and sees the mere will of the one who commands as a sufficient condition or justifica-tion for a command. But in the case of laws the will is only a necessary but not a sufficient condition for the command. What is true of an order is not as a rule true of a law. A pure order requires no justification, and any preliminary reflection is superfluous; furthermore, an order remains in force unless and until it is cancelled or replaced by a different one. It is more appropriate to interpret the notion of law by recourse to Aristotle's

concept of *proairesis*, of decision as voluntary action preceded by deliberation (*Nicomachean Ethics*, book III, chs. 1–7) and to supplement
the voluntaristic dimension of a command with a specifically cognitive
dimension.

We must also object to Hobbes's further claim that it is part of the
definition of a command that it is directed toward the advantage, "benefit," or "good" of the one who commands (L ch. 25: 131–32). Whereas
in the case of "counsel" or advice, the issue is the advantage of the one
who receives counsel rather than that of the one who dispenses it, there
are actually three options open to the one who commands: his own good,
the good of the one who is commanded, and the good of both parties.
The task of the legislator, as Hobbes's construction of the state implies
and subsequently develops, is precisely to care for the welfare or good of
the people (L ch. 30: 175).

It also speaks against this notion of a command as an order that a
demand that springs from pure willfulness is experienced as something
wholly alien. Thus one who is addressed solely by an order cannot recognize his own self in this process, but can only see himself as one who in
Hobbes is merely impotently subjected to an infinitely superior power.
Something of the kind may sometimes occur in obeying a law, but it
is not the rule, and it certainly does not belong to the concept of law
as such. For one can interpret laws in different ways; one can also raise
objections to specific laws, and attempt to persuade the legislator or relevant legislative institution to introduce changes with regard to the laws.

Even if Hobbes had espoused a broader concept of command than
the narrow conception at issue here, this would still be inadequate to
capture the nature of law. We can certainly formulate civil laws as hypothetical commands in the following way: "*assuming* that you wish to do
X, e.g., enter into marriage or draw up a legally binding will, *then* you
must do x, namely fulfill specific formal requirements." But a command
consists in a concrete demand ("Do this," "Refrain from doing that"),
which holds in the judicial field for the conduct of official functionaries
(in the police, in tax agencies, in court procedures), but not for the law
as a general rule.

A command theory is burdened with the further difficulty that while
commands are simply directed toward others, many legal obligations, in
matrimonial law, in contract law, in traffic law, in penal law, also apply
to those who have enacted them. Even if members of Parliament enjoy
a certain legal immunity, this is lifted in the event of more serious cases

of crime. On account of this specifically self-reflexive character, of the fact that enacted laws also apply to the legislators themselves, the binding character of laws are to be understood not as a concrete command ("Do this"), but rather as a rule that governs action in general. This maintains the prescriptive and proscriptive character of legal obligations, their intrinsically normative character, without our being bound to the demands of a particular person or body or to a merely unilateral relationship between the source or author of the commands and those who are addressed by them.

Hobbes's express definition of civil law actually does some justice to these considerations, since it speaks specifically of a "rule" rather than simply of a (concrete) order or command (L ch. 26: 137). Thus the text appears to waver between a problematic command theory of law and a more appropriate theory of rules. If Hobbes had dispensed with the concept of "command" as an order and spoken instead of something like an injunction or commandment, he would have avoided many of these objections.

In the case of a later proponent of the imperativist theory of law, such as John Austin (1832/1954, p. 13ff.), the command aspect is directly linked to the concepts of superior power, of the threat of sanction on the part of the sovereign source of law, of habitual obedience on the part of those addressed by the laws. This approach relinquishes an internal juridical perspective in favor of an external sociological one. Hobbes, on the other hand, does retain this internal perspective, and discovers a distinguishing characteristic that is missing in Austin's analysis of law. Hobbes regards laws as objective obligations, the objectivity of which is determined by a twofold question: What are the conditions that oblige obedience from those addressed by the laws, and what are the conditions that entitle the author of the laws to promulgate them?

Hobbes answers the first question by reference to a preliminary obligation to obedience, which distinguishes law from illegal coercion; he answers the second question by reference to the "person" of the state or commonwealth: the (monarchical, aristocratic, or democratic) sovereign. He also emphasizes two further elements: laws are made known "by word, writing, or other sufficient sign of the will"; and they are concerned with "the distinction of right, and wrong; that is to say, of what is contrary, and what is not contrary to the rule" (L ch. 26: 137).

Hobbes thinks that eight conclusions can be derived "by necessary consequence" from this definition of civil law (L ch. 26: 137–40). In the first place I would simply like to consider his second conclusion. This tells us that the sovereign possesses absolute power in the literal sense of *legibus solutus*. That is to say, his power to make laws or create obligations involves the power to repeal laws or dissolve any such obligation. But this power can only be derived from his definition of civil law by assuming the narrow, purely voluntaristic conception of "command" as an order. This is not the case if we assume the broader conception of law as a "rule." Hobbes's theorem of the absolute sovereignty of the state does not therefore rigorously follow from a concept of law that has been indubitably established on the basis of an unprejudiced examination of the issue.

A further difficulty is presented by common law, which is hardly a peripheral dimension of (positive) law. All law was originally customary or common law, and when it was initially committed to writing, this simply served as an unambiguous record of the law that already prevailed. Common practice of this kind still retains its significance for positive law under the following conditions: (1) where codified law reveals certain gaps and leaves room for further elaboration and application; (2) where there is a reliable and consistent mode of procedure; (3) where the parties involved are convinced that this procedure is just.

When Hobbes's third conclusion defines common as the silent or implicit command of the sovereign, he does do justice to the first condition above that common law today merely supplements statute law, and that the legislative power can always supersede it. Perhaps it also fulfills the second condition, but it violates the third one. For in relation to common law even an absolute sovereign possesses only the limited, secondary, and negative power of being able to supersede it, but not the primary power of being able to create it. In order to counter this objection, one might appeal to the fifth conclusion, which tells us: "For the legislator is he, not by whose authority the laws were first made, but by whose authority they now continue to be laws" (L ch. 26: 139). But apart from the fact that common law knows no explicit legislator, it might be more accurate to recognize the person or persons who first enacted the laws as the legislator.

As far as the authority of the legislator is concerned, Hobbes cannot avoid asking the question regarding the means by which this authority asserts itself if required. The short answer is: by means of the army (B part I, 65). And he is honest enough to ask the further question: "Who shall compel the army?" The fact that the answer offered here, where he refers to the preachers and the universities, is conspicuously absent from Hobbes's argumentation elsewhere points to a basic problem or even incoherence in his position. Hobbes is unable to provide an internally compelling answer to the question concerning the means of asserting and realizing the required authority, a question that arises directly from his own philosophy. The answer we have mentioned even contradicts his fundamental politico-legal thesis that underlies his approach, for the preachers and the universities stand for truth, the very thing that authority was supposed to depose and disempower.

10.4. Laws of Nature as a Corrective?

Many interpreters of Hobbes regard the concept of absolute sovereignty as necessary within his systematic philosophy. But in fact there is an internal problem here that springs from the system itself, for the danger of war which constantly threatens in the state of nature is not actually overcome by the notion of a state power invested with unconditional authority. In his discussion of the division of the sciences in chapter 9 of *Leviathan*, Hobbes already concedes that the sovereign also has duties and the subject also has rights. In chapter 26 Hobbes mentions three fundamental duties in this regard: defense against (external) enemies, protection of industry (crafts, trade, and commerce), and redress for those who have been wronged (L ch. 26: 142). Moreover, he subsequently defends an evidently comprehensive notion of the security or "safety of the people," for "by safety here, is not meant a bare preservation, but also all the other contentments of life, which every man by lawful industry, without danger, or hurt to the commonwealth, shall acquire to himself" (L ch. 30: 175). The laws of nature are required to determine more precisely the legitimate and allegedly absolute character of the sovereign power of the state. The ultimate authority here is "God the creator of this law," and also "conscience," although this only appears in the Latin version of the text (L ch. 25: 79).

If we take all these claims and remarks together, it is clear that we need to correct the view that he should be seen as the original proponent of all modern legal and political positivism, as one who thus simply opposed the idea of critically investigating law and state from a perspective that does not essentially appeal to established purely positive principles and criteria, namely the idea that has long made itself felt in the Western tradition in terms, originally, of "divine law," "the law of nature," and "natural law," and later in terms of "justice." As we have seen, *Leviathan* even dedicates two whole chapters (14 and 15) to what Hobbes calls "laws of nature" or "natural laws," of which indeed he identifies no fewer than nineteen. And in chapter 26 Hobbes also says that it is against the law of nature to punish the innocent (L ch. 26: 144). Finally, in his "Review, and Conclusion" at the end of the book Hobbes also introduces a duty of defense as another law of nature: "every man is bound by nature, as much as in him lieth, to protect in war, the authority, by which he is himself protected in time of peace" (L 390). Thus *Leviathan* contains twenty-one laws of nature in all.

It is also remarkable that Hobbes recognizes laws of nature that apply only to particular groups, and perhaps even only to particular individuals. Thus where a minister or official has no written instructions to follow, "he is obliged to take for instructions the dictates of reason," and as an ambassador in the same situation, "he must take for instruction that which reason dictates to be most conducing to his sovereign's interests" (L ch. 26: 141). The basis here is provided by a moral characteristic, namely the virtue of "fidelity; which is a natural branch of justice."

In the course of chapter 26 Hobbes once again describes these natural laws as moral ones. But they are still merely prudential rules in the service of free self-preservation (as we pointed out in chapter 9.2). That is why they enjoy a somewhat precarious status in two respects. On the one hand, it is true that these laws hold eternally, and are bound up with an obligation to give account of ourselves before God who established them. But they only acquire validity in a state or commonwealth when the sovereign makes them a part of "his" civil laws. To this extent they do not belong to the conditions under which the laws of the state possess validity; thus a law of the state that clearly and emphatically contradicts the laws of nature does not thereby forfeit its validity. One might assume that this situation simply follows from Hobbes's purely voluntaristic definition of law. But the natural laws do have a (quasi) sovereign of their own, namely God or reason, and this sovereign precedes the sovereign power of the state.

On the other hand, according to Hobbes, the content of the laws of nature is also readily accessible to any human being who makes impartial and dispassionate use of natural reason. But since few human beings actually do so, the law of nature has "now become of all laws the most obscure" (L ch. 26: 143). Even with those human beings from whom impartiality is professionally expected, such as judges (L ch. 15: 75ff.), it is to be feared that their judgments may be erroneous (L ch. 26: 144). Nonetheless, in a later passage Hobbes ascribes the task of determining truth specifically to the judges.

But since even those who would be expected by profession to be familiar with the law of nature, namely the moral philosophers (among whom Hobbes counts himself), are incapable of providing an unimpeachable evident knowledge and interpretation of the natural laws, these laws in spite of their universal validity continue to appear private and controversial in character. Since endless conflicts and controversies must be feared as a result, there is a need for persons who are authorized to provide authentic interpretations in order to overcome this situation. These are the judges appointed by the sovereign power who are charged, so far as they are "competent," with examining and determining the truth (L ch. 46: 380).

According to Hobbes, we also need the state, among other things, because conscience is neither so immune from error nor so strong as to insure that moral laws are realized by themselves. But for the same reason, although Hobbes does not recognize this, our responsibility merely before God is not sufficient, so that there remains a fundamental and unresolved tension in the theory of natural laws. Thus in accordance with his rationalistic ideal of science Hobbes makes a strict truth claim on behalf of his assertions. The task of political philosophy is to promote the construction of a "firm and lasting edifice" (L ch. 29: 167). But on account of Hobbes's thesis that the "representative" enjoys unreserved authority (L ch. 16), the assertions concerning the laws of nature are subordinated to the legislative and interpretive monopoly of the sovereign. In the former case, Hobbes's assertions are regarded as unreservedly true, while in the second case they are regarded as proposals, which the sovereign can disregard whenever he sees fit.

10.5. Authorized Power

Whitehead's famous remark that the history of Western philosophy consists in a series of footnotes to Plato seems to apply in a different form to Hobbes's basic juridical thesis: *sed auctoritas, non veritas, facit legem*. For Plato in his *Laws* (book X, 889d–890a) certainly employs the contrast between nature (*phusis*) and art (*technē*), and the course of the discussion shows that nature stands for truth while art stands for the arbitrary and even oppressive enactments of legislators. This may indeed appear to reduce Hobbes's theory of law to a footnote to Plato. But the claim that it is not nature *qua* truth, but art *qua* (legislative) authority that makes a law is only introduced by Plato because he intends to challenge it. It is for this reason, and even more because Plato's political thought is usually discussed solely with reference to dialogues such as the *Crito*, the *Gorgias*, and the *Republic* rather than the *Laws*, that this thesis has proved influential through Hobbes rather than first through Plato. It is above all Hobbes who first treats it as a significant position that fully deserves endorsement.

The slightly fuller English version of *Leviathan* makes clear what Hobbes is really concerned about: "The authority of writers [in moral philosophy], without the authority of the commonwealth, maketh not their opinions law, be they never so true" (L ch. 26: 143). Thus it is the authoritative rather than the authentic interpretation that counts here. It is true that Hobbes is here concerned solely with the legal power of the judges, but this effectively applies to all judicial and political power. In this connection it is clear that Hobbes is not defending a positivistic theory of law, but rather indicating, in a strikingly compressed fashion, three minimal conditions of any genuine theory of law.

Thus, in the first place, legal principles and determinations cannot be treated as purely theoretical objects. Neither laws nor judicial claims are something already given that simply awaits identification or discovery. On the contrary, they are effectively produced ("made") by human beings. But this initial partial thesis only represents a significant insight from a legal-theoretical perspective if the "making" in question is understood in such a broad and at the same time formal sense that it also includes both common law and the law of nature. In this sense the talk of "making" is to be understood in terms of objective validity rather than in terms of some specific historical source or origin. It alludes to a noncognitive dimension, namely that of assent or recognition, which does not create the law out of nothing, as it were, but selects and identifies it out of existing possibilities. Thus the Latin word *facere* here signifies something like selection or nomination.

In the second place, the "truth" that Hobbes rejects as a ground of validity for law is to be understood in this context as objective insight and the kind of argumentation or rational grounding that leads to it. Even in the rare case that moral philosophers were all agreed with regard to the interpretation of the laws of nature, and this interpretation could be regarded as true beyond controversy, this universally shared insight would still not provide a ground of validity. Nor does the information supplied by legal scholars or commentators furnish an authoritative interpretation of the laws (L ch. 26: 145). The decision as to what the law is falls to the judge (L ch. 26: 142). The latter does not even have to be a jurist by profession, for Hobbes endorses the English practice whereby both the lords of Parliament, though "few of them were much versed in the study of the laws," and lay assessors or members of the jury may decide not only on questions of fact but also on those of right (L ch. 26: 146). In repudiating the position that *insight grounds validity*, Hobbes rejects the strict legal moralism that regards mere insight into alleged injustice as a sufficient reason for declaring the relevant law or court sentence to be invalid.

In the third place, Hobbes's own thesis that *authority grounds validity* tacitly operates with a many-faceted concept of authority. Thus the term "authority" refers, in the first instance, to the notion of an "author," namely an original source or will. The term also refers, secondly, to the notion of "power," with which the will realizes itself. But this power does not simply consist in a mere abundance of strength. And thirdly, in contrast to something like organized crime, it involves a sense of authorization that shows why the citizens are already "obliged" to obey the sovereign (L ch. 26: 137). In *Leviathan* this prior obligation even enjoys the status of a "fundamental law," namely one "which being taken away, the commonwealth faileth, and is utterly dissolved; as a building whose foundation is destroyed" (L ch. 26: 150).

Thus the thesis that *authority grounds validity* actually means that *authorized power grounds validity*. That is why the sovereign exercises *potestas* rather than *violentia*, why institutions of right involve legality. The idea that *authorized decision grounds validity* does not imply that rulings or decisions already made are beyond criticism or possible change. Hobbes is perfectly well aware that there can be erroneous and even manifestly unjust judgments. But a judicial decision that has been made remains in force as an element of established law unless and until a new judicial decision has been taken.

In the case of every authority and entitlement the question of its source or origin inevitably arises. In terms of Hobbes's theorem of the authorized representative, it springs neither from "the grace" of the established judicial or political powers, nor from the "grace of God." It arises through "the consent of all concerned." Here, in addition to the aspect of judicial authority or legality, we find a second level of authority that is typically described as "legitimacy" as distinct from "legality." According to *Leviathan* this legitimacy consists in the free recognition afforded by all concerned. Thus when the lapidary formula that *authority grounds validity* is fully explicated, it signifies that *the power authorized by all concerned grounds validity*, or more succinctly that *freely recognized authority grounds validity*, or simply that *consensus ground validity*.

Theories concerned with the validity of law can initially be divided into two basic types: theories of power and theories of consent or recognition. Given his thesis that *power grounds validity*, Hobbes is often counted among the theorists of power. But since the concept of authority involves both aspects—the elements of will and power and the notion of a fundamental recognition on the part of those concerned—Hobbes's position actually involves both types of theory. And since the dimension of entitlement plays a significant role in his account, he should also be included in a third type of approach, which could be described as theories of authorization or empowerment.

The notion of the free recognition of all concerned makes Hobbes's theory of law clearly and directly relevant to the idea of justice. To begin with, this should be understood in the formal sense that every individual person gives his or her free consent. But those concerned only give their consent because they expect an advantage from the establishment of the sovereign, and one that benefits every individual: the reciprocal limitation of freedom for the sake of the reciprocal securing of freedom (cf. the second law of nature in *Leviathan*, ch. 14: 64). Thus since the ultimate legitimating ground of the legal and the political order lies in a material and not merely formal conception of justice, Hobbes's theory of law proves to be clearly anti-positivist in character.

On the other hand, given his theorem of the authorized representative endowed with unlimited power, the laws of nature are permitted no binding political power on their own account. In the end, therefore, justice serves solely to legitimate but not to limit law. Whatever authority may demand, it can never commit "injustice" upon anyone (L ch. 18: 90). It is here once again that a fundamental objection to Hobbes's theory of sovereignty makes itself felt: bound by no conditions whatsoever, the highest authority of the state enjoys complete and unreserved power, although it is meant to guarantee the end or purpose for which it was instituted in the first place. But if the legitimation of sovereignty is not bound up with any corresponding limitation on power, and the subject is not accorded rights as well as duties, then this end or purpose—the free self-preservation of the individual—is itself endangered.

ELEVEN

Religion and the Church

11.1. A Twofold Political Question

In this age of confessional wars and conflicts the place and role of religion in the public context of civil power is an eminently political question. And the complementary question of how the state, the institutional embodiment of civil power itself, should relate to religion is also of decisive political significance. Both issues are so inextricably connected that they are better addressed as a *single* twofold question.

This question is so important to Hobbes that he dedicates considerable space to it in all three of the works that deal with political philosophy and the nature of the state. In the first anthropological part of the *The Elements of Law* (on "Human Nature") the chapter on natural laws is concerned with the "Confirmation of the Same out of the Word of God" (chapter 18). Within the second political part of the same work, the second half of the text addresses the claim "That Subjects are not to follow the Judgment of Any Authority in Controversies of Religion which is not Dependent on the Sovereign Power." Again, in *De Cive*, the last part of his threefold system, Hobbes dedicates chapter 11 to the scriptural justification of "the right of government," and four further chapters (the whole of the last part of the text) to the issue of religion.

Finally, his principal work *Leviathan* evokes the twofold question in its subtitle, which speaks expressly of the "commonwealth ecclesiastical

175

and civil," and dedicates approximately half of the entire text to a discussion of this question, the third part bearing the title "Of a Christian Commonwealth" and the fourth part the title "Of the Kingdom of Darkness." In this latter case Hobbes, as a convinced Anglican, is thinking of the pope and the Catholic Church, but also of the Presbyterians who had become such a significant force in Scotland. The first half of *Leviathan* also contains two explicit discussions of religious questions: the anthropological part has chapter 12 ("Of Religion"), and the political part has chapter 31 ("Of the Kingdom of God by Nature"). And in many other chapters religion plays such a significant role that there is barely a topic in Hobbes's philosophical anthropology ("The First Part") or his political philosophy ("The Second Part") that is discussed without some reference to God, or to the doctrines and figures of the Old and New Testaments. Two examples will suffice here: already in the chapter on "Imagination," Hobbes goes into the question of visions and miracles (L ch. 2; 7f.). And when he discusses belief Hobbes distinguishes between the usual sense in which we believe a trustworthy person and the different sense, specifically reserved for religious texts, where we "believe in" something.

Given the quantitative and qualitative significance of all these references and allusions, and especially given the structure of Hobbes's argumentation itself, it has been argued by A. E. Taylor (1938), and subsequently also by A. P. Martinich (1992, p. 1ff.), that a certain form of theism, namely the conviction that some sort of supreme individual being has created and still governs the world, is absolutely required by Hobbes in order "to make the theory work." According to R. Tuck (1992, p. 114), on the other hand, Hobbes only defends a form of deism in which God is the original source of all things, but is neither a "person," nor intervenes in the course of nature, nor speaks to us through any special revelation. And for Leo Strauss (1936, p. 74f.) Hobbes must ultimately be regarded as an atheist.

A careful and unprejudiced examination of Hobbes actually reveals a theologically inflected system of thought that allows us to recognize the (partial) justice of all three positions here. In the first instance, I would simply like to indicate why we should eschew an overly simplified or rough-hewn interpretation of Hobbes's thought in this regard. If Taylor, Martinich, or Tuck were completely right, this would destroy the fundamental basis of Hobbes's philosophy of the state: the quasi-axioms developed in the opening chapters of *Leviathan*, his theses regarding the human mind (from the account of the senses, of imagery and thought, through to language, reason, and science) would only divert attention from the supposedly theistic or deistic foundation of his philosophy, and perhaps even consciously or unconsciously obscure this foundation. What is more, the engraving on the title page of *Leviathan* already undermines Taylor's position. For while the figure of the sovereign certainly bears the symbol of spiritual power in one hand, the iconographical "explanation" in the five emblematic panels beneath the spiritual arm of the sovereign strictly avoids any suggestion of theism or deism (see chapter 3.2, above). None of the pictorial images presented here symbolizes any genuinely religious notion or idea. All we see are insignia of the Church as a worldly power.

On the other hand, the radically alternative or essentially atheist interpretation defended by Leo Strauss is also unconvincing. The deistic reading seems to be supported by the fact that the idea of God already plays a role in the first part of *Leviathan*, for Hobbes assumes an absolutely original ground, or *causa prima*: "some cause, whereof there is no former cause, but is eternal; which is it men call God" (ch. 11: 51), and which, like Aristotle, he also describes as the "one first mover" (ch. 12: 53). Hobbes also goes further than this, for he says in the introduction that "God hath made" the world (L: 1) and that from "the very creation" God has "reigned over all men . . . by his might" (L ch. 35: 216). And the theistic reading seems to be supported when he accepts "the secret working of God, which men call good luck" (L, ch. 10: 41).

But one should not overestimate the weight of these passages. In the first two "secular" parts of *Leviathan,* remarks such as these do not play any fundamental or even subsidiary role in the development of the argument. For here we must remember Hobbes's telling claim that God "is no fit subject of our philosophy" (Works, vol. V, p. 435). These remarks are only made in passing, and if they were not included in the text Hobbes would not have to change or reject any of his central anthropological or political theses. It is true that there is one significant exception in this regard: Hobbes's theory of religion goes beyond the limits of any purely natural or "heathen" religion insofar as it recognizes a supernatural revelation, and the associated notions of divine calling and witness (L ch. 2: 57ff.). On account of these remarks alone Strauss's claims regarding Hobbes's atheism fail to convince.

Since all of the aforementioned interpretations oversimplify the question at issue, some have adopted an alternative approach here. Thus one could argue that Hobbes wrote the first two parts of *Leviathan* with philosophers in mind, and the last two parts with the (biblically) educated public in mind. But there are also numerous objections to this suggestion, starting with the question as to why, if Hobbes really had two different audiences in view, he didn't simply compose two separate texts. And this idea also seems unconvincing given the fact, as we have already indicated, that theological claims and arguments are strewn throughout the first two parts of *Leviathan*.

In this age of religious wars and conflicts it would be difficult to answer the twofold question solely in terms of political philosophy. But in fact Hobbes's thinking was neither so orthodox in character (as Taylor, Tuck, and Martinich claim) that he had to connect his political philosophy with some form of deism or theism, nor so revolutionary in character that he could regard genuinely theological questions as insignificant or irrelevant, as the atheist reading implies. Kersting (2008, p. 255) argues that Hobbes's philosophy is "the first system of knowledge in western philosophy that no longer has any place for God, that manages without appealing to some original ground, *causa sui*, or ultimate ontological principle." But neither of these claims is strictly true. Since in all of his philosophical writings, even in the work expressly concerned with natural philosophy (*De Corpore*), Hobbes discusses the issue of God, it is impossible to ignore the persisting systematic significance of this issue in his thought.

God is "that invisible power" that all human beings "worship as God; and fear as a revenger of their perfidy" (L ch. 14: 70). Only the "fool hath said in his heart there is no God" (L ch. 15: 72). Moreover, it is only "under the Immortal God" that we owe "our peace and defence" to that Leviathan, which Hobbes describes as a "Mortal God" (L ch. 17: 87). Furthermore the sovereign "receiveth his power *Dei gratia* simply; that is to say, from the favour of none but God" (L ch. 23: 125). And all natural laws are also described as "divine" (L ch. 26: 148). God above is the one whom the sovereign "should stand in fear of, and whose laws he ought to obey" (L ch. 28: 167), for it is to God, the author of the law of nature, that he must render account (L ch. 30: 175). Last but not least, there is one exception with regard to the subject's duty of obedience: this latter must not be "repugnant to the laws of God" (L ch. 31: 186).

On the other hand, we should note that such an outstanding example of Western philosophical thought as Aristotle's *prima philosophia* also contains, in addition to the project of a nontheistic form of theology (*Metaphysics*, book XII), two other projects that belong to what we have called "fundamental philosophy": a theory of the most general principles of thought (ibid., book IV, 3–8 and book XI, 5–6) and a universal science of being (ibid., books VII–IX), neither of which requires reference to the concept of God.

11.2. The Anthropological Foundations of Religion

Hobbes does not discuss the question of religion for external or merely contemporary and historical reasons. On the contrary, in chapter 12 of *Leviathan* he develops an anthropological approach to the issue on the basis of arguments internal to his philosophy as a whole. As a kind of empiricist, Hobbes begins with a factual observation: religion is something we only find among human beings. But as a philosophical theorist he is hardly satisfied with this empirical observation alone. On the assumption that the source or "seed" of religion is only found among human beings, he inquires into the grounds of religion insofar as these lie in the nature of humanity, that is, in the essential properties and characteristics of human beings. He discovers three grounds for the phenomenon of religion, which in part also effectively undermine religion itself. Hobbes's anthropological theory of religion thus involves a significant contribution to what we would today describe as the critique of ideology. In the first place, we seek out the causes behind visible events out of concern for "our own good or evil fortune." In the second place, we assume that there is some cause behind all things that arises and "has a beginning." In the third place, we observe the effects of things, and when we are unable to identify or determine their causes we turn either to the imagination (our "own fancy") or to the authority of other people we are close to or who we consider to be wiser than ourselves (L ch. 12: 52). It is only because Hobbes regards the first human characteristic we have mentioned here as essentially practical, oriented as it is to considerations of happiness or unhappiness, rather than as purely theoretical, as a mere desire for knowledge itself, that he finds the first natural source of religion in our belief in spirits ("our opinion of ghosts"), something he rejects as a heathen belief.

The first two human characteristics we have mentioned serve to produce "anxiety" and "fear." Human beings who are anxious regarding the future will ascribe the causes of things to an invisible power or agent when the true causes remain obscure. The (heathen) Gods thus arise from human fear. But if the third human characteristic comes into play, if we indulge the imagination or trust in the authority of others, this gives rise to a kind of philosophical religion. We come upon the idea of "a first and eternal cause of all things," which we describe "by the name of God" (L ch. 2: 53). Hobbes here evokes the cosmological proof of the existence of God and the merely deistic rather than theistic concept of God that is associated with it. He thereby also makes the notion of God seem a little conceivable to us, in spite of various other remarks of his that emphatically suggest the opposite.

Hobbes identifies three further "natural seeds" of religion: our ignorance of real causes (which leads us to mistake what he calls "casual," i.e., contingent, things for the causes themselves); the tendency to worship or reverence things that we fear; and the tendency to treat things as signs or portents through which "invisible powers declare to men the things which shall hereafter come to pass" (L ch. 12: 54).

Hobbes then proceeds to distinguish two basic forms of religion: the heathen religion of "the Gentiles" and revealed or "supernatural" religion. He justifies this distinction not by recourse to purely anthropological reasoning or arguments solely internal to religion, but by appeal to a politically inflected argument. It is true that he grounds the distinction between these forms of religion in terms of "two sorts of men," but he is not thinking of ordinary individuals here, but rather of their political leaders and governors: while the gentiles devised their own practices, those of revealed religion were traced directly to God's instruction and commandment. In both cases the ultimate purpose is the same, which Hobbes understands in terms that are external rather than internal to religion, namely in political terms, in relation to the principal theme of *Leviathan*. For the political leadership has acted "with a purpose to make those men that relied on them, the more apt to obedience, laws, peace, charity, and civil society" (L ch. 2: 54).

In the first case, which is typical for "all the founders of commonwealths, and the law-givers of the Gentiles," religion is "a part of human politics; and teacheth part of the duty which earthly kings require of their subjects." In the second case, in the one and only "true" religion of revelation, religion is a part of "divine politics." It is through "Abraham, Moses, and our blessed Saviour"—the prophets who were also crucial in ancient Jewish tradition go unmentioned—that we learn the laws of the kingdom of God (ch. 12: 54). Thus Hobbes's secular and "enlightened" approach does not go so far as to assert the priority of natural reason in relation to religion. The idea of revelation accords priority to a supernatural element, which demotes the merely natural reason that is common to all human beings, and qualifies it as simply heathen insofar as it goes beyond (monotheistic) deism.

On his own anthropological assumptions Hobbes could actually have conceded a different meaning to religion. Thus, by proceeding in a more cautious and circumspect manner, with specific reference to some of the natural "seeds" of religion he indicates, Hobbes could have spoken of a human need for religion and thereby suggested that society could benefit from this need. Thus institutionalized society, the commonwealth, could find legitimation in religion, while religion, now as a church, could seek protection within the state. This kind of mutually supportive relationship, established in many continental European territories, is alien to Hobbes. He does not specifically reject it, but never seems to consider this as a possible option either in his anthropological discussion of religion or subsequently in his political philosophy itself.

11.3. The Kingdom of God

In the prophetic writings of the Old Testament, the religious and national ideal of the ancient Israelites found ultimate expression in the idea of an Israelite community under God, and this bears the name of the "Kingdom of God." The New Testament speaks of the "Kingdom of Heaven," and this refers to a form of human society in which God's will prevails (Rom. 4:7). According to Hobbes, as we have pointed out, God announces his laws in two different ways: through the precepts of natural reason and through divine revelation. There are thus also two corresponding forms of the kingdom of God: a natural kingdom and a prophetic kingdom as defined by revelation.

Hobbes is not the first major philosopher who has engaged with the notion of a kingdom of God. In this regard the most influential thinker in the Western philosophical-theological tradition is St. Augustine of Hippo. One of his principal works is expressly entitled *De Civitate Dei*, usually translated in English as *The City of God*. Hobbes did not engage with many previous philosophers, though he does discuss a few, but it is rather surprising that he does not address this text. Whether we are talking about *The Elements of Law*, *De Cive*, or *Leviathan*, Hobbes does not even mention Augustine, either in his theory of the worldly or of the Christian commonwealth.

Given their fundamentally different origin and their equally different character, Hobbes discusses the two forms of the kingdom of God at two different points in his text: the last chapter of the second part (on the commonwealth) deals with what he calls the kingdom of God "by Nature," that is, the kingdom of which we learn through purely natural reason without need of any supernatural revelation. Not all human beings are subjects of this kingdom, for it does not include atheists, or even deists. It includes only theists, namely those "that believe [1] there is a God that [2] governeth the world, and [3] that hath given precepts, and [4] propounded rewards, and punishments to mankind" (L ch. 31: 186–87).

As far as the commands of natural reason are concerned, Hobbes distinguishes two kinds of laws: the natural moral laws (of right), which have already been discussed in the anthropological part of the work (L chs. 4–5), and the laws regarding the honor due to God, which Hobbes goes on to discuss here. These laws include the form of worship, which as the public worship of the commonwealth must assume a uniform character, that of the Church of England. Those who refuse to participate in the Anglican Rite, such as Catholics and certain Protestants, became known as "recusants" (from the Latin verb *recusare*, to dispute). However, Hobbes also recognizes an inner or private form of worship, which is open to the individual. The demand for uniformity of worship is thus significantly qualified; it is important for Hobbes that even in the context of an established or state church, there is an essential sense in which religion still belongs to the inviolable private sphere of the individual.

The third part of *Leviathan* is concerned with the second form of the kingdom of God, namely with the "prophetic" rather than "natural" kingdom of God. But Hobbes already explains the essential difference in this last chapter of the second part: in the prophetic kingdom we are told that God, "having chosen out one peculiar nation (the Jews) for his subjects, he governed them, and none but them." Here God did not limit himself to the precepts of natural reason, but supplemented them "by positive laws, which he gave them by the mouths of his holy prophets" (L ch. 31: 187). This kingdom of God is "a civil commonwealth, where God himself is sovereign, by virtue first of the old, and since of the new covenant, wherein he reigneth by his vicar or lieutenant" (L ch. 38: 241), i.e., through the worldly sovereign.

11.4. The Principles of a Christian Politics

In the third and fourth parts of *Leviathan* Hobbes attempts to confirm and reinforce his conception of sovereignty by reference to the doctrines and teachings of both the Old and the New Testament. Here it is not altogether easy to decide whether he regards these detailed discussions not only as a further confirmation of his earlier construction and foundation of the state, but even as a crucial contribution to the latter. There is no question that he sometimes attempts to exploit these references and discussions in this sense. Thus, for example, he seeks to justify the idea of absolute sovereignty, in the worldly and the spiritual context, on analogy with the covenant that Jahweh established with the people of Israel.

Nonetheless, Hobbes overlooks or underestimates a number of essential differences here. Thus he appeals (L ch. 35: 213) to the Book of Exodus (19:5): "If you will obey my voice indeed, and keep my covenant, then ye shall be a peculiar people to me, for all the earth is mine." Exodus also includes passages that imply that the consent of the people was required for the establishment of the covenant. But Hobbes passes over such passages (for example, 19:8 and 24:3–7), which actually support his own theory of sovereignty. He chooses instead to cite the passage we have just cited; but this expresses an obligation that God lays upon the people of Israel, something which must thus be understood in the opposite and purely theonomous sense (i.e., laid down by God): it is Jahweh, not the people, who establishes the covenant, and it is God, not the people of Israel, who takes Moses as their leader and representative. If we transfer this relationship to the sovereign, then, as we saw before, the sovereign becomes a ruler "by the grace of God."

There is no doubt that Hobbes attempted to provide a Christian confirmation of sovereignty for his own contemporaries, for whom the Christian faith furnished the unquestioned basis of life. But then a second problem emerges here. It is striking that Hobbes pays more attention to the Old Testament than he does to the New Testament as the specifically Christian part of the Bible. The reason lies in the fact that Hobbes, even in religious matters, traces the unlimited power of the sovereign back to the story of the Jewish people. For Hobbes, the covenant of the Israelites with Jahweh is the prototype of a covenant with God, which only acquires a certain modification in the New Testament. But he thereby marginalizes that universalization of the idea of divine election, of the chosen people, which is such a fundamental Christian doctrine. Or does Hobbes wish to compare one small part of Christendom, the Anglican Church, with the covenant of Israel, and thus tacitly ascribe a special historical role to England itself?

As if he were the "principal ideologist" of the Anglican Church, which had split so conspicuously from the Church of Rome, and also the "principal theorist" of the continental European conception of an established or state church, Hobbes uses the third part of *Leviathan*, "Of a Christian Commonwealth," to argue that the political sovereign should also be the head of the church (in each case). This serves at last to elucidate the two insignia that the ruler holds in his hands in the engraving on the title page of *Leviathan*: the sword of worldly power and the bishop's staff of spiritual power. The single person of the sovereign thus exercises both the highest worldly and the highest spiritual power in his office as supreme pastor. But unlike the usual representatives of the church, and indeed like Moses, who was described as the absolute regent of Israel, the sovereign is established not merely by political right but also by divine right, namely by the direct authority of God (L ch. 42: 295–96, and 300).

Those tempted to indulge in quick and easy diagnoses may accuse Hobbes here of falling back into the political mentality of the Middle Ages, of attempting once again to fuse political power with ecclesiastical power. But in this case the fusion is supposed to be accomplished in the opposite direction. Thus an already contested claim to spiritual or papal authority must now yield to the claim to political authority. The relative and differentiated autonomy once focused on distinctive areas of competence must give way to the undifferentiated autonomy of one side and the subordination, even subjugation, of the other side of the relationship.

It is also worth drawing specific attention to a few other aspects of Hobbes's multifaceted observations in this connection. He abjures any sort of appeal to "prophecy" in the present age (L ch. 32: 198), and his implicit reasons here are both theological and political in nature. From the theological perspective, any contemporary appeal to prophecy, namely the idea of some immediate divine calling or direct inspiration from God, is repudiated because it endangers the fundamental claim of Christianity that Jesus is the Christ or Anointed One. From the political perspective, it is rejected because it threatens to create an alternative power to the sovereign, or could at least provide a strong argument for renouncing one's obedience to the sovereign.

Hobbes also addresses a number of complex and difficult theological issues. Thus he inquires into the authentic chronology and authorship of the various books of Holy Scripture, and makes use of extremely modern textual-critical methods in the process. Thus he argues that falsification of the writings of the New Testament is improbable because, among other things, the priests and the church fathers would "surely have made them more favourable to their power . . . than they are" (L ch. 33: 204).

How far Hobbes can meaningfully be described as a Christian was a matter of controversy among his contemporaries, and remains so to this day. He responded to suspicions of atheism with the blunt observation: "Do you think I can be an atheist and not know it" (Works, vol. VII, p. 350). There is no doubt that he regarded himself as a Christian and an Anglican. But it can hardly be said that he subscribes to all of the traditional dogmas or to any of the contested interpretations to which they were subjected by the different Christian confessions. What matters above all to Hobbes is the single fundamental dogma: "The (*unum necessarium*) only article of faith, which the Scripture maketh simply necessary to salvation, is this, that JESUS IS THE CHRIST" (L ch. 43: 324).

Hobbes does recognize a few other elements of Christianity, such as the sacraments of baptism and the Lord's Supper (L ch. 35: 221), and indeed the doctrine of the Trinity, which he interprets in a revolutionary way (L ch. 42: 267–68; see Springborg 1996, p. 360f.).

Nor does Hobbes deny that the commandments of Holy Scripture, given their divine origin, possess a higher authority than those of the state. Like Peter when he was arraigned before the High Council (Acts 4:19), Hobbes emphasizes that we owe obedience to God before obedience to man (L ch. 31: 193). But this observation should hold not only for Christians but also for the adherents of other monotheistic religions. And it was a commitment to this principle that already led the "heathen" Socrates to choose death rather than disobey the divine voice within him (Xenophon, *Memorabilia* IV, 8). Yet this is a principle that seems fatal to Hobbes's theory of the state, for it destroys the basic foundations of his theory of sovereignty: the bearer of civil power, who is supposed to have the last word, according to this principle has only the penultimate word.

In order to avoid this conclusion, Hobbes gives further weight to the penultimate word of the sovereign. He certainly admits the divine origin of biblical pronouncements, but after distinguishing between this origin beyond the state and recognition by the state, he declares that the commandments of Holy Scripture only become laws that bind us publicly and politically, and not merely privately in terms of conscience, when a sovereign accepts and dignifies them as such. Even the question as to which books belong to Holy Scripture and which must be regarded as apocryphal, namely as inauthentic, is for the sovereign to decide (L ch. 33: 199).

But then a new problem arises. Whether for reasons of prudence, in order to reassure his Christian readers, or foolishly for reasons that undermine his own theory, Hobbes describes the ruler who accepts or does not accept certain commandments as a "Christian" ruler, which only prompts the question as to who decides whether the sovereign is really Christian or not. And we must also ask how this decision is made: by reference to the sovereign's understanding of the Christian Gospel, or by reference to how far he conducts himself in at least a minimal Christian manner, in accordance with the pronouncement of the New Testament: "By their fruits shall ye know them" (Matt. 7:16)? What are we then to make of King Henry VIII, the founder of the Anglican Church? He was a fervent Catholic, and personally entered the lists against Luther, but severed the English church from Rome as soon as the pope—presumably in accordance with the traditional Christian understanding of marriage—refused to grant him a divorce from Catherine of Aragon when she failed to bear him the son he so desired.

Hobbes's response to questions of this kind is by no means clear. In the last chapter of the specifically political part of *Leviathan* he claims that what "the entire knowledge of civil duty" still lacks is knowledge of the laws of God. For without that "a man knows not, when he is commanded any thing by the civil power, whether it be contrary to the law of God, or not." And this ignorance creates a danger, for one "either by too much civil obedience, offends the Divine Majesty, or through fear of offending God, transgresses the commandments of the commonwealth" (L ch. 31: 186).

This diagnosis goes precisely to the heart of the problem, but it is still remarkable in three respects. Firstly, it identifies a conflict between ultimate levels of authority, though one which Hobbes strives by all means to prevent because of the danger it poses to peace. Secondly, we can point to the laws of nature, already introduced in chapters 4 and 15 of *Leviathan*, as divine laws relevant to the realm of right and the state, so that we do not require further reflection in this regard, let alone the very extensive discussion that Hobbes undertakes in the third part of *Leviathan*. Thirdly, it is clear that Hobbes nonetheless wishes to make the sovereign responsible for all politically relevant decisions, as well as decisions directly connected with religion.

These questions that arise in relation to the "Christian" ruler are by no means of purely historical interest. It is true that the New Testament offers a paradigmatic solution to the problem with the injunction: "Render to Caesar the things that are Caesar's, and to God the things that are God's" (Mark 12:13–17). If we take this together with the pronouncement, "My kingdom is not of this world" (John 18:36), we could say, in a somewhat simplifying fashion, that religion is concerned with the care of the soul, while the state is concerned with our earthly welfare. But where the care of the soul seems to require some intervention in the earthly world, it must dispense with the typically earthly means of power and concentrate upon "persuasion" instead.

The more serious problem arises where a religion does not recognize the New Testament separation of the worldly sphere (Caesar) from the religious sphere (God), and thus refuses the principle that is defended by Hobbes and recognized by modern states: the idea of the state's monopoly of power and the relinquishment of power on the part of its citizens. A slightly lesser but still significant problem arises when this separation of spheres is recognized, but when the political system is considered so profoundly unjust in the eyes of its citizens that they feel justified in resorting to violent resistance. And another lesser problem arises in connection with the question of civil disobedience: in a political system that is recognized as just in principle, is one justified in resisting political measures or proposals that contradict one's own conscience?

European social and political systems have long since provided an answer that contradicts Hobbes's solution: in contrast to such political absolutism, they have adopted the idea of separated powers, beginning with the well-known separation of the three public powers of the legislature, the executive, and the judiciary, but certainly not stopping there. Even more fundamental is the idea of the separation of church and state, which is implicit in the two biblical passages we have cited and has been broadly realized in liberal political systems. This arrangement requires self-limitation on both sides: the state dispenses with Hobbes's strict Anglican model and concedes full public, and not merely private, freedom of religious worship, and the religious communities concentrate on their properly religious tasks and functions, i.e., matters of rite and liturgy, the cultivation of spirituality, the personal integrity and commitment that is nourished by a particular faith, etc. Furthermore, in liberal states, in spite of certain transitional gray areas, the public and the private spheres are kept separate from one another, while the spheres of the economy, of science, of art, and of culture generally, are separated from that of the state. Last but not least, the public powers are organized in such a way that they serve to balance and limit one another within the sovereignty of the state.

In chapter 42 of *Leviathan*, the longest chapter of the book, Hobbes engages explicitly with Cardinal Bellarmin (1542–1621), who was one of the most important figures of the Counter Reformation. Hobbes vehemently repudiates ideas that Bellarmin defended in his writings on papal power and authority (in 1586 and 1610), and specifically the claim that the pope has the right to excommunicate rulers and princes and to release their subjects from the duty of obedience.

11.5. A Materialistic Theology

In the third and longest part of *Leviathan* ("Of a Christian Commonwealth") Hobbes engages in remarkable detail with a host of specifically theological issues. Here he generally applies his preferred mathematical method, and indeed in an almost scholastic fashion. Thus he begins by defining the fundamental concepts involved, here those of the Bible, and soon shows us that this son of an uneducated country parson was a skillful critical exegete with an exceptionally good knowledge of the Scriptures. The careful and methodical approach he had developed in his humanistic studies of the Greek and Latin authors had prepared him well in this regard. Thus on the basis of his thorough knowledge of the texts Hobbes explicates the different meanings of the relevant words, emphasizes the principal meanings over the less significant ones, and, in accordance with his basic thesis that thinking is nothing but "reckoning," proceeds to draw the necessary conclusions.

But why does Hobbes undertake all this labor in the first place? There seem to be two reasons at work, which correspond to Hobbes's two principal convictions: the universal reign of materialism, which is essential to his "fundamental philosophy," and the necessity of absolute sovereignty, which is central to his theory of the state. Both of these convictions invite obvious religious and theological objections. In order to undermine such objections openly and thoroughly, without "beating around the bush," Hobbes addresses them in detail.

On account of the political importance of these issues Hobbes begins with the "Principles of Christian Politics" (L ch. 32) and the question of the authority of Holy Scripture. On the one hand, for much of the time,

Hobbes offers an interpretation of biblical notions and doctrines that is decidedly non-spiritual or anti-spiritual, one which can be described positively as purely secular and even materialist in character. Thus a sacrament is not some invisible mystery but "a separation of some visible thing from common use, and a consecration of it to God's service" (L ch. 35: 221). And while prophecy is a rare gift, those who claim it are often "worthy to be suspected of ambition and imposture" (L ch. 36: 230). He acknowledges the possibility of miracles in the strict sense, that is, of certain events that are "unnatural" and extraordinary not merely in the eyes of ignorant and superstitious individuals (L ch. 2: 7). But these are accomplished not by men, either by saints or prophets, but only by Him who stands in his omnipotence over and above the laws of nature.

This idea of the omnipotence of God shows there is a clear limit to mechanistic materialism. Hobbes does not indeed deny the existence of God, nor does he reduce God to some purely worldly or ultimately material phenomenon. But according to Hobbes's mechanistic theory of thoughts and representations ("imaginations") we can have "no idea, or conception" of the infinite (L ch. 3: 11). God must therefore be regarded as the wholly Other, something "incomprehensible" to us, and whose greatness and power is literally "unconceivable." Thus, as Hobbes logically and perceptively points out, the "name of God is used, not to make us conceive him . . . but that we may honour him" (L ch. 3: 11; see also ch. 46: 371).

With this notion of God Hobbes thus breaks out of a seamlessly materialist philosophy. Materialism is thereby modified in a theological, or more precisely in a Judeo-Christian sense. Hobbes defends a theologically qualified materialism that is meant to be compatible with Christianity. At the same time, he ascribes a unique and wholly overpowering spiritual character to God. Since "the nature of God is incomprehensible," Hobbes says that "we understand nothing of what he is, but only that he is" (L ch. 34: 208). In spite of this, Hobbes specifically ascribes creative power to him (L ch. 31: 187), as well as omnipotence, both directly, when he speaks of his "irresistible power" (ibid.), and indirectly, when he simply speaks of "God Almighty" (ibid., and L ch. 38: 244). So Hobbes does say something about God's nature after all. And it certainly goes beyond that minimal claim without which we could not even assert the actual existence of the divine being.

Apart from God, Hobbes claims that the only things that exist are corporeal substances. Whereas the scholastics had spoken of "incorporeal substances," Hobbes argues that the two words "substance" and "incorporeal" are mutually incompatible, so that we might just as well speak of "incorporeal bodies" (L ch. 34: 207). Even angels are no exception here, for they are messengers of God who make his extraordinary presence known to us in dreams and visions. Hobbes does not deny that these messengers of God are often described in Scripture as "spirits." But such spirits are not "incorporeal substances" but merely "subtle bodies" that are invisible because they are so "thin," but which have "the same dimensions that are in grosser bodies" (L ch. 34: 210–11). In short, apart from God himself, the only things that exist are extended bodies that stand in the same material continuum to which human beings also belong.

Does this materialistic reconstruction of Judeo-Christian theologoumena also apply to the notions of eternal life, of hell, of the next life, etc.? From the biblical point of view, it is precisely these things that pose the greatest challenge to a materialist position. Hobbes accepts the challenge, ascribing a this-worldly meaning to all these notions; but he does so not simply by providing a profane reinterpretation of these notions but rather, once again, by offering a detailed interpretation of all the relevant biblical passages. The place where human beings enjoy eternal life is here on earth (L ch. 38: 239). "As the kingdom of God, and eternal life, so also God's enemies, and their torments after judgment, appear . . . to have their place on earth" (L ch. 38: 242). The kingdom of Satan, "the Enemy, the Accuser, and Destroyer," is "on earth also" (L ch. 38: 244). The "torments of hell," expressed among other things by "weeping, and gnashing of teeth," all "design metaphorically a grief, and discontent of mind" (ibid.). And "the joys of life eternal," which are "comprehended all under the name of salvation," consist in the liberation from sin and "from all the evil, and calamities which sin hath brought upon us" (L ch. 38: 245).

Thus Hobbes remains faithful to his philosophical materialism. He even reinforces the plausibility of this materialism by upholding it even where it would seem to encounter insuperable limits and difficulties, in the field of religion itself. On the other hand, this materialist reconstruction of Christianity amounts, politically speaking, to a form of secularization: if someone like Hobbes, who is neither a cleric nor a theologian, can interpret the Bible in such a well-informed manner, it is clear that no one requires any special expertise beyond a close textual knowledge of the Bible and the use of common human reason. And this also furnishes an indirect argument for the spiritual authority of the political sovereign. As the representative of the citizens, given the range of potentially conflicting views that may be expected under Protestantism, the sovereign can also assume responsibility for spiritual questions to the extent that they have a public rather than a private significance. For it is only when it comes to the open "confession" of faith that "private reason must submit to the public," but this is none other than the "lieutenant of God, and the head of the church" (L ch. 37: 238).

11.6. Hobbes's Critique of Other Churches

In the four chapters that make up the last part of Leviathan, Hobbes extends the critique of ideology that he began in his anthropology of religion. In an account brimming with sarcastic observations, Hobbes paints a dark picture of the antithesis of the Christian kingdom, which he defends with rational arguments in the second part and with biblical arguments in the third part of his book. With true biblical pathos he describes this antithetic vision as "the kingdom of darkness," and claims that it arises from a "confederacy of deceivers" who attempt "to obtain dominion over men in this present world" (L ch. 44: 333) by identifying the kingdom of God with "the present Church" in the world, and thus asserting that a supreme earthly representative is necessary to rule the world in the name of the transcendent God. In his self-appointed role as chief ideologist of the Anglican Church, Hobbes finds pagan and super-stitious elements (such as the invocation of spirits) in both Catholic and Presbyterian doctrines. And he identifies the scholastic traditions in the universities, including the University of Oxford where he originally stud-ied, as the breeding ground of these false and dangerous beliefs, although the Anglican Church had deep roots in these institutions as well. Hobbes held the priests and popes to be ultimately responsible on account of the way in which they secured special advantages for themselves by falsifying the truth of the Bible.

TWELVE

An Excursus

Hobbes's Critique of Aristotle

The question concerning the extent and character of Hobbes's relation to classical thought and literature has often been discussed (see Leijenhorst 1988, for example). Of course, with such a self-reflective and independent thinker as Hobbes there is no straightforward answer to this question. Thoroughly grounded from early on in Latin and Greek, the young Hobbes translated Thucydides, and subsequently excerpts from Aristotle's *Rhetoric* and, in his last years, both of Homer's great epics. Other classical writings are obviously more important for the philosophical analysis of the state, which was his central concern. But here Hobbes's ambition to renew political philosophy, even to establish it for the first time as a genuine science, effectively pushes all earlier philosophical contributions aside as ultimately irrelevant to his own project.

12.1. The "Vain Philosophy" of Aristotle

Aristotle is the real founder of "political philosophy" as an independent discipline and has been the source of inspiration for the development of a "science of politics" that was still unknown in the High Middle Ages. And among the philosophers Aristotle is also the most important interlocutor as far as Hobbes is concerned, though more as an exemplary opponent than as a model to be imitated. In the foreword "To the Readers" of his translation of Thucydides, it is quite true that Hobbes accords "primacy" to Aristotle among the philosophers, just as Homer is acknowledged first among the poets. And from *The Elements of Law* onward, Hobbes's first contribution to political philosophy, Aristotle is indeed the philosopher who is cited more frequently than any other. But from then on, especially in *De Cive*, and again later in *Leviathan* and *De Corpore*, he is also the thinker who is most severely criticized and attacked. In terms of frequency of mention and direct philosophical engagement, Plato and Cicero still come some way behind Aristotle.

Since Aristotle's political philosophy is still very much a positive influence for someone like Athusius (1557–1638), the work of Hobbes clearly reveals how the intellectual relevance and potential of Aristotle's thought had begun to ebb within a single generation or two. His influence did not of course wane altogether. Critics of Hobbes such as Clarendon continued to uphold various Aristotelian ideas (see chapter 14.1, below). And in a way Aristotle's thought still showed its power precisely through Hobbes's strongly articulated criticisms of the Aristotelian tradition and the alternative approach that he developed in response to that tradition.

In *Leviathan* Hobbes's critique of Aristotle is not restricted to the political sphere but is truly comprehensive in character and concerns the essential underlying principles. And as well as the expressly philosophical and political arguments he presents, Hobbes also brings theological arguments and considerations of ecclesiastical politics into play. Thus the anti-Catholic sentiment that dominates the fourth part of *Leviathan*, Hobbes's militantly antipapal outlook, also rebounds on Aristotle, the philosopher he also associates with the antimonarchical "sovereignty of Rome" (L ch. 21: 111).

Barely a decade earlier, in *De Cive* of 1642, the issues were presented slightly differently. In the preface to that work Hobbes positively recognizes Aristotle as one of the ancient philosophers who expressly attempted to develop a philosophical science of the state. In the course of the text, however, numerous Aristotelian doctrines are subjected to criticism, although this itself clearly documents Hobbes's close familiarity with Aristotle's *Politics*. Thus he rejects the supposedly natural origin of the state (C ch. 1, §2, footnote), along with the view that some human beings are slaves by nature (C ch. 3, §13); he repudiates the idea that man is a political being by nature (C ch. 5, §5); that we can distinguish systems of government in terms of whether they serve the interests of the ruler or the subjects (C ch. 10, §2); that tyrannicide is permissible (C ch. 12, §3); and, lastly, that the weakness of human beings requires that law be the supreme authority in the state (C ch. 12, §4; for further criticisms of Aristotle, see also C ch. 14, §2 and ch. 17, §12). Hobbes's own counter-arguments are based partly upon experience and partly upon the law of nature that we must consider every human being as more or less equal with every other (C ch. 3, §13); and his arguments emphasize the rivalry that accompanies the pursuit of honor and dignity and the fact that agreement among human beings, based as it is "only on contract" (*pactitia tantum*), must be regarded as artificial rather than natural (C ch. 5, §5).

In *Leviathan* Hobbes reproduces these specific criticisms of Aristotelian thought. Chapter 15 repeats the critique of Aristotle's theory of slavery, chapter 17 that of his political anthropology, and chapter 26 that of his notion of the priority of law. However, when it comes to showing "not what is law here, and there; but what is law" itself, the same chapter invokes Aristotle, along with Plato and Cicero (L ch. 26: 137). But all three examples simply show that the philosopher does not have to be a jurist or legal expert in order to express a view about laws in general.

Hobbes's comprehensive critique already begins in the opening chapter of *Leviathan*, which is directed against Aristotle as the ultimate philosophical authority acknowledged in the universities of the time. In the following chapters Hobbes attacks "the Schools" for encouraging obscurantist and superstitious doctrines rather than exposing them (L ch. 2), and accuses misleading scholastic thinkers of uncritically adopting absurd and meaningless expressions (L ch. 3). The high point of Hobbes's critique is clearly expressed in the fourth part of *Leviathan*, where Aristotle's thought is roundly repudiated as "vain philosophy" (L ch. 46: 373) as far as his natural philosophy, his metaphysics, and his moral and political philosophy are concerned. But those parts of Aristotle's philosophy that Hobbes could have acknowledged and appreciated in certain respects he simply passes over in silence. This includes aspects of Aristotle's logical theory and his account of scientific knowledge, the biological investigations that constitute the larger part of his natural philosophy, the highly convincing parts of his ethical theory such as his account of voluntary and involuntary action (along with his example of the captain in the storm and his account of weakness of will), and the reflections on the nature of art and poetry. This is also true for Aristotle's contributions to rhetoric, even though Hobbes himself translated the *Rhetoric*, a text he claims to have held in high regard.

Even Hobbes's more detailed and specific criticisms of Aristotle can hardly be said to do him justice. The hierarchical structure of what we could describe as Hobbes's "phenomenology of mind," with its stages of sensation, conception and imagination, memory, experience, and understanding, does not simply vaguely recall the series of stages presented in the opening chapter of Aristotle's *Metaphysics*, but is basically the same. And of course the distinction between the knowledge *that* something is so and the knowledge *why* it is so can also be found in the philosopher who is the privileged object of his critique. It is true that Hobbes is more concerned with the effects or "consequences" of things than with their causes, and whereas Aristotle introduces four kinds of cause, only one of these corresponds to Hobbes's understanding of causal relations. And where effects are concerned, Hobbes lays greater emphasis upon the deliberate production of these effects and their utility for us. Where Hobbes deploys a techno-practical or utilitarian conception of science and knowledge, Aristotle defends an idea of knowledge that is principally, if not wholly exclusively, theoretical in character, and springs from an all-encompassing kind of intellectual curiosity that effectively marginalizes considerations of utility or practical application.

If we consider all of the numerous passages relevant to Hobbes's view of Aristotle, we can interpret his far-from-gentle critique in terms of three levels. In the first place, Aristotle is seen as the principal representative of the philosophy that prevails in the universities of the time and is all too respectful of tradition. Hence Hobbes can say that "since the authority of Aristotle is only current there, that study is not properly philosophy, (the nature whereof dependeth not on authors,) but *Aristotelity*" (L ch. 46: 370). Nonetheless, it is also true that in some passages Hobbes defends Aristotle against the scholastic tradition itself (L ch. 46: 378).

This first level of critique is not really directed against Aristotle himself but against those who profess to follow him and revere his authority. But in the second place, Hobbes also holds Aristotle's thought to be problematic as a whole precisely because it has created spurious and meaningless distinctions in the fields of metaphysics, ethics, and politics. And in the third place, within the context of this general criticism, Aristotle's political philosophy is specifically rejected as fundamentally mistaken.

In the last part of *Leviathan*, where Aristotle is subjected to the harshest criticism, Hobbes initially describes Plato as "the best philosopher of the Greeks" and praises him because he "forbad entrance into his School, to all that were not already in some measure geometricians" (L ch. 46:

369; he is alluding to the *Republic*, book VII, 527a–b). But with regard
to Aristotle, whom Hobbes regards as principally responsible for the tradition of "vain philosophy," his verdict is unremittingly negative. Not
content with simply rejecting Aristotle's political philosophy, Hobbes
repudiates his thought as a whole: "I believe that scarce anything can be
more absurdly said in natural philosophy, than that which now is called
Aristotle's Metaphysics; nor more repugnant to government, than much of
that he hath said in his *Politics*; nor more ignorantly, than a great part of
his *Ethics*" (L ch. 26: 370).

Hobbes is well aware that the title of Aristotle's *Metaphysics* literally
refers to the "books written or placed after his natural philosophy," but
in a sense the schools were not wrong in regarding them as "books of
supernatural philosophy" since "that which is there written, is for the
most part so far from the possibility of being understood" (L ch. 26: 371).
Hobbes completely overlooks the fact that Aristotle distinguishes between
substance in the "primary" sense and substance in the "secondary" sense,
the former denoting a concrete individual such as Socrates, the latter an
essential and generic characterization such as "a living being endowed
with reason." For Aristotle this essential character does not exist separately
or independently of the individual body, and in fact Hobbes's own conception of the living being and the specific characteristics of the human
being also acknowledges this essential character. All that Hobbes's critique
actually requires in this connection is the clear rejection of supernatural
essences or substances such as disembodied spirits.

Thus it is not entirely easy to understand why Hobbes so roundly
rejects every aspect of Aristotle's rich and suggestive conception of metaphysics, why he did not direct his critique of "separated essences" specifically at Plato's doctrine of ideas rather than at Aristotle's teaching, and
why in a political theory of the state such as *Leviathan* he should lay so
much emphasis on ontology (as a theory of objective reality). One basic
reason for the vehemence of his critique lies in the philosophical materialism that he defends with an almost missionary fervor: "every part of the
universe, is body, and that which is not body, is no part of the universe"
(L ch. 26: 371). And here we must also recognize, however difficult it is
for us to appreciate, Hobbes's specifically political fear that the doctrine of
"separated essences" might frighten human beings from "obeying the laws
of their country, with empty names" (L ch. 26: 373). But how could the
political authority of a state that is legitimated on the basis of our interest
in peace and self-preservation possibly be endangered by a (supposedly)

false theory of objective reality? It is obvious that a host of politically relevant theological and ecclesiastical considerations, as well as various other concerns, are all obscurely in play here.

In his anthropological reflections on religion in chapter 12, Hobbes had already identified two reasons why "the religion of the church of Rome . . . was abolished in England, and many other parts of Christendom." Along with the eminently practical and religious reason that "the failing of virtue in the pastors, maketh faith fail in the people," Hobbes also mentions a specifically philosophical and theological reason, namely the "bringing of the philosophy, and doctrine of Aristotle into religion, by the Schoolmen; from whence there arose so many contradictions, and absurdities, as brought the clergy into a reputation both of ignorance, and of fraudulent intention" (L ch. 12: 59). Though here again, Hobbes's objections in this passage seem to be directed not so much at Aristotle himself as at the subsequent conflation and combination of Aristotelian and Christian philosophy.

12.2. An Aristotelian in Spite of Himself

It is not strictly true that Hobbes's political philosophy is simply anti-Aristotelian. On the contrary, it remains faithful to a remarkably large number of Aristotelian ideas. Like Aristotle, Hobbes also connects political philosophy directly with moral philosophy or ethics, and treats the latter first. Before he goes on to speak of law and the state, Hobbes discusses the most basic ethical concepts, and indeed those with which we are already familiar from the work of Aristotle, even if they are now radically redefined: the good and the bad, pleasure, aversion, and desire, the range of the passions, the process of deliberation, the nature of the will, and of happiness (L ch. 6), and also the concepts of virtue, and specifically the intellectual virtues (L ch. 8), as well as the concepts of power, worth, dignity, honor, and worthiness (L ch. 10), and finally and clearly the issue of differing customs and practices, what Hobbes calls "the difference of manners" (L ch. 11). And the "natural laws" that precede the state, being laws, belong together with the concept of justice (L chs. 14 and 15) to the realm of "ethics" rather than "politics" in the Aristotelian sense of these terms.

Both thinkers agree on the need to provide an emphatically practical, and specifically political, philosophy as such (see *Nicomachean Ethics* book I, ch. 1, 1095a5f.). Again, like Aristotle, Hobbes seeks to accomplish this goal not in the immediate terms of moral warning or direct ethical and political intervention, but rather *modo philosophico*, namely by means of conceptual analysis and clarification, of discursive criticism and argumentation. It is really only in the fourth and final part of *Leviathan* that his practical and political interests reveal themselves explicitly and all too directly.

As far as the details of the argument are concerned, however, Hobbes differs significantly from Aristotle in both substantive and methodological terms. The difference here arises from the distinctive practical and political challenge with which Hobbes found himself confronted. His *Leviathan* was prompted by the fundamental political crisis of the early modern age, namely by the religiously inspired civil wars of the epoch. Whereas Aristotle could still more or less presuppose the existence of an established and generally recognized legal and political order, Hobbes's predicament was quite different. Thus he attempts to overcome the actual experience or imminent threat of anarchy and procure a secure and peaceful order by appeal to the anthropological basis of our human desire for self-preservation. Whereas Aristotle regards happiness as the highest end as such, Hobbes defines it naturalistically as the satisfaction of our particular needs and interests (L ch. 6). This is certainly unsatisfactory from the perspective of moral philosophy, for it underestimates the very different ways in which needs and interests are capable of producing happiness, but Hobbes's approach is appropriate as far as the task of legitimating law and the state are concerned, since it leaves each individual to decide where or how he is to seek his own happiness.

On the cognitive side, Hobbes's concept of prudence corresponds to his naturalistic definition of happiness. As in Aristotle, prudence is concerned with the question of finding the appropriate means for desired ends, but, in contrast to Aristotle, prudence for Hobbes is concerned with the means for satisfying needs rather than the means for attaining the highest human end as such. The task of prudence in the usual sense (L ch. 5) is to estimate the particular means for attaining the happiness of particular individuals. But prudence in the universal sense, which is decisive for Hobbes—namely, "experience; which equal time, equally bestows on all men, in those things they equally apply themselves unto" (L ch. 13: 60–61)—is what grounds the state as the universally valid precondition for any particular attempts to secure happiness.

In order to promote and extend this second-level prudential knowledge Hobbes adopts the axiomatic-deductive method as his ideal of exact science (L ch. 5). Although Hobbes's political philosophy strives to emulate the theoretical sciences in this regard, it also remains true to another idea that is familiar from Aristotle's methodological reflections on "typological" knowledge (*Nicomachean Ethics* book I, ch. 1, 1094b20). For political philosophy itself only develops certain fundamental principles, while the question as to what a specific order of law and the state would look like in concrete detail is left open. This openness is recognized as what is appropriate and precisely required in the nature of the case. For the legal-positivist and absolutist elements of *Leviathan* leave it to the sovereign power to decide how the order of law and the state is to be organized and arranged in specific detail.

There are other points of affinity with Aristotle that Hobbes is just as incapable of recognizing as the ones we have already mentioned. Thus, like Aristotle, Hobbes finds his starting point in a concept of "motion" (*kinēsis* in Aristotle), which is drawn from natural philosophy, and develops and supplements this idea in the case of man with the same capacities of reason and language. And while Hobbes's motto, *auctoritas, non veritas, facit legem,* certainly allows us to regard him as a precursor of modern legal positivism, he must also be recognized in two respects as a defender of the competing tradition of "natural law." For in the first place, like Aristotle, he seeks to discover the truth regarding the political community or the state by means of natural reason. And in the second place, like Aristotle, he attempts to ground this truth in terms of the ultimate and irreducible presuppositions of human action, in terms of human nature itself. Like the tradition of natural law theory, Hobbes also bases his philosophy of the state essentially on anthropological premises.

Hobbes even recognizes certain normative natural laws that we cannot find in Aristotle's admittedly sparse observations on that which is just "by nature" (*Nicomachean Ethics*, book VI, ch. 10, 1134b18ff.). Finally, we should also note that both Hobbes and Aristotle employ a similar resoluto-compositive method: in each case the political community or state to be legitimated is broken down into its component parts, although the two philosophers adopt a different starting point. If we leave aside the *resolutio* that Hobbes employs in the context of natural philosophy, we can see that he begins with the individual human being in a pre-political condition independent of the state. Aristotle, on the other hand, conducts his analysis in a twofold fashion. He begins with human beings prior to or independent of the state, but who are already social beings, who, as male or female and as master or slave, are already related to and dependent upon one another (*Politics*, book I, ch. 2). But again, like Hobbes, he also considers the citizen as the minimal component of the political community or the state.

12.3. Inevitable Strife or the Social Nature of Man?

The crucial difference between Hobbes and Aristotle in their respective philosophies of the state lies not in their contrasting theories of reality (in the questions of ontology or metaphysics), nor in their respective philosophies of nature, of mind, or language, but in their different approaches to philosophical anthropology. One of Aristotle's most celebrated doctrines furnishes the basic thesis of political anthropology, namely the claim that a human being is by nature a political animal (*phusei politikon zōon*). At the beginning of *Politics* (book I, ch. 2, 1253a2f.) this is directly linked to three other claims: that the *polis* is a complete community (1252b28), that it is a natural community (1253a2; cf. 1253a18f.), and that it is to be considered as by nature prior to the household and to the individuals that constitute it (1253a19; see also 1253a25). These claims had been recognized and accepted without contradiction for centuries, but they were finally subjected by Hobbes to such a trenchant and historically influential critique that this entire Aristotelian approach would come to be regarded derogatively as the *via antiqua* destined to be superseded by the *via moderna* of Hobbes's theory of the state.

For Hobbes, human beings are not intrinsically political beings; and the reason for this lies not in any specific conditions of early modern society, but in the nature of human beings themselves. Hobbes's own systematic alternative to Aristotle's political anthropology is presented in chapter 13 of *Leviathan*. In this alternative account human beings are not essentially social beings but beings that are prone to conflict, as we have seen, for three principal reasons: rivalry or competition, mutual mistrust, and concern for honor or reputation. We merely note in passing the remarkable fact that in this connection Hobbes does not mention the conflict regarding true religion, which was certainly one of the essential causes behind the civil wars of the period. In his discussion here Hobbes does not even attempt to explain this confessional conflict, the "epochal" source of conflict with which he was confronted, in terms of his three "anthropological" causes of human conflict.

When he begins to present his expressly *political* anthropology in chapter 17 of *Leviathan*, Hobbes agrees with Aristotle and concedes that it "is true, that certain living creatures, as bees, and ants, live sociably one with another, (which are therefore by Aristotle numbered amongst political creatures)" (L ch. 17: 86; see Aristotle, *Historia animalium,* book I, ch. 1). But here Hobbes is ultimately interested only in the difference between human beings and other creatures: animals promote the "common good" or benefit by pursuing their "private" or individual good, whereas human beings are caught up in a constant competitive struggle for honor and respect. Hence Hobbes clearly argues against Aristotle that "the agreement of these creatures [i.e., bees and ants] is natural; that of men, is by covenant only, which is artificial" (L ch. 17: 87). Hobbes had already argued in *De Cive* that political communities or "civil societies are not mere meetings, but bonds, to the making whereof faith and compacts are necessary" (C ch. I, §2, footnote). And the introduction to *Leviathan* explicitly describes the state or commonwealth as something that is created by "art" rather than nature.

In order to understand the contrasting claim of Aristotle here, we must bear in mind his underlying concept of nature. In contrast to the static concept of nature as defined by physics, the paradigm of natural science in the early modern era, it is an essentially dynamic concept of biological nature that underlies Aristotle's political anthropology. Conceived in the light of biological processes, Aristotle's concept of nature involves a notion of development that must be interpreted in terms of four perspectives: the beginning, the efficient cause, the end, and the unfolding of the process. Although Aristotle understands nature in relation to the essential nature of human beings and the idea of human self-realization, he does not claim that humanity has always fundamentally organized its social and political life in the form of republican city-states. But he does make two specific claims in this regard: firstly, that the characteristic achievement of human beings (the *ergon tou anthrōpou*), being grounded in the human capacity for reason and language, can only fully be realized within the social-political community (the *polis*); and secondly, that the beginning, cause, and unfolding of this development is also essentially connected with the nature of human beings as such (see Höffe 2006, ch. 15).

When Hobbes declares that the state is "artificial," he may be attempting to avert the alternative Aristotelian position because he fears that it implies a kind of "biological fallacy": the idea that political communities arise spontaneously or "of themselves" in the same way as plants do, without any deliberate contribution on the part of human beings themselves, or that such communities are sustained of themselves in the same way as the animal communities of ants and bees are. But such an understanding of nature actually contradicts the way in which Aristotle speaks of a "benefactor" who first brought the *polis* into being, and who must thus be regarded as the source of the greatest human benefits (*Politics*, book I, ch. 2, 1253a31).

Aristotle would have no difficulty, therefore, in conceding an aspect of truth to Hobbes's idea of the artificial character of the state. But he rejects the notion that the political domain is artificial in the sense that it impedes or frustrates the essential vocation of human beings. Thus both thinkers are opposed to the view that the state or political community is something that alienates human beings from their own character, either through the growth of luxury or degeneration (the second level in Plato's analysis of the emergence of the *polis*; cf. *Republic*, book II, 372cff.), or through an exclusive preoccupation with the protection of property (as Rousseau claims in the second *Discourse on the Inequality of Man*), or through an inappropriate and unjustified restriction of human freedom (as philosophical anarchism maintains). On the contrary, both thinkers regard the state as a social form of life that helps human beings to realize their own potential. In this quite fundamental respect we can say, once again, that Hobbes is an Aristotelian in spite of himself.

In his critique of Aristotelian philosophy Hobbes overlooks an important point. In the introductory chapter of his *Historia animalium*, Aristotle distinguishes between the solitary animals and those that live in herds or groups, and in this latter category he distinguishes between creatures that roam and those he calls "political" animals; as examples of political animals he mentions the human being, the bee, the wasp, the ant, and the crane, and identifies the underlying feature here as a certain shared accomplishment (a *koinon ergon*; see 487b33–488a10). In his discussion in the *Politics* (book I, ch. 2), Aristotle does not repudiate this biological approach, but he supplements it by emphasizing that the human being, comparatively speaking, is more of a political animal (*politicon . . . mallon*) than the bee or any other animal that lives in groups (1253a8f.). Here he focuses on the *koinon ergon* that is already contained in his biological conception of the social animals, implicitly paying less attention to the reliability of social cooperation, which is what matters to Hobbes, than to the quality of this cooperation, something Hobbes does not discuss in chapter 7 of *Leviathan*.

Hobbes is right in holding that human beings, given the endless conflicts to which they are prone, are less cooperative than bees and ants.

But Aristotle is interested in something else here, namely that nonhuman animals are essentially concerned simply with living as such (*zēn*), whereas human beings in communities are concerned with maintaining a good rather than simply an agreeable life, namely with living well (*eu zen*). Hobbes does not consider this qualitative intensification of the social-political dimension, nor does he address Aristotle's arguments in favor of the political nature of human beings. In contrast to Hobbes's "three principal causes of quarrel"—competition, mistrust, and desire for honor—Aristotle identifies what we could call "three principal causes of cooperation": human sexuality, the helplessness and vulnerability of the human infant, and different human aptitudes in terms of skill and labor, along with the advantages deriving from the social division of labor. (Hobbes does not of course specifically deny any of these factors, but he ascribes no significance to them in his crucial claim concerning the state of nature in chapter 13 of *Leviathan*.)

Here we may pass over Aristotle's second line of argument for the essentially political character of human beings, namely the possession of reason and language, and focus directly on his third line of argument, which Hobbes overlooks. This is Aristotle's claim that the human being who lives outside or independent of the *polis* is "ready for war," is indeed a "wild beast," and that nothing is worse than injustice backed by armed force (*Politics*, book I, ch. 2, 253a6, a29, a33ff.). These arguments anticipate in part Hobbes's own account of "the war of all against all" and his description of the human being as a "wolf" to his fellow men. And since Aristotle argues that the human being in the *polis* is the best of all living beings, whereas torn away from law and right the human being is the worst of all beings (*Politics*, book I, ch. 2, 1253a3–33), he even anticipates the dual character of humanity that Hobbes emphasizes when he says in *De Cive* that the human being is both "a kind of God" (in the political condition) and "an arrant wolf" (in the natural condition) (C, the dedication, p. 90).

Thus we can describe Hobbes as an Aristotelian despite himself in a further respect, and at the same time reject the one-sided interpretation of Aristotle's political anthropology, which lays an exclusive emphasis upon the positively social nature of human beings. But unlike Hobbes, Aristotle recognizes more than simply *one* remedy for the danger of war. Friendship is at least as important to Aristotle as law, justice, and the state. For friendship, in accordance with its various kinds and levels, is what holds political communities together, which is why lawgivers show more concern for friendship even than for justice (*Nicomachean Ethics*, book VIII, ch. 1, 1155a22–24). In contrast to Hobbes's claim that "men have no pleasure, (but on the contrary a great deal of grief) in keeping company," Aristotle's chapters on friendship furnish abundant counter-examples drawn directly from concrete human experience, and without feeling the need to add Hobbes's own qualification: "where there is no power able to overawe them all" (L ch. 13: 61).

If we bear all these observations in mind, Hobbes appears as a dogmatic proponent of modernity who relates to Aristotle rather as the warring confessions of his time related to each other: fixated on an abstract either-or, he sees Aristotle as (almost) nothing but an intellectual opponent, and with his talk of "vain philosophy" even simply as an enemy deserving of nothing but full frontal assault. Instead of sometimes learning from Aristotle, and admitting it when he does so, and instead of recognizing Aristotle at least as a valuable interlocutor, Hobbes prefers to engage in a negative and purely destructive critique.

Finally there is one other respect in which Hobbes can be called an Aristotelian in spite of himself. Whereas Plato had invoked the philosopher as the ideal ruler (*Republic*, book V, 473c–d), according to both Hobbes and Aristotle the philosopher may act solely as advisor or counselor, but certainly not as ruler. At a prominent point of the text, in the concluding paragraph of the second part of *Leviathan* ("Of Commonwealth"), Hobbes expresses the hope that his book "may fall into the hands of a sovereign, who will consider it himself . . . without the help of any interested, or envious interpreter; and by the exercise of entire sovereignty, in protecting the public teaching of it, convert this truth of speculation, into the utility of practice" (L 31: 193). In claiming a practical and political value for his theoretical reflections on the state in this way, and without putting himself forward as any kind of ruler or expecting any special philosophical expertise on the part of the actual ruler, Hobbes contents himself, like Aristotle before him, with the role of advisor. The surprising conclusion to be drawn from all this is that Hobbes, despite his own philosophical self-understanding, is in certain methodological, substantive, and indeed functional respects a kind of Aristotelian, albeit a highly reluctant one.

There are basically two reasons for this remarkable finding with regard to *Leviathan*. In the first place, it seems as if Hobbes did retain something of his earlier evaluation of Aristotle and had taken over the corresponding ideas from his own earlier writings. And in the second place, the most emphatically anti-Aristotelian passages in the text appear to be specifically directed against the Scholastic tradition and also to express an explicitly anti-Catholic position in matters of ecclesiastical politics. It is to be regretted that Hobbes was unable to draw a clear and fair distinction between these two aspects of the issue, between a genuine respect for Aristotle as a philosopher and the repudiation of a scholastically ossified and authoritarian Aristotelianism that lent itself so easily to misuse in the area of ecclesiastical politics.

THIRTEEN

History

It is rather remarkable how many of the leading thinkers of the Enlightenment, such as Voltaire, Leibniz, and Hume, also made a name for themselves as historians. Hobbes, who must be recognized as an early philosopher of the Enlightenment, proved to be a model and precursor in this regard as well, for he made contributions to ecclesiastical and political history, composed an autobiography, and early in his career translated the Greek historian Thucydides. In marked contrast to other contemporary or near contemporary thinkers such as Descartes, Pascal, and Leibniz, one cannot say that Hobbes excelled in mathematics, the discipline he took to be the very ideal of science. But in the field of history, the "knowledge of fact" specifically concerned with "the voluntary actions of men" (L ch. 9: 40), Hobbes does fulfill the criterion for a good historian that he himself sets up: "In good history, the judgment must be eminent [in comparison with the power of imagination or "fancy" required in poetry]; because the goodness consisteth, in the method, in the truth, and in the choice of actions that are most profitable to be known" (L ch. 8: 33).

13.1. Translating Thucydides

Even before *A Short Treatise on First Principles* (1630), the "private" publication of *The Elements of Law* (1640), and the appearance of *De Cive*

207

(1642), Hobbes's very first publication was his translation of the most important historical work of ancient Greece, namely Thucydides' *History of the Peloponnesian War* (431–404 B.C.E; abbreviated as PW; Hobbes's translation of 1629 is cited from Works, vol. VIII). Hobbes was proud to be the first person to translate Thucydides into English "immediately from the Greek" rather than from the standard Latin version of the text (Works, vol. VIII, ix).

In his prefatory remarks "To the Readers," Hobbes explains that what he particularly admires in Thucydides is the author's narrative style. Above all, according to Hobbes, the Greek historian avoids moralizing digressions and allows the events in question to speak for themselves. Hobbes also includes a few textual-critical observations regarding the quality of the existing translations of the text and praises the veracity and linguistic facility, the "truth and elocution," of Thucydides: "For in truth consisteth the soul, and in elocution the body of history" (Works, vol. VIII, xx). The alleged purpose of Thucydides' work will also govern Hobbes's own writings on history, and indeed his entire philosophy of the state: that of enlightening people about the past in order that they may live wisely in the present and take due care for the future. But if Hobbes entertained any hope that his translation of Thucydides might help to lessen the contemporary tensions between the king and Parliament, it was of course not to be, and it was just the same with his analogous hopes in the case of the later explicitly political writings.

There is no doubt that Hobbes felt he had discovered a kindred spirit in Thucydides. For his version of the *History* already reveals certain essential elements of his own later convictions regarding the state, convictions which seem to be continuous not only with *The Elements of Law* of 1640, but with this work of eleven years before. What Hobbes particularly values in Thucydides is the writer's sober perspective on the permanent realities of human nature, a view that is free from the distortions of wishful thinking (cf. PW III, 82; Works, vol. VIII, p. 348; cf. also PW I, 22; Works, vol. VIII, p. 25), as well as the recognition that states conduct their relations with one another in terms of self-interest rather than justice. There are also a couple of passages that seem to anticipate Hobbes's subsequent description of the condition of nature: "The cause of all this [civil war and its attendant excesses] is desire of rule, out of avarice and ambition; and the zeal of contention from those two proceeding. For such as were of authority . . . though in words they seemed to be servants of the public, they made it in effect but the prize of their contention: and striving by whatever means to overcome, both ventured on most horrible outrages and prosecuted their revenges still farther, without any regard of justice or the common good" (PW III, 82; Works, vol. VIII, p. 350). And in a passage in chapter 1 we already seem to meet Hobbes's thesis of the restless human striving after power, for although Agamemnon "exceeded the rest in power," he still sought to augment it further. We also read that the Athenians advanced their dominion on the basis of three basic motivations: "chiefly for fear, next for honour, and lastly for profit" (PW I, 75; Works, vol. VIII, p. 81). This is reflected, albeit in a different order, in Hobbes's own later reflections on the principal causes of human conflict: "competition" or rivalry (profit), "diffidence" or mistrust (fear), and "glory" or reputation (honor) (L ch. 13: 61).

The differences that nonetheless exist between the two writers, with regard to their respective views of democracy for example, should not be exaggerated. In what is probably the most celebrated passage of his work Thucydides certainly allows Pericles to sing the praises of Athenian democracy, but he also adds: "It was in name, a state democratical; but in fact, a government of the principal man" (PW II, 65; Works, vol. VIII, p. 221). Hobbes also suggests a certain further personal affinity with his author, one with implications for his own account of religion, when he points out in the biographical observations ("Of the Life and History of Thucydides") with which he introduced his translation that the historian himself was "by some reputed an atheist" since he was quite capable of recognizing the "vain and superstitious" character of the heathen religion of the Greeks (Works, vol. III, p. xv).

13.2. The History of the Church and the Kingdom of God

A year after the publication of *De Homine* (1659), the third part of his encyclopedic system of philosophy, Hobbes composed his *Historia Ecclesiastica*. But this history of the church, recounted in 2,242 Latin verses, was only published in 1688, a decade after his death. Neither the appearance of this work, nor that of an English paraphrase of the text in 1711, made any significant difference to the image of Hobbes, which had already been established by this time.

Hobbes's *Historia*, a dialogue in verse form, furnishes an interpretation of the Judeo-Christian tradition from Moses up until the Reformation. The central part of the work is principally concerned with the decisions and pronouncements of the early Christian councils and the interpretation of the Trinity. Once again, Hobbes traces the disputes regarding the nature of the Trinity back to the influence of Greek philosophy, the doctrines of which have distorted the core meaning of the Christian conception of faith and given rise to heretical views of one kind or another. The Christian conception of faith has thus been transformed by personal and philosophical notions that are quite alien to it.

Hobbes's schema of world history as "the story of salvation" is of more interest and significance for the interpretation of politics and the church. In his reflections on the kingdom of God Hobbes raises the political and also religious question whether there is a conflict of obedience where the demands of human and divine laws are concerned. Hobbes pursues a twofold interest here. On the one hand he wants to support the orthodox idea that there is such a thing as the kingdom of God, while on the other he wishes to obviate the danger that this idea could destabilize the political realm itself. And to this end he develops a biblically grounded history of the human relationship to God. He divides this history into four epochs, as follows: (1) in the time from Adam and Eve up to Moses or Abraham there is as yet no kingdom of God; (2) from Abraham or Moses up to the time of Saul we have "the Kingdom of God under the Old Covenant" (to cite the title of chapter 16 of *De Cive*); (3) from the time of Saul through to the end of the present world there is no kingdom of God; (4) the kingdom of God then lasts from the end of this world into all eternity. As far as Hobbes's philosophy of the state is concerned, it is the third epoch that is the decisive one. It is quite true that *De Cive* speaks of "the Kingdom of God by the New Covenant" (in the title of chapter 17), but Hobbes makes it clear that what Christ establishes is a "heavenly" kingdom, which "is not properly a kingdom or dominion, but a pastoral charge," for "God the Father gave him not a power to judge of *meum* and *tuum*, as he doth to kings of the earth" (C ch. 17, §6, p. 336; and in a similar vein, L ch. 41: 263).

13.3. Behemoth

Hobbes was already approaching his eightieth year when he composed a history of the English Civil War, with the subtitle of "The Long Parliament," referring to the period between November 3, 1640 and March 16, 1660. The actual title of the work, *Behemoth*, evokes another monster from the Bible. This of course only emphasizes the intimate connection between Hobbes's philosophical masterpiece, *Leviathan*, and his most important historical work. Yet the later text of Behemoth did not attract anything like the amount of attention as the earlier book. The reason for this can hardly lie in the fact that the work, which was probably begun in 1665, was refused the necessary license for publication when it was completed three years later, with a first unauthorized version appearing a good ten years later in the year of Hobbes's death, and the first edition proper seeing the light of day only three years after that in 1682.

The reason for this neglect lies rather in the fact that this work, an exemplary study of the pathologies of political communities, makes no significant additions to Hobbes's existing theory of the state and undertakes no major revision in the basic structure of that theory. In contrast to the more theoretical construction provided by *Leviathan*, the text of *Behemoth*, being an explicitly historical work, is certainly more empirical in orientation. A comparison with the work of contemporaries who offer an alternative diagnosis of the Civil War (see chapter 14.1 below), such as Edward Hyde, the first earl of Clarendon (1609–1674), and James Harrington (1611–1677), shows that it was just as important for Hobbes himself to communicate and substantiate his own trenchant judgment concerning the political predicament of the time. He does not even try and reproduce the straightforward and non-moralizing presentation of the events themselves that he praised in the work of Thucydides, and this may be another reason for the relative neglect of this work on the part of posterity. Although it is rich in concrete empirical observations, in *Behemoth* Hobbes makes no attempt to offer a description of the historical events independent of subjective evaluations of his own.

The text consists of four dialogues that can barely claim any literary or artistic value. In the ensuing conversations the dominant partner, designated simply as "A," who shows considerable knowledge of current social and political conditions, instructs the other less informed party, designated as "B," about that high point of history "which passed between 1640 and 1660." Thus Hobbes writes: "He that thence, as from the Devil's Mountain, should have looked upon the world and observed the actions of men, especially in England, might have had a prospect of all kinds of injustice, and of all kinds of folly, that the world could afford" (B, Works, vol. 6, p. 165). Hobbes makes his own perspective on all these matters clear right from the start, describing King Charles I as an exemplary ruler, as "a man that wanted no virtue, either of body or mind, nor endeavoured anything more than to discharge his duty towards God, in the well governing of his subjects." Hobbes claims, by contrast, that "the people were corrupted generally, and disobedient persons esteemed the best patriots" (B, p. 166).

All of the culprits already encountered in *Leviathan* duly reappear here, "seducers" such as the clerics or "ministers, as they called themselves, of Christ" who pretended "to have a right from God to govern every one his parish, and their assembly the whole nation" (B, p. 167), and likewise the "Papists" who remained faithful to the authority of the Catholic Church. Again, as in his critical observations in the *Historia Ecclesiastica*, Hobbes singles out those scholars and thinkers who called upon "the famous men of the ancient Grecian and Roman commonwealths" in the "glorious name of liberty" and thus defended the rule of the people against the idea of a "monarchy disgraced by the name of tyranny" (B, p. 168). And once again Hobbes charges the Aristotelian tradition of the universities with indulging in pointless conceptual hairsplitting and intellectual pseudo-problems. Hobbes also makes no secret of the fact that, unlike Aristotle, he has no interest in expounding an ethics appropriate for citizens who are equally entitled to participate in political life, whether we are speaking of the governing or the governed, for he is concerned with "the ethics of subjects" rather than "the ethics of sovereigns" (B, p. 219).

Toward the end of the first dialogue Hobbes accuses the universities of constituting the "core of rebellion," of failing to teach "true politics," namely Hobbes's own demand for unconditional obedience. For we must "make men know, that it is their duty to obey all laws whatsoever that shall by the authority of the King be enacted" (B, p. 236). Hobbes here shows himself as a doctrinaire thinker in the genuine sense of the term, as an uncompromising defender of a strict and narrowly conceived doctrine.

Among the enemies of his own theory he also includes "the city of London and other great towns of trade," which viewed with "admiration the prosperity of the Low Countries after they had revolted from their monarch, the King of Spain" (B, p. 168). Hobbes wished to show these merchants and traders that they were thereby deceiving themselves with regard to their own long-term interests. For it is better to place one's trust in a powerful sovereign who can strengthen the power of civil authority required by all instead of encouraging the forces of social and political unrest and rebellion. The lesson of the English Civil War was something that Hobbes had already defined as the center of his political philosophy from the time of *The Elements of Law* onward: only a sovereign endowed with absolute power is capable of reliably meeting the constant threat of falling back into the condition of nature, i.e., is capable of preventing the experience of civil war.

III

THE INFLUENCE OF HOBBES

Hobbes was well aware of the originality and importance of his own work for political philosophy and the theory of the state. His claim that there was no such thing as "civil philosophy" before the appearance of his own *De Cive* is certainly a case of rhetorical exaggeration, especially given the fact that predecessors such as Socrates, Plato, Aristotle, and Cicero are all mentioned in the preface to this work. But there is no doubt that Hobbes must be regarded as one of the greatest philosophers of law and the state there has ever been.

FOURTEEN

From His Age to Our Own

At first Hobbes was only known simply as a translator of Thucydides and as an active participant in the contemporary debates regarding the character and status of the natural sciences. But once he had presented his theory of the state and of political authority he rapidly acquired renown in the broader philosophical context of scientific and political thought. His work has continued to exert considerable influence through the period of the Enlightenment all the way down to our own time. In Britain one witnessed the appearance of the literary and cultural figure of the "Hobbist," one who dared to defend Hobbes's often highly controversial views. Leading intellectuals of the time such as James Harrington and Edward Hyde, earl of Clarendon, John Selden, and Anthony Ashley-Cooper (one of the founders of the Whig party and subsequently the first earl of Shaftesbury) all revealed their respect for Hobbes by engaging explicitly and intensively with his work. From expressly political and ecclesiastical quarters, on the other hand, Hobbes encountered the most vehement criticism.

14.1. The Early Reception and Critique of Hobbes's Work

Hobbes's polemic against the prevailing theory and practice of English law, and his criticisms of Sir Edward Coke, a prominent defender of

217

that tradition and still regarded as one of the most important figures of English jurisprudence, provoked a sharp response from Chief Justice Mathew Hale (1609–1676), the greatest English legal theorist of the time and a defender of the idea of the constitutional state. In his work entitled *Reflections on Hobbes's 'Dialogue on Laws'* (a response to *A Dialogue between a Philosopher and a Student of the Common Laws of England*) and again later in his *History of the Common Law of England*, Hale followed Coke in acknowledging and celebrating the experience of earlier generations that had come to be embodied in the common law tradition. According to Hale, it was this experience that had helped to secure for the country the long-lasting order of civil peace, which was Hobbes's own fundamental concern. In view of the numerous wars and conflicts that had marked English and British history, Hobbes would naturally cast considerable doubt on this diagnosis of a successfully established peaceful order of life. Coke, on the other hand, would object that the relevant threats to the peace of the realm sprang not from the structure of common law itself but rather from the kind of politics that saw itself as beyond such law.

In terms of the arguments he presents, especially with regard to the importance of security, Hale is actually closer to Hobbes than to Coke. For, like Hobbes, he claims that the lack of stability or security in maintaining and enforcing the legal order is a much graver problem than that of injustice in relation to particular laws. What is more, as if he had never read Hobbes's own criticisms of the attempt to ground law on the basis of reason, either in the individual or the collective sense, Hale specifically emphasizes the dangerously unreliable character of appeals to rational knowledge. But like Coke, and in opposition to Hobbes, he places his trust not in the sovereign authority of the state but in the insight of the wise who in all times have agreed upon certain reliable laws, rules, and methods in the administration of the common law (see Holdsworth 1924, vol. 5, p. 503).

In relation to Hobbes's criticisms of Coke, Sir William Blackstone (1723–1780), a fundamental authority on modern constitutional law, also made a contribution to the debate. Blackstone defends a quite particular halfway position of his own with regard to the theory of law. For in opposition to both Coke and Hobbes he claims that natural right, being as old as humanity and dictated by God himself, naturally stands above any other in terms of its obligatory power (see Blackstone 1893, vol. I, p. 41). This approach harbors a revolutionary potential as far as established positive law is concerned, since it does not merely permit but even commands the judge not to pursue a certain course if it obviously contradicts divine law. On the other hand, Blackstone does not entirely share Coke's optimistic view that reason is effectively realized in the law, for he argues only for an assumption of reasonableness, which can in principle be challenged, although we should respect earlier ages enough not to assume that they always acted without due reflection (ibid., vol. I, p. 70).

This position, which might be described as a positivist version of natural law theory, was completely rejected by Jeremy Bentham (1748–1832), who adopted a consistently positivist approach to law and subjected Blackstone's uncertain and wavering position to ruthless criticism. He strongly insisted on the dangers inherent in the revolutionary potential of Blackstone's approach: "The denying the validity of a Law of which they like not the contents is a common expedient of popular impatience" (Bentham 1774–75/1977, p. 54). But what is more important, as far as the subsequent influence of Hobbes is concerned, is of course the fact that Bentham takes up the earlier thinker's command theory of law, although he does not actually mention the original father of this approach in his own relevant work, *Of Laws in General* (1782).

The legal theorist John Austin (1790–1859), who was a student of Bentham's, went on to introduce certain sociological elements into the command theory of law in his highly influential work *The Province of Jurisprudence Determined* (1832). And this theory, under the authoritative triumvirate of Hobbes, Bentham, and Austin, would subsequently dominate English jurisprudence over many generations.

Particularly after the English Restoration, with the reestablishment of the monarchy in 1660, and up to and far beyond the year of Hobbes's death in 1679, we find a plethora of pamphlets composed by clerics and other interested parties with the sole purpose of attacking the work of this "arch-atheist and materialist," while almost no one was prepared to defend him (Mintz 1962, pp. 157ff.). Certain bishops even contended that the prominent "heretic" should be publicly burned at the stake. Fortunately for Hobbes, the situation did not actually exceed the limits of an intellectual witch-hunt. Thus John Bramhall (1594–1663), the bishop of Derry, produced a work, brimming with odium, which was directed specifically at the doctrines propounded in *Leviathan*. And the earl of Clarendon, who was lord chancellor for almost a decade (1658–1667), thus serving as minister of justice under King Charles II, launched a vehement general attack on Hobbes for trumpeting rebellion, and argued that *Leviathan* should be denounced and burned in public.

The sometimes savage attacks on Hobbes that came from ecclesi-astical quarters were directed against his absolutist conception of state sovereignty, but even more against his repudiation of political claims on the part of the churches and against his attempt to provide a moral theory that was largely emancipated from and independent of religion. Even before Hobbes's death, the writings of this ferociously anti–Roman Catholic thinker had been placed on the Index of Prohibited Books by the Catholic Church.

In 1683, three and a half years after the philosopher's death, the Uni-versity of Oxford, where Hobbes had studied, issued a "Judgement and Decree" condemning "certain pernicious books and damnable doctrines destructive to the sacred persons of princes, their state and government, and of all humane society" (Parkin 2007, p. 372). At the top of the list we find Hobbes's two most important contributions to political philoso-phy, *De Cive* and *Leviathan*. Many teachers, clerics, and students took part in the ensuing book-burning ceremony, which was arranged by the university itself. Hobbes had expected reactions of this kind. If a thinker questions the structure of power, human beings do not think of the laws but merely cry: "Crucify him!" (*An Historical Narration Concerning Her-esy, and the Punishment Thereof*, in: Works, vol. IV, p. 407).

The critics and opponents who were motivated more by specifically intellectual considerations rather than by narrowly political ones did not confine themselves to explicit criticisms of Hobbes's texts. The earl of Clarendon, for example, wrote a lengthy and detailed *History of the Rebel-lion and Civil War in England* (completed in 1672, but published posthu-mously in 1702). In explicit contrast to Hobbes's account in *Behemoth*, Clarendon told the story from the perspective of the moderate royalists. Influenced in this regard by Aristotle, Clarendon defended the cause of a "mixed monarchy"; and while Hobbes had rejected Aristotle's idea of the rule and supremacy of the laws (L ch. 46: 377–78), Clarendon regarded the king's duty to observe the law as the strongest source and support of his power (Clarendon 1676, p. 49f. and 55f.).

How far Hobbes has influenced the notion of an established state church that has been so important in many Protestant countries is a question that still requires further investigation. If we consider the gen-eral development of British constitutional history, and set aside the fact that the monarch here is both the head of state as well as the head of the established church, namely the Anglican Church, it can hardly be said that the political system of Great Britain has followed Hobbes's own recommendations. For the British political system has followed the path of recognizing fundamental civil rights and the principle of the separation of powers. The conception of political authority that this implies clearly contradicts Hobbes's views in this regard. Instead of the absolute authority of the sovereign we are presented with a normatively limited and regulated system with several related but relatively independent levels of authority: the Monarch, the Upper House, the Lower House, and the Judiciary.

Even before the appearance of Hobbes's *Behemoth*, one of the philosopher's intellectual rivals, James Harrington, a highly regarded political thinker in his time, had published another alternative diagnosis of the causes of the English Civil War. His work *Commonwealth Oceana* (1656), which belongs to the genre of utopian literature, argued that the war had an essentially economic and political cause, namely the destruction of the English feudal order that was accomplished during the reigns of Henry VII and Henry VIII. For with the dissolution of the monasteries and the threats that were posed to the great aristocratic landowners, according to Harrington, the monarchy came to lose its own natural sources of support. In spite of this analysis, Harrington did not plead for a return to the old structures and patterns of ownership, but actually argued for a more equitable distribution of property.

14.2. A Continuing Debate

The violent and widespread repudiation of *Leviathan* was not of course without consequences for the book and its reputation. After the first English edition of the work appeared in 1651 (the Latin version was published in 1668) Hobbes's famous book had to wait almost two hundred years to be republished in England. It was only much later that Hobbes was acknowledged in England as the greatest and undoubtedly the most original and thought-provoking political thinker of his country (Holdsworth 1924, vol. V, p. 294).

In the intervening period, Hobbes's theory of the state had been overshadowed by the influence of Locke's political thought. Although in his unpublished *Two Tracts on Government* of 1661 Locke himself had initially defended an autocratic conception of the state resembling that of Hobbes, his *Letter Concerning Toleration*, composed around 1667, shows him already turning toward political liberalism, the position which was definitively expressed in his most important work on political philosophy, the second of the *Two Treatises of Government* that appeared in 1690, more than a decade after Hobbes's death. Here he claims that to accept the doctrine of Hobbes's *Leviathan* is "to think that men are so foolish that they take care to avoid what mischiefs may be done to them by polecats and foxes, but are content, nay, think it safety, to be devoured by lions" (ch. 7, § 93).

The philosopher Joseph Butler (1692–1752), later Bishop Butler, would also publish an influential critique of Hobbes's moral theory. On the European continent Hobbes's political philosophy certainly began to exert an influence, although it also met with considerable criticism. Thus Spinoza, Pufendorf, and Leibniz, Thomasius, Rousseau, and Kant, and Hegel too, took over from Hobbes at least the basic idea that the state of nature must be abandoned for a state of right with publicly recognized structures of law and authority. It is worth indicating a few key stations in the history of this critical reception of Hobbes's thought. Thus it was no less a figure than Gottfried Wilhelm Leibniz (1646–1716), universal scholar and leading thinker of the German Enlightenment, who was more than ready to praise Hobbes's achievement. In Leibniz's view, the English philosopher had certainly undertaken the most thorough investigation of the basic principles of all things, and was the first to apply the right method of argument and demonstration in the field of the philosophy of law and the state (*Philosophischer Briefwechsel* I, p. 94). In spite of his appreciation for *Leviathan*, in a letter to Hobbes himself Leibniz expressed his fear that the giant figure exalted in the image of Leviathan might abuse and monopolize power rather than establish and secure it (*Philosophischer Briefwechsel* I, pp. 56ff.).

In his *Discourse on the Arts and Sciences* (1750), a work that made him famous throughout Europe, Rousseau spoke of the "pernicious reflections of Hobbes" (p. 24). In the second discourse, *A Discourse on the Origin of Inequality* (1775), the English philosopher had claimed, according to Rousseau, that "man is bold by nature and seeks only to assail and attack other men." In certain later passages of the text Rousseau also anticipates the thesis, defended in modern times by Franz Borkenau and Crawford Macpherson, that Hobbes attributed to man in the state of nature certain passions, which have actually only emerged in the context of society. In particular Rousseau reproaches Hobbes for regarding man as "evil by nature" because man possesses no natural idea of goodness, as subject to vice because he has no conception of virtue, as reluctant to help others because he owes nothing to his fellow human beings. Rousseau himself insists, by contrast, that one must distinguish the original love of self (*amour de soi*) as a natural feeling from that artificial pride or selfishness (*amour-propre*), which has emerged in society. It follows from this that in the true state of nature, understood as an early form of human community, such selfishness did not actually exist.

In *The Social Contract* (1762) the first chapter begins dramatically with the famous claim: "Man is born free; and everywhere he is in chains," a phrase that may recall Hobbes's remark that men "have made artificial chains" for themselves called civil laws (L ch. 21: 109-09). In the next chapter Rousseau implicitly contrasts Hobbes with Locke. Rousseau remarks that according to Hobbes, as for Grotius (*De jure belli ac pacis*, book I, ch. 3, § 8), it is "doubtful whether the human race belongs to a hundred men, or that hundred men to the human race. . . . On this showing, the human species is divided into so many herds of cattle, each with its ruler, who keeps guard over them for the purpose of devouring them" (*The Social Contract*, book I, ch. 2, p. 167).

Hobbes also remained an important point of reference for Kant and Hegel in the context of political philosophy and the theory of the state. In the *Critique of Pure Reason* (B779f.), Kant compares the "endless disputes of a merely dogmatic reason" with Hobbes's "state of nature," which is a "state of injustice and violence," so that, just as Hobbes says, "we have no option save to abandon it and submit ourselves to the constraint of law," and thereby to recognize, as Kant says, "the critique of pure reason" as "the true tribunal for all disputes of pure reason."

In Kant's essay *On the Common Saying 'That May be Correct in Theory, but it is of no Use in Practice'* (1793), the second part entitled "On the Relation of Theory to Practice in the Right of the State" carries the subtitle "(Against Hobbes)." Kant maintains in contrast to Hobbes that the public "has its inalienable rights against the head of state, although these cannot be coercive rights" (*Werke*, vol. VIII, 303).

It might be objected, on behalf of Hobbes, that he does recognize certain moral laws, namely the laws of nature that are valid even in the pre-political condition and imply certain rights in relation to the sovereign; and it might be argued that he is more rigorous and consistent than Kant insofar as Hobbes holds that rights that cannot be realized or enforced (which are not "coercive rights") have precious little value. But in contrast to Hobbes, the moral laws recognized by Kant have a categorical rather than a merely functional character, and precisely for that reason are "inalienable." Any community that can claim an even basic or minimal legitimacy has to recognize these inalienable rights. The citizen is treated unjustly if such recognition is withheld. Hobbes takes the contrary view. In *De Cive* (C ch. 7, §14) he declares that since "they who have gotten the *supreme command*, are by no compacts obliged to any man, it necessarily follows, that they can do no *injury* to the subjects." Nonetheless, without explicitly mentioning Hobbes in this regard, Kant does follow him in two specific respects, namely in arguing that the state of nature is a state of war, and that the state of peace is something that must be "established" (Kant, *Toward Perpetual Peace*, sect. II, *Werke*, vol. VIII, 348f.).

In Hegel's principal contribution to political thought, the *Outlines of the Philosophy of Right* (1821), Hobbes is mentioned in the handwritten notes that Hegel made in his copy of the text. Thus in relation to §71 ("Transition from property to contract") we read: "I am master over my life—everyone else likewise—*Hobbes*: each individual can do away with another, —all human beings are therefore equal—I alone have the *true* judgement—each judges for himself whether I deserve to live" (*Werke*, vol. VII, p. 153). And in his *Lectures on the History of Philosophy* Hegel provides a many-sided critical account of Hobbes's philosophy (*Werke*, vol. XX, pp. 225–29). At the beginning of his discussion Hegel observes that "Hobbes is well-known and famous on account of the originality of his views." Hegel mentions *De Cive* "and also his *Leviathan*, a most notorious work," although he then goes on to praise them: "With regard to the nature of society and government they contain sounder ideas than some which are still current." This initial praise is nonetheless qualified as he proceeds: "But there is nothing truly speculative or genuinely philosophical in them." And toward the end of his discussion he says that "thus on the basis of a quite correct view, since the general will has been located in the will of a single individual, the monarch, there arises a condition of absolute rule, a condition of complete despotism." But as far as Hobbes's philosophical method and its originality is concerned, Hegel rightly points out: "In the past ideals were set up, or one appealed to Scripture, or to positive law; but Hobbes attempted to trace the unity of the state, the nature of civil power, back to principles which lie within ourselves, which we are able to recognize as our own" (*Vorlesungen über die Geschichte der Philosophie*, *Werke*, vol. XX, p. 226). Hegel thus clearly recognized that Hobbes's moral and political philosophy was not in the last analysis theonomous in nature, but rather autonomous in character, albeit in a somewhat qualified sense.

Before Kant and Hegel, of course, the materialists and encyclopedists of the French Enlightenment had discovered the significance of Hobbes's critique of ecclesiastical religion, and they also felt a strong affinity with his mechanistic philosophy of nature and anthropology. Thus Denis Diderot (1713–1784), initially a coeditor but eventually the sole editor of the legendary *Encyclopédie*, wrote of Baron d'Holbach's partial translation of Hobbes's *Elements*: "*C'est un livre à lire et à commenter toute sa vie*" ("This is a book that one could spend a lifetime reading and interpreting"; D. Diderot, *Oeuvres*, vol. XV, p. 124). And elsewhere he writes: "*C'est un chef d'oeuvre de logique et de raison*" ("It is a masterpiece of logic and reason"; *Oeuvres*, vol. III, p. 466). And finally, in his article on "Liberty" in the *Encyclopédie*, Diderot includes Hobbes along with Spinoza among the "fatalists," while going on to reject their respective arguments against the freedom of the will (*Oeuvres*, vol. XV, pp. 480ff.).

At the beginning of the nineteenth century Hobbes was effectively rediscovered in Great Britain itself, and his radical philosophy of law and the state exerted great influence on Utilitarianism and on the analytical legal positivism of Jeremy Bentham, James Mill, and John Austin, an approach that rejected all issues of substantive truth in relation to the force or validity of positive law, albeit not in relation to the question of legislation and the political debates surrounding it. And indeed William Molesworth, the editor of Hobbes's *Complete Works* (London 1839–45), belonged himself to this tradition of thought. Even before, however, it cannot be said that Hobbes was ever entirely forgotten, for in his voluminous work on *The Wealth of Nations* (1776, book I, ch. 5) we also find Adam Smith alluding to Hobbes's view that wealth is power (L ch. 10: 41, "Also riches joined with liberality is power.").

14.3. The Modern Discussion

In more recent times it was above all the writings of Ferdinand Tönnies (1855–1936) that helped to bring the English philosopher to fresh attention. It is often overlooked that Tönnies, a sociologist principally known on account of his famous book *Gemeinschaft und Gesellschaft* (*Community and Society*) of 1888, was also a significant contributor to the field of Hobbes scholarship. In 1889 he published an edition of the English text of *The Elements of Law*, Hobbes's early contribution to political philosophy and a work that had long been forgotten, and in 1926 he published a German translation of the same work. He also edited the English text of *Behemoth* in 1927. In his foreword to his edition of the *Elements*, Tönnies cited the remarks of Diderot, which we have mentioned above. Not long after producing this edition Tönnies presented and examined Hobbes's theory of law and the state in the substantial monograph *Thomas Hobbes. Leben und Lehre (Thomas Hobbes. His Life and His Thought)* in 1896. Gustav Adolph Walz, a theorist of constitutional and international law who was influenced by Carl Schmitt, acknowledged the importance of this line of interpretation, which saw Hobbes principally as a theorist of positive constitutional law, when he wrote: "Basically speaking, Hobbes simply undertakes to furnish a rational theory of the positive constitutional state, and a theory which is entirely free of political dogmas" (Walz 1930, p. 9).

One could also describe the sociologist and historian Max Weber (1864–1920) as a crypto-Hobbesian thinker. For in the famous definition of dominion or political power presented in his principal work, *Economy and Society* (§16, p. 53), he effectively takes up Hobbes's command theory and reformulates it in social-theoretical terms: "'Domination' (*Herrschaft*) is the probability that a command with a given specific content will be obeyed by a given group of persons." In spite of this he does not actually mention Hobbes by name in this seminal text.

The great legal theorist Hans Kelsen (1881–1973) concluded the second edition of his principal work, *The Pure Theory of Law* (1960^2), with an essay on "The Problem of Justice." Here he praises Hobbes for eliminating any conflict between natural right and positive law. Kelsen appeals specifically to *De Cive* (ch. 14, §10) and *Leviathan* (ch. 26), arguing that natural right contains positive law and positive law is a part of natural right. Obedience with respect to positive law is a demand of natural right itself (Kelsen 1960^2, p. 439; the essay was not included in the English translation of the work).

In his voluminous and comprehensive work *The Principle of Hope* (composed between 1938 and 1947, and published between 1954 and 1959), Ernst Bloch also discussed Hobbes's work in the section of his text entitled "Social Utopias and Classical Natural Right," where he rightly describes the English philosopher as "the fiercest champion of absolute central power and yet—a democrat" (1986, vol. II, p. 536).

Another much-discussed twentieth-century interpretation of Hobbes stems from the work of Leo Strauss (1899–1973), a conservative social and political philosopher who had studied under the leading thinkers of the time, such as Edmund Husserl, Ernst Cassirer, and Martin Heidegger.

Strauss was not content with simply supplementing or slightly correcting the currently prevailing image of Hobbes but attempted to transform our understanding of his thought in a quite fundamental way. In the process he characterizes Hobbes's image of humanity as asocial and reduces it to the level of individual vanity, while remarkably downplaying the elements of power, mistrust, and rivalry. In seeking to identify the origin of Hobbes's image of man Strauss ignores the resoluto-composite method of his "natural scientific" approach, as well as the "mechanistic psychology" that led him to deny the freedom of the will. According to Strauss, behind Hobbes's "theoretical" approach we can detect another philosopher who was still strongly marked by the hated Aristotle of his youth. For the philosophy of Aristotle was almost hammered into Hobbes in his earlier years. Strauss does not however deny the other aspect of the asocial human being, namely the "social" fear of violent death, which actually serves to promote peace. The human being thus exhibits an antithetic moral character, an opposition between the fundamentally unjust character of vanity on the one hand and the fundamentally just, since wholly justified, fear of violent death on the other.

Not unlike Tönnies in this regard, Strauss regarded Hobbes as a founding thinker of political liberalism (*The Political Philosophy of Hobbes*, 1936). Although this interpretation is plausible only in rather limited terms, it is certainly true that Hobbes's "commonwealth" does not furnish a pattern for the totalitarian state. For in the totalitarian political systems of the twentieth century the apparatus of the state is controlled by groups that mount absolute claims to truth, by parties sustained by secularized versions of religious ideology, namely by the kind of groups that Hobbes certainly did not wish to see in positions of power.

Whereas Leo Strauss saw Hobbes as a cardinal figure in the liberal tradition of natural law theory, in his book *Der Leviathan in der Staatslehre des Thomas Hobbes* (*The Leviathan in Hobbes's Doctrine of the State*) of 1938, the legal theorist Carl Schmitt was openly impressed by Hobbes's anti-liberal approach and expressed his support for the Leviathan itself: for the unambiguous monopoly of power in contrast to the diffusion of power exemplified by pluralistic democracy, for the correlation between protection (provided by the sovereign) and absolute obedience (on the part of the citizen), for the replacement of parliamentary debate by a supposed sense for the truly political, for the exercise of admittedly arbitrary yet absolutely sovereign decision. Schmitt's later "conversion" to a more liberal style of interpretation, his altered emphasis upon Hobbes's "strong sense of individual liberty," and his claim that Hobbes's "ultimate concern is not with mathematics and geometry, but with attempting to define the unity of a Christian commonwealth," as he argues in *Die vollendete Reformation* (*The Completed Reformation*) of 1965, all this has hardly been acknowledged in the context of the general political reception of Schmitt's work.

The Canadian political theorist C. B. Macpherson offered an interpretation of Hobbes that is very different from, and indeed almost diametrically opposed to, that proposed by Strauss. Effectively following in the footsteps of two authors he does not specifically mention, namely Rousseau and Franz Borkenau, a social theorist associated with the Frankfurt School, Macpherson offers a reading of Hobbes that clearly reveals the influence of Marxian thought. But in his study *The Political Theory of Possessive Individualism* (1962), as the subtitle "Hobbes to Locke" already indicates, he does not simply restrict himself to the author of *Leviathan*. The basic thesis of the book is that English political philosophy from the seventeenth to the eighteenth century shares a common concern with basic socio-economic issues and endorses a conception of possessive individualism that accounts for certain fundamental difficulties in liberal-democratic thought from J. S. Mill onward.

From a methodological point of view Macpherson detects various logical problems in Hobbes's argument, although he sometimes proceeds too quickly in this regard. For he mistakenly supposes that Hobbes's notion of the condition of nature is derived from a historical condition of society, whereas in fact it is developed by reference to fundamental characteristics of human beings inasmuch as they do not live a solitary life but enter into relations with their fellow human beings.

But Macpherson is not really concerned with resolving the problems he claims to identify. On the contrary, he attempts to explain them in ideological terms in relation to the social and economic conditions of the emerging "market society" of Hobbes's time, a society that contradicted the assumptions of an older and more traditional social order with different conceptions of rank and status. In this interpretation of Hobbes's thought the state is not actually derived from a basic concept of natural philosophy, namely "matter in motion," but rather from what Macpherson calls "social motion," namely the "civilized passions," or the desires and motivations that have developed under the specific conditions of a modern market society. This argument has important consequences, for in that case Hobbes's state is not something that is absolutely necessary for human beings as such, but only for human beings as citizens in the context of specific property and exchange relations. It seems to me that such a thesis applies more convincingly to Locke than it does to Hobbes, who never directly discusses the economy in its own right (though it surfaces indirectly in Hobbes's critical remarks on Dutch merchants in *A Dialogue*). Nor can this thesis be integrated within Hobbes's theory of the state except at the cost of considerable interpretive violence. What is remarkable about Macpherson's approach is the degree to which it marginalizes the actual historical circumstances that prompted Hobbes to develop his thought as he did, namely the Civil War with its attendant religious disputes and the conflict between the king and Parliament.

In terms of content Macpherson's interpretation of Hobbes is certainly very different from that presented by Strauss, but they are much the same from a formal perspective. Both writers approach Hobbes with strong political, even ideological, preconceptions, so that the texts of the philosophy in question are basically reduced to a quarry to be exploited for specific systematic interests.

Although it has received little attention in the secondary literature on Hobbes at least, Jürgen Habermas also offered a convincing interpretation of *Leviathan* at around the same time as Macpherson's book. With specific reference to Hobbes, Habermas claims: "In its role as the science of the state of nature, a modern physics of human nature replaces the classical ethics of Natural Law" (*Theory and Practice*, p. 64). Above all, Habermas explores two antinomies here, which he describes respectively as "the sacrifice of the liberal context in favor of the absolute form of its sanction" (p. 67) and "the practical impotence of the science of power as social technique" (p. 70). In his later "Contributions towards a Discourse Theory of Law and of the Democratic State based on Law" (see *Faktizität und Geltung*, 1992, p. 118), Habermas "looks back at Hobbes from a Kantian perspective" and, correcting the earlier interpretation, recognizes that "Hobbes is more a theorist of the bourgeois constitutional state without democracy than an apologist of unrestrained absolutism."

Since the 1970s there has been something of a renaissance in social contract theory, something hardly conceivable without the contribution of Thomas Hobbes as its first modern proponent. It is quite true that the principal modern defender of social contract theory, John Rawls (*A Theory of Justice*, 1971), along with the author of the present work (Höffe 2003), owe far more to Kant than they do to Hobbes. But the thought experiment of envisaging an original condition or "position" of equality and developing normative principles on the basis of this thought experiment remains indebted to the beginnings of modern contract theory in Hobbes. Another author who expressly refers back to Hobbes is James Buchanan (*The Limits of Liberty. Between Anarchy and Leviathan*, 1975), while a third social contract theorist, Robert Nozick (*Anarchy, State and Utopia*, 1974), has built on Locke, and a fourth, David Gauthier, has drawn on his own interpretation of Hobbes (*The Logic of Leviathan*, 1969) to develop a contract-theoretical account of morality (*Morals by Agreement*, 1986).

From the abundance of scholarly literature on Hobbes it may suffice here to draw attention to certain leading lines of inquiry. Thus there are studies that focus on the systematically scientific character of Hobbes's thought (e.g., Weiss 1980); explorations of his moral philosophy (e.g., Warrender 1957) or of the socio-economic context of his work (e.g., Macpherson 1960), not forgetting the earlier investigations of his theory of law and the state (Tönnies 1896, Hönigswald 1924, Schmitt 1938), as well as the more recent contributions (Willms 1987 and Bühler 2007). Apart from the journal *Hobbes Studies* and various recent collections (Höffe 1981, Bermbach/Kodalle 1982, Bernhardt 1990, Sorell 1996, Hüning 2005, Springborg 2007), there have been numerous monographs dealing with particular themes and specific works (Braun 1960, Gauthier 1969, Oakeshott 1975, Hampton 1986, Martinich 1992 and 2008). Finally we should mention the works that undertake to provide a comprehensive account of Hobbes's work as a whole (Schelsky 1940/1981, Polin 1981, Tuck 1989, Terrel 1994, Martinich 2005, Ottmann 2006, Gert 2010).

Such an original and important thinker as Hobbes has also of course made his presence felt in allusions within the literary field, of which I simply offer a few examples here. Thus in Schiller's drama *William Tell* (act 4, scene 3), the line "his sting is also given to the weak" recalls Hobbes's remark that "the weakest has strength enough to kill the strongest" (L ch. 13: 60). In his novel *Königliche Hoheit* Thomas Mann describes Samuel Spoelman, the millionaire who has emigrated from the United States, as a "Leviathan" on account of the power he wields through his enormous wealth. And J. M. Coetzee, a winner of the Nobel Prize for literature, has even drawn directly on Hobbes's account of the state in his *Diary of a Bad Year*.

The extraordinary influence of Hobbes's thought derives to a significant degree from the inherent power of the symbol of the Leviathan itself and the striking quality of the illustration that introduces his book. One can say without exaggeration that this must indeed be the most impressive title page of any work of political philosophy.

But what is it that really accounts for the persisting relevance of Hobbes's philosophy, and specifically of his theory of the state? This can only be explained by the fact that, while it certainly arose from a very specific historical situation, this philosophy, with all its achievements and its shortcomings, reaches far beyond that situation. As a philosopher Hobbes effectively formulated the particular challenge of his own time as a universal and fundamental question that every political theory must address: Why, and in what form, is an institutional political order, a state, required in the first place? Since Hobbes's own answer is also framed in terms of universal claims, of genuine principles, Hobbes's question, and the solution he proposes, transcends the historical context of the English Civil War and the conditions of early bourgeois market society.

Thus the condition of peace that Hobbes insists we must establish is indispensible for the full development of our material, cultural, and intellectual powers generally, and not merely in the context of the bourgeois socio-economic order. Moreover, the English Civil War is merely one of many horrific examples of politico-religious and confessional wars in Europe during the sixteenth and seventeenth centuries. Thus only two generations before, the Huguenot wars in France had led Jean Bodin to compose his *Six Livres de la République* of 1576 (see chapter 1.1, above).

If it was the rival and absolute claims of religious confessions and political authorities that paved the way for civil war in the early modern period, since the beginning of the twentieth century we have often enough seen how the exclusive claims of political as well as religious conviction have led to similar results. One only has to think of the struggle between the Bolsheviks and the anti-Bolsheviks, of Spain before the Second World War, of China and Korea, of Ireland, Vietnam, and Lebanon, and more recently of certain violent Islamicist ideologies.

Finally, as we already indicated in chapter 1.1, Hobbes's philosophy of the state is not relevant merely to the historical situation of civil war. On the contrary, the thesis of the absolute and undivided sovereignty of the state proves inadequate not only in more settled and peaceful times, but also in times of civil war. The task of securing and guaranteeing human freedom, which Hobbes ascribes to political absolutism, is precisely what absolutism itself is unable to accomplish. Thus Hobbes's philosophy of the state can illustrate the continuing relevance of the thesis that the elementary human interest in free self-preservation represents both the

authorization and the content, and thereby also the normative criterion
and the limit, of the power of the state.

In short, a structure of political order is required if human beings
are to lead their lives in conditions of security. But if we are to enjoy this
security not only in relation to our fellow human beings but also in relation to the state, there can be no such political absolutism. After Hitler,
Stalin, Mao Tse Tung, after Idi Armin and the Kmer Rouge, the regime
in North Korea, the Revolutionary Councils in Khomeini's Iran, and a
plethora of other political rulers such as Mugabe, there is one thing that
we know only too clearly. For, in contrast to Hobbes, we recognize that
human existence is fundamentally threatened not only in the stateless
condition of nature, or the condition of anarchy, but also in the despotic
situation, whether latent or acute, of omnipotent state sovereignty.

Chronology of Hobbes's Life and Work

1588   April 5: Thomas Hobbes born in Westport, near
     Malmesbury.

     The Spanish Armada sails up the English Channel but is
     defeated and dispersed.

1596–1602 Hobbes is brought up in the household of his uncle
     Francis Hobbes; the young Hobbes attends local schools
     in Westport and Malmesbury and acquires a good
     grounding in Latin and Greek.

1603   Hobbes begins his studies at Magdalen Hall, Oxford;
     focuses on logic and physics.

     Death of Queen Elizabeth I, who has reigned since 1558;
     Elizabeth is succeeded by the Stuart king James I.

1605   Exposure of the Catholic Gunpowder Plot against the
     king and Parliament.

1608   February: Hobbes acquires his Baccalaureus Artium
     (B.A.); enters the service of the aristocratic Cavendish
     family as private tutor; he maintains close links with the
     family for the rest of his life.

1610–15 Hobbes accompanies the young William Cavendish on a
     cultural and educational journey to France, Germany, and
     Italy.

1623   Hobbes becomes secretary to Francis Bacon.

1625   James I is succeeded by his son Charles I.

1629   Hobbes translates Thucydides's *History of the Peloponnesian War*; accompanies Sir Gervaise Clifton during a one-and-a-half-year trip to France, and visits Geneva; he reads Euclid's *Elements* and occupies himself with scientific and mathematical studies.

            Charles I dissolves Parliament and rules for eleven years without recourse to Parliament.

1630   Hobbes writes *A Short Tract on First Principles*; he is once again in the service of the Cavendish family, from 1631 as private tutor.

1634–36   Hobbes accompanies William Cavendish, third earl of Devonshire, on an educational journey to France and Italy; in Paris (1635) Hobbes meets Marin Mersenne, Pierre Gassendi, and René Descartes, and in Florence (1636) meets Galileo Galilei.

1637   Anonymous publication of *A Briefe of the Art of Rhetorique* (a translation of an abridged version of Aristotle's *Rhetoric*).

1640   *The Elements of Law, Natural and Politic* circulates in manuscript copies; in November Hobbes immigrates to Paris, where he resumes contact with Mersenne and Gassendi.

1640–41   Hobbes corresponds with Descartes regarding the latter's *Discourse on Method* (1637); produces his own *Optics*.

1641   Hobbes submits, in Latin, his *Objections to the Meditations of Descartes*.

1642   March: outbreak of the English Civil War; April: *De Cive* (= Part III of the projected *Elementae Philosophiae*) privately published in Paris.

1644   *Tractatus opticus.*

1645   Hobbes engages in polemical exchanges with Bishop Bramhall on the subject of the freedom of the will.

1646   In Paris Hobbes teaches mathematics to the future King
            Charles II of England.

1647   Hobbes falls seriously ill; publishes a second edition of *De
            Cive*.

1649   Public execution of King Charles I; England declared a
            republic.

1650   *Answer to Devenant's Preface Before Gondibert.*

1651   Publishes *Leviathan, or The Matter, Forme, & Power of A
            Common-Wealth Ecclessiasticall and Civill*, and an English
            translation of *De Cive*.

1652   February: Hobbes returns from exile to England; once
            again in the service of the Cavendish family.

1654   *De Cive* is placed on the Vatican's Index of Prohibited
            Books.

1655   *De Corpore* (= Part I of the *Elementa Philosophiae*); an
            English version is published in 1659.

1658   *De Homine* (= Part II of the *Elementa Philosophiae*);
            Bishop Bramhall publishes his *Castigations of Mr. Hobbes*,
            with an appendix entitled "The Catching of Leviathan."

1659   Hobbes composes his *Historia Ecclessiastica*; published
            posthumously in 1688.

1660   The Stuarts return to England; King Charles II awards
            Hobbes an annual pension of £100.

1661   Hobbes attacks the physicist and chemist Robert Boyle
            and publishes *Dialogus Physicus, sive de Natura*.

1666   Parliamentary investigation and condemnation of
            Hobbes's *Leviathan*; Hobbes works on his *Dialogue
            between a Philosopher and a Student of the Common Laws
            of England* (published in 1681).

1668–70   Hobbes works on his history of the English Civil War:
            Behemoth, or The Long Parliament; the text is refused a
            licence for publication and only appears posthumously in
            1679.

1669   Hobbes publishes *Quadratura Circuli, breviter demonstrata.*

1675–76   Hobbes produces a verse translation of Homer's *Odyssey* and *Iliad.*

1679   December 4: Hobbes dies in Hardwick Hall, Derbyshire; he is buried in accordance with the Anglican Rite.

1685   Hobbes's political writings are condemned and publically burned under the auspices of the University of Oxford.

Bibliography

1. Primary Texts

1.1. Complete Editions

Thomae Hobbes Malmesburiensis Opera philosophica quae latine scripsit omnia. In unum corpus nunc primum collecta studio et labore G. Molesworth, London 1839–45, 5 vols.

The English Works of Thomas Hobbes of Malmesbury, now first collected and edited by Sir W. Molesworth, London 1839–45, 11 vols.

The Collected Works of Thomas Hobbes, 11 vols.; Thoemes Press reprint of the *The English Works,* edited by W. Molesworth, Bristol 1992.

The Clarendon Edition of the Works of Thomas Hobbes, edited by H. Warrender et al., Oxford 1983ff.

1.2. Editions of Individual Texts

Leviathan, or The Matter, Forme & Power of a Common-Wealth Ecclesiasticall and Civill, London 1651.

Leviathan sive de material, forma & potestate ecclesiasticae et civilis, Amsterdan 1668.

Leviathan, ed. with an Introduction by M. Oakeshott, Oxford 1946 (reprinted 1952 and 1957).

Leviathan, ed. with an Introduction by C. B. Macpherson, London 1968.

Leviathan, ed. by Richard Tuck, Cambridge 1991.

237

Leviathan, ed. with an Introduction by J. C. A. Gaskill, Oxford 1996.
Leviathan, 3 vols. (the English and Latin version), introduced and edited by Noel Malcolm, vols. 3–5 of the *Clarendon Edition of the Works of Thomas Hobbes*, Oxford.
De corpore, Elementorum philosophiae sectio prima, in: *Opera philosophica*, London 1839, vol. I, pp. 1–431.
De homine, Elementarum philosophiae sectio prima, in: *Opera philosophica*, London 1839, vol. II, pp. 1–132.
Man and Citizen (De Homine and De Cive), ed. with an Introduction by B. Gert, Indianapolis / Cambridge 1998.
The Elements of Law, Natural and Politic, Part I *Human Nature*, Part II *De Corpore Politico*, ed. by J. C. A. Gaskill, Oxford 1994.

2. Bibliographies and Reference Sources

Brown, K. C. (ed.) 1965: *Hobbes-Studies*, Cambridge, Mass.
Curley, E. 1939: "Reflections on Hobbes: Recent Work on His Moral and Political Philosophy," in: *Journal of Philosophical Research* 15, pp. 170–249.
Garcia, A. 1986: *Thomas Hobbes. Bibliographie Internationale de 1620 à 1986*, Caen.
MacDonald, H. / Hargreaves, M. 1952: *Thomas Hobbes. A Bibliography*, London.
Martinich, A. P. 1995: *A Hobbes Dictionary*, Cambridge, Mass.
Sacksteder, W. 1982: *Hobbes Studies 1879–1979. A Bibliography*, Bowling Green, Ky.
Willms, B. 1979: "Der Weg des Leviathan. Die Hobbesforschung von 1968–1978" (*Der Staat*, Beiheft 3), Berlin.

3. Secondary Literature

3.1. Introductions

Bagby, L. 2007: *Hobbes' Leviathan*, London.
Condren, C. 2000: *Thomas Hobbes*, New York.
Flathman, R. D. 1993: *Thomas Hobbes: Skepticism, Individuality and Chastened Politics*, Newbury Park / London.

Gert, B. 2010: *Hobbes. Prince of Peace*, Cambridge, Mass.
Kersting, W. 1992: *Thomas Hobbes zur Einführung*, Hamburg.
Martinich, A. P. 1997: *Thomas Hobbes*, Basingstoke.
Münkler, H. 2001²: *Thomas Hobbes*, Frankfurt.
Newey, G. 2008: *The Routledge Philosophical Guidebook to Hobbes and Leviathan*, London.
Peters, R. S. 1956: *Hobbes*, Harmondsworth.
Raphael, D. D. 1977: *Hobbes. Morals and Politics*, London.
Sorell, T. 1986: *Hobbes*, London.
Robertson, G. C. 1886: *Hobbes*, Edinburgh (reprinted London / New York 1995).
Tuck, R. 1989: *Hobbes*, Oxford.

3.2. Edited Collections

Bernbach, U. / Kodalle, K-M. (eds.) 1982: *Furcht und Freiheit. Leviathan-Diskussion 30 Jahre nach Thomas Hobbes*, Opladen.
Bernhardt, J. (ed.) 1990: *Hobbes oggi*. Atti del Convegno Internazionale di Studi Promosso da Ariggi Pacchi, Milan.
Brown, K. C. (ed.) 1965: *Hobbes-Studies*, Cambridge, Mass.
Cranston, M. / Peters, R. S. (eds.) 1972: *Hobbes and Rousseau. A Collection of Critical Essays*, Garden City, N.Y.
Dietz, M. F. (ed.) 1990: *Thomas Hobbes and Political Theory*, Lawrence, Kans.
Dunn, J. / Harris, I. (eds.) 1997: *Hobbes*, 3 vols., Cheltenham.
Höffe, O. (ed.) 1981: *Thomas Hobbes: Anthropologie und Staatsphilosophie*, Freiburg, Switzerland.
Hüning, D. (ed.) 2005: *Der lange Schatten des Leviathan. Hobbes' politische Philosophie nach 350 Jahren*, Berlin.
Kersting, W. (ed.) 20082: *Thomas Hobbes. Leviathan oder Stoff, Form und Gewalt eines kirchlichen und bürgerlichen Staates*, (= *Klassiker Auslegen*, vol. 5), Berlin.
King, P. (ed.) 1993: *Thomas Hobbes. Critical Assessments*, 4 vols., London / New York.
Koselleck, R. / Schnur, R. (eds.) 1969: *Hobbes-Forschungen*, Berlin.
Rogers, G. A. J. (ed.) 1995: *Leviathan. Contemporary Responses to the Political Theory of Thomas Hobbes*, Bristol.
Rogers, G. A. J. / Ryan, A. (eds.) 1988: *Perspectives on Hobbes*, Oxford.

Ross, R. et al. (eds.) 1974: *Hobbes in His Time*, Minneapolis, Minn.

Sorell, T. (ed.) 1996: *The Cambridge Companion to Hobbes*, Cambridge, Mass.

Springborg, P. (ed.) 2007: *The Cambridge Companion to Hobbes' Leviathan*, Cambridge, Mass.

Van der Bernd, J. G. (ed.) 1982: *Thomas Hobbes. His View of Man*, Amsterdam.

Voigt, R. (ed.) 2000: *Der Leviathan*, Baden-Baden.

Walton, C. / Johnson, P. J. (eds.) 1987: *Hobbes's "Science of Natural Justice,"* Dordrecht.

Zarka, J. C. (ed.) 1992: *Hobbes et son vocabulaire*, Paris.

Zarka, J. C. / Bernhardt, J. (eds.) 1990: *Thomas Hobbes. Philosophie première, théorie de la science et politique*, Paris.

3.3. Essays and Monographs

Adam, A. 1999: *Despotie der Vernunft?*, Freiburg / Munich.

Angoulvent, A-L. 1992: *Hobbes ou la crise de l'Etat baroque*, Paris.

Aubrey, J. 1987: 'Thomas Hobbes', in: Aubrey, J., *Brief Lives*, ed. with an introduction by O. L. Dick, pp. 226–38, London.

Baumgold, D. 1988: *Hobbes' Political Theory*, Cambridge, Mass.

Bertmann, M. A. 1981: *Hobbes. The Nature and the Artefacted God*, Bern.

Bobbio, N. 1993: Thomas Hobbes and the Natural Law Tradition, Chicago.

Boonin-Vail, D. 1994: *Thomas Hobbes and the Science of Moral Virtue*, Cambridge, Mass.

Borkenau, F. 1934: *Der Übergang vom feudalen zum bürgerlichen Weltbild. Studien zur Geschichte der Philosophie der Manufakturperiode*, Paris (reprinted 1988, Darmstadt).

Bowle, J. 1951: *Hobbes and his critics. A Study in Seventeenth-Century Constitutionalism*, London.

Brandon, E. 2007: *The Coherence of Hobbes' Leviathan. Civil and Religious Authority Combined*, London / New York.

Brandt, F. 1928: *Thomas Hobbes' Mechanical Conception of Nature*, London.

Brandt, F. 1982: "Das Titelblatt des *Leviathan* und Goyas *El Gigante*," in: Bermbach / Kodalle 1982, pp. 201–31.

Braun, D. 1960: *Der sterbliche Gott oder Leviathan gegen Behemoth*, 2 vols., Zürich.

Bredekamp, H. 1999: *Thomas Hobbes' visuelle Strategien. Der Leviathan: Das Urbild des modernen Staates*, Werkillustrationen und Portraits, Berlin.

Bühler, J. 2007: *Thomas Hobbes in den internationalen Beziehungen. Zur Existenz eines zwischenstaatlichen Naturzustandes in der politischen Philosophie von Thomas Hobbes*, Saarbrücken.

Burger, R. 2005: "Der sterbliche Gott. Eine Bildbetrachtung," in: *Merkur* 59/11, pp. 1032–42.

Campagna, N. 1998: "Leviathan und Rechtsstaat," in: *Archiv für Rechts- und Sozialphilosophie*, 84, pp. 340–53.

Collins, J. R. 2005: *The Allegiance of Thomas Hobbes*, Oxford.

Cooke, P. D. 1996: *Hobbes and Christianity. Reassessing the Bible in Leviathan*, Lanham.

Covell, C. 2004: *Hobbes, Realism, and the Tradition of International Law*, Basingstoke.

Deigh, J. 1996: "Reason and Ethics in Hobbes's Leviathan," in: *Journal of the History of Philosophy*, 34/1, pp. 33–60.

Esfeld, M. 1995: *Mechanismus und Subjektivität in der Philosophie von Thomas Hobbes*, Stuttgart-Bad Canstatt.

Fiebig, H. 1973: *Erkenntnis und technische Erzeugung. Hobbes' operationale Philosophie der Wissenschaft*, Meisenheim.

Finkelstein, C. O. 2005: *Hobbes on Law*, Aldershot.

Gebauer, A. K. 2005: 'Der "unzähmbare" Leviathan. Rechtsstaatlichkeit und natürliche Gesetze bei Thomas Hobbes', in: *Archiv für Rechts- und Sozialphilosophie*, 91, pp. 239–55.

Gauthier, D. 1969: *The Logic of Leviathan. The Moral and Political Theory of Thomas Hobbes*, Oxford.

Goldsmith, M. M. 1966: *Hobbes' Science of Politics*, New York.

Goyard-Fabre, S. 1975: *Le droit et la loi dans la philosophie de Thomas Hobbes*, Paris.

Grant, H. 1996: "Hobbes and Mathematics," in: Sorell 1996, pp. 108–28.

Green, A. W. 1993: *Hobbes on Human Nature*, New Brunswick, N.J.

Großheim, M. 2008²: "Religion und Politik. Die Teile III und IV des Leviathan," in: Kersting 2008², pp. 283–316.

Hampton, J. 1986: *Hobbes and the Social Contract Tradition*, Cambridge, Mass.

Höffe, O. 2008[2]: "Zur vertragstheoretischen Begründung politischer Gerechtigkeit: Hobbes, Kant und Rawls im Vergleich," in: O. Höffe, *Ethik und Politik*, ch. 6, Frankfurt a. M.

Hoekstra, K. 2003: "Hobbes on Law, Nature and Reason," in: *Journal of the History of Philosophy*, 41/1, pp. 111–20.

Hoekstra, K. 2006: "The End of Philosophy (The Case of Hobbes)," in: *Proceedings of the Aristotelian Society*, 106/1, pp. 23–60.

Hönigswald, R. 1924: *Hobbes und die Staatsphilosophie*, Munich.

Hofmann, H. 2005: "Zur politischen Theologie von Thomas Hobbes," in: R. M. Kiesow, R. Ogorek, S. Simitis (eds.), *Summa. Festschrift für Dieter Simon*, Frankfurt a. M., pp. 283–96.

Horstmann, F. 2006: *Nachträge zu Betrachtungen über Hobbes' Optik*, Berlin.

Hünning, D. 1998: *Freiheit und Herrschaft in der Rechtsphilosophie des Thomas Hobbes*, Berlin.

Hood, F. C. 1964: *The Divine Politics of Thomas Hobbes. An Interpretation of Leviathan*, Oxford.

Isermann, M. 1991: *Die Sprachtheorie im Werk von Thomas Hobbes*, Münster.

Johnston, D. 1998: *The Rhetoric of Leviathan. Thomas Hobbes and the Politics of Cultural Transformations*, Princeton, N.J.

Kavka, G. S. 1986: *Hobbesian Moral and Political Theory*, Princeton, N.J.

Klenner, H. 1996: "Einführung," in: *Thomas Hobbes. Leviathan*, edited and introduced by H. Klenner, translated by H. Schlösser, pp. xiii–xli, Meiner, Hamburg.

Kodalle, K.-M. 1996: "Thomas Hobbes (1588–1679)," in Tilman Borsche (ed.), *Klassiker der Sprachphilosophie*, Munich 1996, pp. 111–31.

Kodalle, K.-M. 1972: *Thomas Hobbes. Logik der Herrschaft und Vernunft des Friedens*, Munich.

Koselleck, R. 1959: *Kritik und Krise. Ein Beitrag zur Pathogenese der bürgerlichen Welt*, Freiburg / Munich.

Krause, J. 2006: "Der Bund im Alten Testament und bei Hobbes. Eine Perspective auf den Leviathan," in: Karl Graf Ballestrem et al. (eds.), *Politisches Denken*. Jahrbuch 2006, Berlin.

Leijenhorst, C. 1998: *Hobbes and the Aristotelians. The Aristotelian Setting of Thomas Hobbes's Natural Philosophy*, Utrecht.

Lloyd, S. A. 1992: *Ideals as Interests in Hobbes's Leviathan*, Cambridge, Mass.

Ludwig, B. 1998: *Die Wiederentdeckung des Epikureischen Naturrechts. Zu*

Thomas Hobbes philosophischer Entwicklung von De Cive zum Leviathan im Pariser Exil 1640–1651, Frankfurt a. M.

MacNeilly, F. S. 1968: *The Anatomy of Leviathan*, London.

Macpherson, C. B. 1962: *The Political Theory of Possessive Individualism*, Oxford.

Malcolm, N. (ed.) 2002: *Aspects of Hobbes*, Oxford.

Malcolm, N. 1988: "Hobbes and the Royal Society," in: Rogers / Ryan 1988, pp. 43–66.

Malherbe, M. 1984: *Thomas Hobbes ou l'oeuvre de la raison*, Paris.

Martinich, A. P. 1992: *The Two Gods of Leviathan*, Cambridge, Mass.

Metzger, H.-D. 1991: *Thomas Hobbes und die Englische Revolution 1640–1660*, Stuttgart-Bad Cannstatt.

Mintz, S. I. (ed.) 1962: *The Hunting of Leviathan. Seventeenth-Century Reactions to the Materialism and Moral Philosophy of Thomas Hobbes*, Cambridge.

Missner, M. 1977: "Hobbes's Method in Leviathan," in: *Journal of the History of Ideas*, 38, pp. 607–21.

Mohrs, Th. 1995: *Vom Weltstaat. Hobbes' Sozialphilosophie, Sozialbiologie, Realpolitik*, Berlin.

Oakeshott, M. 1975: *Hobbes on Civil Association*, Berkley, Calif.

Ottmann, H. 2006: "Thomas Hobbes (1588–1679)," in: *Geschichte des Politischen Denkens. Die Neuzeit*, vol. 3.1, pp. 265–321, Stuttgart.

Pagallo, U. 1998: "Bacon, Hobbes and the *homo homini deus* formula," in: *Hobbes Studies* 11, pp. 61–69.

Parkin, J. 2007: *Taming the Leviathan. The Reception of the Political and Religious Ideas of Thomas Hobbes in England, 1640–1799*, Cambridge, Mass.

Pettit, P. 2008: *Made with Words. Hobbes on Language, Mind, and Politics*, Princeton, N.J.

Polin, R. 1981: *Hobbes, Dieu et les hommes*, Paris.

Prins, J. 1996: "Hobbes on Light and Vision," in: Sorrel 1996, pp. 129–56.

Rhodes, R. 2002: "Obligation and Assent in Hobbes's Moral Philosophy," in: *Hobbes Studies* 15, pp. 45–67.

Rolle, H. 1980: "Hobbes' *Leviathan*—Der Staat als Maschine," in: *Deutsche Zeitschrift für Philosophie* 28, pp. 934–42.

Rottleuthner, H. 1983: "Leviathan oder Behemoth? Zur Hobbes-Rezeption im Nationalsozialismus und ihre Neuauflage," in: *Archiv für Rechts- und Sozialphilosophie* 69, pp. 247–65.

Schelsky, H. 1937: "Die Totalität des Staates bei Hobbes," in: *Archiv für Rechts- und Sozialphilosophie* 31, pp. 176–93.

Schelsky, H. 1981: *Thomas Hobbes—Eine politische Lehre*, Berlin.

Schmitt, C. 1938: *Der Leviathan in der Staatslehre des Thomas Hobbes*, Hamburg.

Shelton, G. 1992: *Morality and Sovereignty in the Philosophy of Hobbes*, Basingstoke.

Skinner, Q. 1966: "The Ideological Context of Hobbes' Political Thought," in: *The Historical Journal* 9, pp. 286–317.

Skinner, Q. 1996: *Reason and Rhetoric in the Philosophy of Hobbes*, Cambridge, Mass.

Skinner, Q. 2008: *Freiheit und Pflicht—Thomas Hobbes' politische Theorie* (Frankfurter Adorno-Vorlesungen 2005).

Skinner, Q. 2008b: *Hobbes and Republican Liberty*, Cambridge, Mass.

Sommerville, J. 1992: *Thomas Hobbes. Political Ideas in Historical Context*, New York.

Spragens, Th. 1973: *The Politics of Motion. The World of Thomas Hobbes*, Lexington.

Sprute, J. 2002: "Moralphilosophie bei Hobbes," in: *Deutsche Zeitschrift für Philosophie* 50/6, pp. 833–53.

Steinberg, J. 1988: *The Obsession of Thomas Hobbes. The English Civil War in Hobbes' Political Philosophy*, New York.

Strauss, L. 1936: *The Political Philosophy of Hobbes*, Oxford.

Taylor, A. E. 1938: "The Ethical Doctrine of Hobbes," in: *Philosophy* 13, pp. 406–24.

Terrel, J. 1994: *Hobbes, matérialisme et politique*, Paris.

Thornton, H. 2005: *State of Nature or Eden? Thomas Hobbes and his Contemporaries on the natural Condition of Human Beings*, Rochester, N.Y.

Tönnies, F. 1896: *Thomas Hobbes. Leben und Lehre*, Stuttgart-Bad Cannstatt.

Tuck, R. 1992: "The 'Christian Atheism' of Thomas Hobbes," in: M. Hunter / D. Wooten, *Atheism from the Reformation to the Enlightenment*, pp. 111–30, Oxford.

Van Mill, D. 2000: *Liberty, Rationality and Agency in Hobbes' Leviathan*, Albany, N.Y.

Vialatoux, J. 1952²: *La cité de Hobbes. Théorie de l'État totalitaire. Essai sur la théorie naturaliste de la civilisation*, Paris / Lyon.

Waas, L. R. 2002: "Der gezähmte Leviathan des Thomas Hobbes oder: Ist der Theoretiker des Absolutismus eigentlich als Vordenker der liberalen Demokratie zu verstehen?," in: *Archiv für Rechts- und Sozialphilosophie* 88, pp. 155–77.

Warrender, H. 1957: *The Political Philosophy of Thomas Hobbes. His Theory of Obligation*, Oxford.

Watkins, J. W. N. 1973²: *Hobbes' System of Ideas*, London.

Weiss, U. 1978: "Hobbes' Rationalismus. Aspekte der neueren deutschen Hobbes-Rezeption," in: *Philosophisches Jahrbuch der Görres-Gesellschaft* 85, pp. 167–96.

Weiss, U. 1980: *Das philosophische System von Thomas Hobbes*, Stuttgart-Bad Cannstatt.

Willms, B. 1970: *Die Antwort des Leviathan. Thomas Hobbes' politische Philosophie*, Neuwied / Berlin.

Willms, B. 1980: "Tendenzen der gegenwärtigen Hobbes-Forschung," in: *Zeitschrift für Philosophische Forschung* 34, pp.442–53.

Willms, B. 1987: *Thomas Hobbes. Das Reich des Leviathan*, Munich.

Wright, G. 2006: *Religion, Politics and Thomas Hobbes*, Dordrecht.

Wolfers, B. 1991: *"Geschwätzige Philosophie." Thomas Hobbes' Kritik an Aristoteles*, Würzburg.

Zarka, Y. C. 1987: *La décision métaphysique de Hobbes. Conditions de la politique*, Paris.

4. Further Literature

Aristotle, *The Complete Works of Aristotle*, the Revised Oxford Translation, 2 vols., edited and revised by Jonathan Barnes, Bollingen Series LXXI: 2, Princeton, N.J., 1985.

Austin, J. 1832: *The Providence of Jurisprudence Determined*, London.

Bacon, F.: *The Works of Francis Bacon*, collected and edited by J. Spedding, D. D. Heath, and R. L. Ellies (=SHE), 14 vols., London, 1857–74.

Bacon, F.: *De augmentis scientiarum*, in: *The Works of Francis Bacon*, vol. 1, pp. 423–844.

Bentham, J. 1774–75: *A Comment on the Commentaries. A Criticism of William Blackstone's Commentaries on the Laws of England*, in: H. Burns and H. L. A. Hart (eds.), *Comment on the Commentaries and A Fragment on Government*, London, 1977, pp. 1–389.

Blackstone, W. 1765–69: *Commentaries on the Laws of England*, 4 vols., Oxford (reprinted Philadelphia 1893, 2 vols.).

Bodin, J. *The Six Books of a Commonweale*, translated by Richard Knolles, 1606; reprinted, edited by K. D. McRae, Cambridge, Mass., 1962.

Boyle, R. 2000: *The Works of Robert Boyle*, edited by Michael Hunter and Edward P. Davis, Posthumous Publications 1692–1744, vol. 12, London.

Bramhall, J.: *A Defence of True Liberty*, London, 1665; reprinted in: *Early Responses to Hobbes*, 6 vols., London, 1996 (vol. 1).

Bramhall, J.: *Castigations of Mr. Hobbes* (London 1658), reprinted New York, 1997.

Brugger, B. 1999: *Republican Theory in Political Thought: Virtuous or Virtual*, Basingstoke.

Buchanan, J. 1975: *The Limits of Liberty. Between Anarchy and Utopia*, Chicago.

Clarendon, First Earl of (Sir Edward Hyde), 1676: *A Brief View and Survey of the Dangerous and Pernicious Errors to Church and State, in Mr. Hobbes's Book, Entitled Leviathan*, London; reprinted in: *Early Responses to Hobbes*, 6 vols., London, 1996 (vol. 6).

Clarendon, First Earl of, 1786: *State Papers*, collected by Edward, Earl of Clarendon, 3 vols., Oxford.

Descartes, R.: *Oeuvres de Descartes*, edited by C. Adam and P. Tannery (=AT), 11 vols., Paris 1974–87.

Descartes, R.: *The Philosophical Writings of Descartes*, edited by J. Cottingham et al., 3 vols., 1985 and 1991, Cambridge, Mass.

Diderot, D.: *Oeuvres complètes de Diderot*, edited by J. Assézat, 20 vols., Paris 1875ff.

Filmer, R. 1652: 'Observations on Mr. Hob's his Leviathan', in: *Patriarcha and Other Writings*, edited by J. P. Sommerville, Cambridge Texts in the History of Political Thought, Cambridge, Mass., 1999.

Grotius, H. 1625: *De Jure Belli ac Pacis Libri Tres*, Paris; De Jure Belli ac Pacis Libri Tres, translated from the edition of 1646 by F. H. Kelsey et al, Oxford, 1925.

Habermas, J. 19714: *Theorie und Praxis. Sozialphilosophische Studien*, Frankfurt a. M.; *Theory and Practice*, translated by John Viertel, London, 1974.

Habermas, J. 1992: *Faktizität und Geltung*, Frankfurt a. M.; *Between Facts and Norms. Contributions to a Discourse Theory of Law and Democracy*, translated by W. Regh, Cambridge, Mass., 1996.

Hegel, G. W. F. *Werke* (TWA), edited by E. Moldenhauer and K. Michel, 2 vols., Frankfurt a. M., 1969–72.

Hegel, G. W. F.: *Phänomenologie des Geistes*, in: *Werke*, vol, 3; *Phenomenology of Spirit*, translated by A. V. Milller, Oxford, 1977.

Hegel, G. W. F.: *Grundlinien der Philosophie des Rechts*, in: *Werke*, vol. 7; *Outlines of the Philosophy of Right*, translated by M. Knox, edited and revised by S. Houlgate, Oxford, 2008.

Hegel, G. W. F.: *Vorlesungen zur Geschichte der Philosophie*, in: Werke, vol. 20; *Lectures on the History of Philosophy*, translated by Robert Brown, 3 vols., Berkeley, Calif., 1990.

Höffe, O. 1991: *Gerechtigkeit als Tausch? Zum politischen Projekt der Moderne*, Baden-Baden.

Höffe, O. 2003[4]: *Politische Gerechtigkeit. Grundlegung einer kritischen Philosophie von Recht und Staat*, Frankfurt a. M.

Höffe, O. 2005[2]: "Zur Analogie von Individuum und Polis," in: O. Höffe (ed.), *Platon. Politeia*, pp. 69–94 (Klassiker Auslegen, vol. 4), Berlin.

Höffe, O. 2006[3]: *Aristoteles*, Munich; *Aristotle*, translated by C. Salazar, Albany, N.Y., 2003.

Höffe, O. 2008[3]: *Praktische Philosophie. Das Modell des Aristoteles*, Berlin.

Holdsworth, W. S. 1924: *A History of English Law*, 12 vols., London.

Imschodt, P. v. / Horning, C. 2008: "Leviathan," in: *Reallexikon für Antike und Christentum*, edited by G. Schölgen et al., vol. 22, pp. 1245–51, Stuttgart.

Kant, I.: *Gesammelte Schriften* (Akademie-Ausgabe), Berlin, 1900ff. (reprinted Berlin, 1968ff.).

Kant, I. *Kritik der reinen Vernunft* (Akademie-Ausgabe, vols. 3–4); *Critique of Pure Reason*, translated by N. Kemp Smith, London, 1933[2].

Kant, I.: *Metaphysik der Sitten* (Akademie-Ausgabe, vol. 6, pp. 203–493); *The metaphysics of morals*, translated by M. J. Gregor, in: I. Kant, *Practical Philosophy*, pp. 353–603, Cambridge, Mass., 1996.

Kant, I.: *Über den Gemeinspruch: das mag in der Theorie richtig sein, taught aber nicht für die Praxis* (Akademie-Ausgabe, vol. 8, pp. 273–314); *On the common saying: That may be correct in theory, but it is of no use in practice*, translated by M. J. Gregor, in: I. Kant, *Practical Philosophy*, pp. 273–309, Cambridge, Mass., 1996.

Kant, I.: *Zum ewigen Frieden* (Akademie-Ausgabe, vol. 8, pp. 342–86); *Toward perpetual peace*, translated by M. J. Gregor, in: I. Kant, *Practical Philosophy*, pp. 311–51, Cambridge, Mass., 1996.

La Mettrie, J. O. de: *Machine man and other writings*, translated by A. Thompson, Cambridge, Mass., 1996.

Leibniz, G. W.: *Sämtliche Schriften und Briefe* (Deutsche Akademie der Wissenschaften), Reihe I, Band 1: *Allgemeiner politischer und historischer Briefwechsel 1668–1676*, Berlin, 1976.

Leibniz, G. W.: *Philosophical Papers and Letters*, edited by L. F. Loemker, Dordrect, 1999.

Locke, J. 1661: *Two Tracts on Government*, edited and introduced by P. Abrams, Cambridge, Mass., 1967.

More, H. 1653: *An Antidote against Atheism. Or, An appeal to the naturall faculties of the minde of man*, London.

Nozick, R. 1974: *Anarchy, State and Utopia*, Oxford.

Owens, J. *Epigrammata, Libri I–III*, edited and introduced by J. R. C. Martyn, Leiden, 1976.

Plato, *The Collected Dialogues*, edited by E. Hamilton and H. Cairns, Bollingen Series LXXI: 1, Princeton, N.J., 1961.

Plautus, *The Comedies*, edited by D. R. Slavitt and P. Bovie, Baltimore / London, 1995.

Rawls, J. 1971: *A Theory of Justice*, Cambridge, Mass.

Ross, A. 1653: *Leviathan drawn out with a hook, or Animadversions upon Mr. Hobbs his Leviathan*, London.

Rousseau, J.-J. 1750: *Discours qui a remporté le prix à l'académie de Dijon*, in: *Oeuvres complètes*, Paris, 1959ff., vol. 3, pp. 1–30; *A Discourse on the Arts and Sciences*, in: J.-J. Rousseau, *The Social Contract and Discourses*, translated by G. D. H. Cole, pp. 1–26, London, 1973.

Rousseau, J.-J. 1755: *Discours sur l'origine et les fondements de l'inégalité parmi des homes*, in *Oeuvres complètes*, Paris, 1959ff., vol. 3, pp. 111–237; *A Discourse on the Origin of Inequality*, in: J.-J. Rousseau, *The Social Contract and Discourses*, translated by G. D. H. Cole, pp. 27–113, London, 1973.

Rousseau, J.-J. 1762: *Du contrat social ou principles du droit politiques*, in: *Oeuvres complètes*, Paris, 1959ff., vol. 3, pp. 347–470; *The Social Contract*, in: *The Social Contract and Discourses*, translated by G. D. H. Cole, pp. 164–278, London, 1973.

Schiller, F.: *Wilhelm Tell*, in: *Schillers Werke*, Band 2: *Dramen*, Frankfurt a. M., 1966; "William Tell," in: *Friedrich Schiller. Poet of Freedom*, vol. II, pp. 59–178, Washington 1988.

Schmitt, C. 1965: "Die vollendete Revolution," in: *Der Staat*, 4, pp. 51–69.

Schmökel, H. 1985[2]: "Mesopotamische Texte," in: W. Beyerlin (ed.), *Religionsgeschichtliches Textbuch zum Alten Testament*, pp. 95–168, Göttingen.

Seneca, *Selected Philosophical Letters*, translated with an introduction by B. Inwood, Oxford, 2007.

Smith, A. 1776: *The Wealth of Nations*, introduction by R. Reich, New York, 2000.

Spinoza, B. de: *The Collected Works of Spinoza*, edited and translated by Edwin Curley, vol. I, Princeton, N.J., 1985.

Springborg, P. 1996: "Thomas Hobbes on Religion," in: Sorell 1996, pp. 346–80.

Stollberg-Rillinger, B. 1986: *Der Staat als Maschine. Zur politischen Metaphorik des absoluten Fürstenstaates*, Berlin.

Sutter, A. 1988: *Göttliche Maschinen. Die Automaten für Lebendiges*, Frankfurt a. M.

Tepl, J. v. *Der Ackermann und der Tod*, Stuttgart, 1984.

Tönnies, F. 1991: *Gemeinschaft und Gesellschaft: Grundbegriffe der reinen Soziologie*, Darmstadt.

Wallis, J. 1655: *Elenchus geometricae hobbianae*; reprinted London, 1999.

Walz, G. A. 1930: *Wesen des Völkerrechts und Kritik der Völkerrechtsleugner*, Stuttgart.

Weber, M. 1985: *Wirtschaft und Gesellschaft. Grundriss der verstehenden Soziologie*, edited by J. Winckelmann, Tübingen / Berlin; *Economy and Society. An Outline of Interpretive Sociology*, edited by G. Roth and C. Wittich, New York, 1968.

Xenophon, *Conversations of Socrates*, translated by H. Treddenick and R. Westerfield, London, 1998.

Name Index

Aaron, 8
Abraham, 180, 210
Adam, 8, 95, 210
Aquinas, Saint Thomas, 102, 104
Aristotle, 9, 13, 18, 28; *Rhetoric,* 30, 38,
 39, 61, 55; *Nicomachean Ethics,* 66–67;
 De Anima, 69, 82; *Politics,* 74, 79;
 Metaphysics, 83; on first philosophy,
 178; on the prime mover, 177; on
 theory, 87; on the will, 86, 102, 104,
 110, 115, 127, 141, 164; Hobbes's
 general critique of, 193–206, 212, 215,
 220, 227, 234
Ashley-Cooper, Anthony, 217
Aubrey, John, 24, 52
Augustine, Saint, 9, 181–82
Augustus, Emperor, 24

Bacon, Francis, 22, 23; on knowledge as
 power, 57, 78, 104, 119, 126; on law,
 160, 234
Bentham, Jeremy, 112, 219, 225
Bermbach, Udo, 230, 239
Bernhardt, Joseph, 230
Bloch, Ernst, 226
Bodin, Jean, 5, 26, 231
Borkenau, Franz, 4, 70, 222, 228
Boyle, Robert, 50
Bramhall, John, 50, 153, 219, 234, 235

Braun, Dietrich, 230
Buchanan, James, 12, 230
Bühler, Joachim, 230

Calvin, John, 29
Cassirer, Ernst, 226
Cavendish, William Lord, 23, 233–34
Cicero, 9, 51, 102, 104, 164, 194–95,
 215
Coke, Edward, 159, 160, 217–19
Cromwell, Oliver, 30, 49

David, 8
Descartes, René, 2, 4, 23, 25–26, 33–34,
 51, 69, 80, 82–84, 102, 104, 207, 234
Donne, John, 22

Elizabeth I, Queen, 22, 28–29, 233
Euchner, Walter, 110
Euclid, 10, 14; Hobbes's debt to, 25–27,
 32, 39–39, 82, 234
Euripides, 38
Eve, 210

Filmer, Robert, 49

Galilei, Galileo, 10, 25–26, 32, 74, 80,
 104, 234
Gassendi, Pierre, 25, 33, 104, 234

251

Gauthier, David, 230
Gert, Bernard, 230
Gondibert, 34, 235
Grotius, Hugo, 25, 138, 223

Hale, Mathew, 218
Hampton, Jean, 153, 230
Harrington, James, 211, 217, 221
Harvey, William, 22, 75
Hegel, Georg Wilhelm Friedrich, 133,
   222–25
Henry VIII, King, 29, 186, 221
Hüning, Dieter, 230
Hitler, Adolf, 232
Höffe, Otfried, 18, 43, 66, 132, 292,
   229–30
Hönigswald, Richard, 230
d'Holbach, Baron, 225
Homer, 9, 38, 51, 107, 193–94, 236
Hume, David, 9, 11, 23, 123, 207
Husserl, Edmund, 226
Huygens, Christian, 25
Hyde, Edward, 34, 211, 217

James I, King, 28, 29, 233–34
Jesus Christ, 105, 184–85, 210, 212
John the Baptist, 9
Johnston, David, 38
Justinian, Emperor, 9
Juvenal, 9, 161

Kant, Immanuel, 12, 16, 18, 59, 81,
   136–37, 140–42, 156, 222–25, 229
Charles I, King, 22, 29, 49, 159, 211,
   234, 235
Charles II, King, 34, 46, 50, 53, 219, 235
Kelsen, Hans, 226
Kepler, Johannes, 78, 80, 135
Khomeinei, 232
Kodalle, Klaus-Michael, 92, 139, 230

La Mettrie, Julien Offray de, 67
Leibniz, Gottfried Wilhelm, 25, 33–34,
   51, 80, 207, 222
Littleton, John, 160

Locke, John, 11, 12, 23, 25, 221, 223,
   228–30

Machiavelli, Niccolò, 5, 24, 26
Macpherson, Crawford, 4, 70, 222,
   228–30
Mao, Tse-Tung, 232
Martinich, Aloysius P., 34, 142, 176, 178,
   290
Mersenne, Marin, 24, 25, 33–34, 104,
   234
Mill, James, 225
Mill, John Stuart, 228
More, Henri, 49
Moses, 9, 180, 183–84, 209–10
Mugabe, Robert, 232

Newton, Isaac, 51, 80–81
Nozick, Robert, 12, 230

Oakeshott, Michael, 230
Ottmann, Henning, 152, 230
Owens, John, 126

Pascal, Blaise, 33–34, 61, 207
Paul, Saint, 9
Pericles, 209
Peter, the Apostle, 9, 185
Plato, 9, 16, 39, 111; the *Laws*, 127; on
   the philosopher king, 46; *Protagoras*,
   94, 112; the *Republic*, 43, 46, 74,
   149, 164, 179, 194, 195–97, 203,
   205, 215
Plautus, 126
Polin, Raymond, 230
Pufendorf, Samuel, 25, 222

Rawls, John, 12, 59, 229
Roberval, Gilles Personne de, 25
Ross, Alexander, 49
Rousseau, Jean-Jacques, 4, 12, 133, 156,
   203, 222–23, 228

Solomon, King, 9
Samuel, 9

Saul, 9, 210
Schelsky, Helmut, 230
Schiller, Friedrich, 230
Schmitt, Carl, 5, 42, 44, 226–28, 230
Selden, John, 217
Seneca, 160
Shaftesbury, Earl of, 217
Shakespeare, William, 22, 149
Skinner, Quentin, 15, 38
Smith, Adam, 225
Socrates, 185, 197, 215
Sorell, Tom, 230
Spinoza, Baruch de, 6, 23, 25–56, 222, 225
Springborg, Patricia, 185, 230
Stalin, Joseph, 232

Strauss, Leo, 152, 155, 176, 177, 226–29
Stuart, Mary, 28

Tacitus, 24
Terrel, Jean, 230
Thucydides, 5, 9, 24, 38, 39, 52, 193–94, 207–09, 211, 217, 234
Tönnies, Ferdinand, 225–27, 230
Tuck, Richard, 176, 178, 230

Voltaire, 207

Wallis, John, 38, 51
Weber, Max, 118, 226

Xenophon, 185

Subject Index

accidents, 98, 104

atheism, 22, 17, 176, 178, 182, 185, 209, 219

anarchy, anarchism, 52, 146, 150, 155, 157, 199, 203, 232

angels, 190

animals, 10, 77f., 86–89, 93, 96, 111–13, 202f.

Antichrist, 48. *See also* atheism

aristocracy, 147, 166

arithmetic, 6, 7, 60, 64, 70, 101, 103f.

art, 34, 55, 105

artifice, artificial, 43, 45, 60, 67–69, 75, 105, 126, 170–71, 202–03

authority, 7–9, 12–13, 17–18, 38, 44, 49, 59, 72, 78, 108, 116, 118, 122–5, 128, 132, 135, 145–48, 150–51, 154, 159–61, 167–175, 179–80, 184–88, 190, 195–7, 208, 212, 221–22. *See also* sovereign

Behemoth (Hobbes), 30, 15, 51–52, 156, 210–11, 220–21, 226

the Bible, 3, 13, 29, 44, 52, 68, 183, 188, 190, 211. *See also* God, Christianity, interpretation, revelation, Scripture

body, 10, 27, 57, 68, 75, 77, 79, 98, 104, 107

Catholicism, 29, 32, 34, 49, 52, 176, 182, 186, 191, 206, 212, 220

cause, 10, 27, 57, 60, 75, 85–86, 102, 109, 117, 125, 129, 141, 177, 179–80, 196, 201–02, 204, 208–09, 221

Christianity, 105, 142–43, 163, 183–87, 189–90, 199, 209–10

the churches, 29, 32, 37, 49, 53, 176–77, 181–82, 184, 186–87, 191, 198, 209–10, 212, 220

civil war, 1, 3, 6, 28–33, 41, 46–47, 51–52, 55, 58, 66, 72, 75, 96, 116, 128, 131, 155, 161, 199, 201, 208, 210–13, 220–21, 229, 231

clerics, 44, 212, 219–20

commands, 92, 93, 98, 154, 160–67, 219, 226. *See also* law, order, counsel

commonwealth, 4, 11, 15, 35, 41, 44–46, 58, 68, 95, 121–22, 126, 128, 138, 144, 147, 161–63, 166, 168–72, 175, 180–82, 186, 202, 227

community, 7, 35, 45, 66, 69, 200–203, 223–25

255

concept, 74, 77, 85, 91, 93, 97–99, 101.
    See also name
conscience, 44, 95, 138–39, 142, 145,
    152, 168, 170, 185, 187
contract, 12, 13, 43, 48, 70, 95, 108,
    118, 123, 135, 137, 143–52, 195
counsel, 91–92, 100, 104, 164–65
covenant. *See* contract
crime, 93, 163, 166, 172

death, 22, 58–9, 72, 118, 122, 130, 132,
    227
decision, 123, 144, 165, 172, 186, 227
De Cive (Hobbes), 9, 15, 26, 28, 30,
    33–34, 39, 41, 49, 58–59, 63–64, 71,
    73, 101, 119, 123, 131, 134, 148, 175,
    181, 194, 202, 204, 207, 210, 215,
    220
De Corpore (Hobbes), 9, 16, 18, 23, 26,
    31, 33, 49, 69, 74, 78, 82, 84, 90–91
De Homine (Hobbes), 9, 26, 33, 50, 69,
    90–91, 110–11, 116, 209
deism, 176–78, 181
deliberation, 112–13, 117, 124, 132,
    165, 196
democracy, 30, 147, 149, 209, 227, 229
demonstration, 4, 104, 222
desire, 11, 57, 72, 74, 79, 86, 91, 96,
    100, 105, 110–118, 120, 122, 125,
    130, 133, 198–99, 223
Dialogue (Hobbes), 15, 51, 101, 160,
    218, 229
dignity, 125, 136, 195, 198
dreams, 84–85, 190

The Elements of Law (Hobbes), 4, 6, 15,
    22, 26, 30–31, 34, 39, 58–59, 61, 64,
    69, 73, 84, 90, 101, 107, 110, 131,
    148, 175, 225
eloquence. *See* rhetoric
error, 79, 94, 99, 102, 104
essence, 10, 97
ethics, 110–11, 116, 139, 141–43, 198,
    212, 229
experience, 3, 6, 62, 68, 73, 77–78, 83,
    86, 87, 89, 97, 112, 160, 196, 199

faith, 143, 260, 185, 187, 191
fancy, 98, 107, 179, 207
fear, 21–22, 43, 65, 72, 85, 112, 114,
    117–19, 125, 130–31, 151, 178–80,
    209, 227
freedom (liberty), 7–8, 12–13, 15, 30,
    44–45, 50–52, 55, 62, 92–93, 115–17,
    123–25, 129, 131–32, 137, 140,
    142–43, 148–50, 156, 173, 187, 212,
    225, 227–28, 230–31
the future, 75, 87, 111, 118, 122, 129,
    137, 179, 208

generosity (liberality), 141, 113, 119,
    141, 225
geometry, 6, 10, 23, 25–26, 51, 60,
    63–65, 73
glory, love of, 43, 100, 125, 129, 209,
    138–40
God, 43–45, 48, 85, 90, 93–94, 103,
    138–43, 154, 168, 170, 176–91, 210,
    218
the Golden Rule, 9, 139, 126, 143
the Good, 6, 11, 59, 110–11, 113, 165,
    198
gratitude, 137, 140–41

happiness (felicity), 11, 58, 74, 86,
    110–11, 113, 120, 125, 128–29, 147,
    179, 198–99
Historia Ecclesiastica (Hobbes), 209, 212
history, 26, 30, 51–52, 106
homo homini lupus, 9, 100, 126
homo homini deus, 126
honor, 117, 148, 189, 209, 201–02, 204,
    182, 195, 198

imagination, 16, 47, 70, 78–80, 82–83,
    85, 111–12, 176, 179–80, 189, 196,
    207
imperatives, 136, 139, 142, 152, 164. *See
    also* commands
the infinite, 85, 97, 189
injustice, 58, 108, 138, 140, 154,
    172–73, 204, 211, 218, 223
interests, 66, 71, 87, 100, 112, 199

international law, 5, 14, 25, 138, 226

judgment, capacity for, 86–87, 107, 161, 170, 172, 207
judges, 69, 159, 161, 169, 170–71
jurisprudence, 13, 164, 218–19
jurists, 160, 164
justice, 43, 52, 58–59, 86, 96, 108, 137–38, 140–41, 144, 150, 169, 173, 198, 205, 208–89, 226

kings and kingship, 149, 180, 210
Kingdom of Darkness, 29, 176, 191
Kingdom of God, 180, 182, 191, 210
Kingdom of Heaven, 81
knowledge, 3, 5–6, 10, 16, 23, 31, 57–58, 61, 64, 66, 77–87, 90–93, 99–100, 102–03, 106, 119, 162, 196, 199–200

language, 40, 89–96, 78, 88, 97–107, 109, 115–16, 162, 202
law, 13, 38, 44, 122–24, 135, 159–75, 195, 218–25
laws of nature, 59, 134–43, 150, 164, 168–71, 173, 186, 189, 223
Leviathan, figure of, 38–48, 68, 75
love of one's neighbour, 113–14, 180

machine, image of, 27–28, 40, 43, 48, 60, 67–69, 73
manners (customs), 61, 121–22, 131, 198
materialism, 10, 32, 53, 107, 188–90, 197
mathematics, 2–4, 6, 10, 15, 26, 32, 41, 50–51, 60, 62–64, 103, 119, 207
matter, 27, 74, 79, 83, 93, 107
memory, 77–78, 80, 82–84, 89, 106
metaphor, 39–40, 42, 67–69, 100, 104–05, 127, 190
metaphysics, 60–62, 107, 195, 197
mind, 10, 47, 57, 77–85, 92, 99, 102, 196
miracles, 189
mistrust (diffidence), 125, 201, 204, 209, 227

monarch, monarchy, 29, 32, 51, 147–49, 155, 212
moral philosophy, 63, 138–42, 171, 198–89, 230
motion, 10, 27, 41, 73–75, 79–83, 93, 110–12, 116, 200, 228

names, 12, 90–102, 104–5, 136, 132. See also words
naturalism, 6, 10–11, 55, 60, 82, 92, 99, 109–12, 136, 143, 199
natural law, 13, 25, 44, 108, 113, 122, 142, 151, 159–64, 200, 219, 227, 229
nature, 6, 10, 15–16, 27, 60, 62–63, 67–74, 78–79, 97, 116–18, 124, 126–28, 135–36, 170, 176, 194, 200–04
nominalism, 96–98
nonsense, 10, 94, 98

obedience, 44, 85, 91, 158, 161–63, 166, 178, 180, 184–88, 210, 212, 226–27
opinion, 39, 64, 113

Parliament, 155, 159, 165, 172, 208
the passions, 41, 65, 96, 109–17, 124, 128–32, 138, 153, 156
the past, 86–87, 208
peace, 31, 33, 41, 47, 55, 57–59, 64, 69, 71–73, 75, 92, 95–96, 121–22, 129–34, 137–42, 148, 150, 152, 156, 169, 186, 218, 224
person, impersonation, 43, 118, 146–48, 151
poetry, 34, 55, 85, 107, 195, 207
the Pope, 176, 186, 188
poverty, 131
power, 11–13, 23, 31–32, 40, 43–48, 57, 61, 70, 74–75, 86, 93–95, 108, 117–20, 122–24, 128, 135, 145–57, 160, 165–73, 184–89, 205, 209, 213
Presbyterians, 12, 29–30, 50, 52, 176, 191
pride, 43–44, 126, 140
prophecy, prophets, 184, 182, 189
proof of the existence of God, 180, 189

property, 137, 149, 151–52, 203, 221, 224, 229
prudence, 77, 83, 85–89, 136, 199
punishment, 68, 137, 182

reason, 26, 31, 40, 42, 57, 59, 62–68, 78–79, 89–93, 98–99, 101–13, 129–32, 136, 141–42, 159, 161–62, 169, 182, 197
regicide, 95
religion, 175–85, 198, 220
representation (political), 70–71, 144, 147
representation (mental), 6, 27, 83, 92, 97, 99, 101, 111, 189
representative, 43, 45, 62, 122, 144, 147–50, 155, 170, 172–73, 183–84, 190–91
resistance, right to, 153–54, 187, 158
revelation, 46, 62, 143
rhetoric, 14–15, 21, 30, 38–42, 63, 100, 108, 126, 195
rivalry (competition), 100, 122, 125, 129, 195, 201, 204, 209, 227
rules, 24, 31, 66, 93, 102, 105, 123, 137, 166, 169, 218

safety (security), 7, 13, 15, 31, 96, 125, 130, 151, 161, 168, 232
Scholasticism, 2, 23, 47, 78, 83, 90, 97–98, 105, 113, 189, 191, 195–96, 206
the Schools, 161, 195, 197
science, 26, 57–79, 89–90, 102–119
self-preservation, 10, 15, 17, 74, 113, 115–17, 124–32, 137, 141, 143, 145–56, 150–55, 173, 197, 231
sensation, 75, 77–78, 80–83, 89, 106, 109, 196
sensationalism, 27, 80–82, 86, 92, 107, 112, 115, 130
sense perception, 27, 78, 80, 82–84, 98
separation of powers, 17, 32, 150, 156, 221
signs, 79, 88, 91–92, 97, 99–100, 114, 162, 166

sin, 93, 190
social contract, 4, 12, 229–30
society, 92, 95, 116, 129, 180–81, 222–23
sovereignty and the sovereign, 13, 15, 17, 43, 49, 72, 92–93, 105, 117–19, 122, 135–36, 144–57, 162, 167–78, 182–88, 191, 205, 212–13
the state (commonwealth), 11, 35, 58, 71, 95, 126, 128, 138, 144, 161–63, 171–72
the state (condition) of nature, 58, 61, 123–29, 131–39, 143–46, 150, 223
the state (condition) of war, 14, 59, 122, 129–30, 138, 143, 224
substance, concept of, 189–90, 197
superstition, 2, 195

theism, 47, 176–78, 180
theory of knowledge, 6, 61, 79–87, 99, 115
thought, 65, 78, 82–83, 86, 91–94, 97, 99–105, 109, 112, 189
trust, 13, 113, 144, 153, 212
truth, 41, 65–66, 98–99, 102, 104, 109, 113, 159–61, 208
tyranny, 95, 155, 212
the universities, 23, 82–83, 191, 195–96, 212

virtue, 86–87, 89, 117–18, 139, 141–42, 146, 169, 198
visions, 85, 176, 190

war, 3, 58–59, 64–66, 75, 115, 121–22, 127–31, 138–40, 144–45, 150–51, 161, 168–69, 204, 210–13
wealth, 117, 225
the will, 86, 79, 113, 117, 124, 162, 164, 172, 198
wisdom, 89, 94, 96, 153, 160–61
words, 40, 42, 62, 90–98, 99–105. See also names